DATE DUE			

Conceptions
of Kinship

Conceptions
of Kinship

Bernard Farber

Elsevier · New York
New York · Oxford

Exclusive Distribution
throughout the World by
Greenwood Press, Westport,
Ct. U.S.A.

Elsevier North Holland, Inc.
52 Vanderbilt Avenue, New York, New York 10017

Distributors outside the United States and Canada:
Elsevier/North-Holland
335 Jan van Galenstraat, P.O. Box 211
Amsterdam, The Netherlands

Library of Congress Cataloging in Publication Data

Farber, Bernard.
    Conceptions of kinship.

    Includes index.
    1. Kinship. 2. Kinship—United States. I. Title.
GN487.F37   306.8′3   80-16712
ISBN 0-444-99076-3

Desk Editor   Robert Glasgow
Design   Edmée Froment
Art Editors   Glen Burris & Aimee Kudlak
Mechanicals/Opening pages   José Garcia
Production Manager   Joanne Jay
Compositor   Crestwood Press
Printer   Haddon Craftsmen

Manufactured in the United States of America

Contents

Preface

Perhaps the title of this monograph should be *Conceptions of Collaterality*. The term *collaterality* refers to aspects of kinship ties associated with genealogical distances among relatives. George Peter Murdock (1949, p. 103) has identified collaterality as a basic dimension in determining relationships among kin:

> The criterion of collaterality rests on the biological fact that among consanguineal relatives of the same generation and sex, some will be more closely akin to Ego than others. A direct ancestor, for example, will be more nearly related than his sibling or cousin, and a lineal descendant than the descendant of a sibling or cousin. Our own kinship system consistently recognizes the criterion of collaterality and, with the sole exceptions of 'cousin', never employs the same term for consanguineal kinsmen related to Ego in different degrees.

This book is based on the premises that (1) any major subsystem of a society (like kinship) can be examined as a means for gaining insight into the character of that society; (2) since, as far as we know, certain attributes of kinship—like collaterality—are universal, kinship seems to provide an appropriate means for the study of modern society; (3) unlike other dimensions of kinship, collaterality lends itself to precise formulations that permit measurement of diversity in a population; and (4) inasmuch as collaterality appears to be a basis for mobilization of action by relatives and for significant rules regarding marriage and inheritance, it appears to provide an effective perspective from which to study the relationship between family and society.

In particular, collaterality seems to be related to the extent that pluralism is significant in structuring of society. A pluralistic ideology is one that values the principle that the collective welfare of a society is best served by promoting the special interests of its particular components defined by race, religion, economic role, status in the socioeconomic stratification system, and/or ethnicity. Kinship may be regarded as a vehicle for perpetuating group identities associated with these special interests—religious sectarianism, socioeconomic position, and ethnic distinctiveness. Presumably some relatives are more closely identified than other kin with these special interests. Collaterality serves to designate the shading among relatives of their relevance to these concerns. One would then anticipate that populations with a pluralistic ideology would develop family and kinship norms that reflect their needs.

By way of contrast, in populations that foster universalism and consider the perpetuation of pluralist ideologies as destructive to the common welfare, kinship is used differently. Here the ideology champions either individualism or "totalitarianism." That is, kinship is intended to serve the individual or the nation as a whole: it is no longer a vehicle of a special interest. Under these conditions, the role of kinship (including family) is to provide personnel exclusively for the society and its duty is to keep them as happy, healthy, and generally proficient as possible. Consequently, this state of affairs demands a different configuration in collaterality.

The monograph elaborates upon various implications of the above distinctions and reports the findings of an empirical investigation which, to some extent, tests the hypothetical statements derived. The propositions examined in the Phoenix study are that spatial metaphors symbolized by the components of models of collaterality are isomorphic with communal versus pluralist distinction in religion, ethnic, and socioeconomic settings in the social structure and that these components are associated with particular kinship norms and values relevant to the communal-pluralist dichotomy.

Many sociologists and anthropologists have written about kinship in ways that contribute significantly to the understanding of the relationship between collaterality and social structure. However, this concern with collaterality has generally been peripheral. Focusing on the work from the perspective of collaterality in this book may give a description of their positions a strange cast—a view of their writings that they had not intended. Of course, this description does not touch the core of their work, but hopefully it does reveal implications of their conceptions for collaterality.

The research in this monograph was undertaken with a grant from the National Science Foundation (SOC76-21110). I am particularly thankful to Professor John Atkins, University of Washington, for his extensive suggestions and criticisms regarding my discussions of models of collaterality. His comments have contributed significantly to the monograph. In addition, I profited much from the comments on earlier drafts of chapters and introductions to chapters by Professors G. N. Ramu and Nicholas Tavuchis of the University of Manitoba and the late Louis Schneider of the University of Texas at Austin. Their sharp criticisms were indeed expressions of friendship. I appreciate also the review of the final chapter by Professors Joan Aldous of Notre Dame University and Robert Lewis of Arizona State University. Mrs. Temtlin of Temple Beth Israel Library was exceptionally kind in providing materials pertaining to Jewish law and kinship. Finally, I thank my associates Morris Axelrod, Edward Greenberg, and Kenneth Andersen for participating with me in this adventure. All three of them have made this an exciting enterprise.

But above all I am grateful to my *mischpokhe* and to my dear wife Rosanna most especially for inspiration, patience, and gentle counsel.

Bernard Farber

Conceptions
of Kinship

Introduction: Popular and Legal Conceptions of Kinship

1

Studies of American kinship have been limited in the kinds of insights they have yielded. For the most part, they have been concerned with the extent to which the nuclear family has become "structurally isolated" in different segments of society and various consequences of this isolation. This concern has stimulated research on patterns of interaction and assistance among relatives, feelings of attachment, and kinds of personal obligations. To a lesser extent, investigators have treated kinship as a cultural phenomenon, dealing with kinship nomenclature and the meanings of consanguinity and affinity in American society. In any case, there seems to be an implicit assumption that American kinship is some sort of vestige of an institution that *used* to be important for maintaining social structure but now serves mainly as an appendage to the nuclear family or as an ephemeral connection between families.

Yet, kinship organization is expressed not only through day-to-day interactions among relatives but also through legal norms that govern such matters as the definition of incestuous marriage, the priorities of succession when intestacy occurs, and rights and obligations pertaining to support and guardianship. Presumably, these legal formulations follow conceptions about kinship ties that are currently in the population. However, family laws often conflict with one another even with regard to such elementary matters as who of a person's relatives are closer and who are more distant. The historical models that provide the basis for computing kinship distances and priorities in modern law differ from each other in significant ways in their ordering of relatives. Comparatively little is understood about these models and their assumptions about the nature of family life. The analysis reported in this monograph is concerned with the extent to which people's ideas about kinship ties conform to the various models for computing kinship distances and the implications of holding these ideas for family life and kinship interaction.

In exploring the implications of different modes of handling collaterality, I deal with several questions with regard to kinship as a mechanism for maintaining social continuity. Under what circumstances do people regard kinship as a corporate-like "reality" by means of which "the important things in life'' are perpetuated? What evidence is there that people in American society organize kinship ties in ways that reflect this "reality?" How is this conception of kinship related to such matters as courtship patterns, marital norms, fertility, socialization of children, and so on? What might knowledge about these matters suggest about future trends in family life and changes in American legal codes?

This book reports the findings of a social survey designed to answer these questions. The target group consisted of residents of Phoenix, Arizona who have ever been married and who are between the ages of 18 and 45. The 772 cases which were studied had two components, a probability sample of Phoenix and a supplementary sample of Jewish households. The field techniques are described in Appendix B, Method of Data Collection.

LEGAL MODELS OF KINSHIP

Inasmuch as legal models of kinship play an important role in the analysis, they should be described first. These models are related to, but are not identical with, systems of terms by which an individual's relatives are designated—parents, uncles, aunts, cousins, and so on. A matrix of terminology describing kinship statuses in a particular culture can be regarded as a table of organization. As such, the table expresses the rights and obligations which, at one time or another in a society's history, people have developed to organize their relationships. The biological similarity of reproduction for all humans makes it possible to compare one table or organization with another. Lewis Morgan, in his analysis of *Systems of Consanguinity and Affinity of the Human Family,* has suggested that:

> In every supposable plan of consanguinity, where marriage between pairs exists, there must be a lineal and several collateral lines. Each person, also, in constructing his own table becomes the central point, or *EGO,* from whom outward is reckoned the degree of relationship of each kinsman, and to whom the relationship returns. His position is necessarily in the lineal line. In a chart of relationships this line is vertical. Upon it may be inscribed, above and below any given person, his several ancestors and descendants in a direct series from father to son, and these persons together will constitute his right lineal male line, which is also called the trunk, or common stock of descent. Out of this trunk line emerge the several collateral lines, males and female, which are numbered outwardly. . . .The first collateral line, male, consists of my brother and his descendants, and the first, female, of my sister and her descendants. The second collateral line, male, on the father's side, consists of my father's brother and his descendants, and the second, female, of my father's sister and her descendants; the second collateral line, male, on the mother's side, is composed of my mother's brother and his descendants, and the second, female, of my mother's sister, and her descendants. The third collateral line, male, on

the father's side, consists of my grandfather's brother and his descendants, and the third, female, of my father's sister and her descendants; on the mother's side, the same line, male, is composed of my grandmother's brother and his descendants, and the same, female, of my grandmother's sister and her descendants (Morgan, 1871, pp. 17–18).

Morgan continues in this manner through the fifth collateral line consisting of the siblings of the great-great-grandparent and their descendants. Analyses of kinship terminology are aimed at determining how the relatives who constitute the person's kindred are grouped by kinship nomenclature to designate the pattern of relationships that one has with relatives. George Peter Murdock has proposed that this grouping can be made on the basis of sex of relatives, generation in relation to Ego, relative age of kin, consanguinity versus affinity, degree of collaterality, and so on (Murdock, 1949, pp. 136ff). Together, these patterns or groupings constitute tables of kinship organization.

Whereas a table of organization based on kinship nomenclature implies a series of rights and obligations pertaining to each relationship, it does not provide a clue to the relative strengths of these obligations to various kin. The table of organization of kinship nomenclature is much like a set of statutes that has evolved over a period of time. There are times when laws conflict and decisions must be made with regard to priorities. Because of these conflicts, nomenclature must be supplemented by other means for designating priorities. The history of legal codes governing intestacy laws indicates that these laws were formulated following periods of conflict (usually between social classes). In complex societies, such as urban civilizations, city states (and dynastic empires, e.g., Feng, 1937), diverse segments of the population differ in ranking which relatives precede others in rights and obligations. Presumably the legal models express popular conceptions about priorities or "proximities" of relatives. The sections below describe the characteristics of the legal models for determining priorities among relatives. The social contexts in which these models emerged will be discussed later.

The legal models for determining priorities among consanguineal relatives share some characteristics. Indeed, study of the historical contexts indicates that, in temporal sequence, the Parentela Orders procedure seems to have arisen first; the Civil Law model represents a modification of the Parentela Orders; and the Canon Law method revises the Civil Law approach. Because of this relatedness in history, despite differences in organizing principles, the three models express similarities in ways of counting the number of parent-child links from one relative to another. Like the Genetic model, which is also described below, all three models assume that rights and duties of "closer" relatives have a priority over those of more distant ones. They differ only in the way by which they count the parent-child links between relatives. (See Atkins, 1974.)

Parentela Orders Model

The Parentela Orders model for computing priorities in the rights and obligations of relatives has had a long history. According to Lewis H. Morgan (1871, p. 34), the term *parentela* was applied by the fifth century Helvetians in their domestic laws to refer to "a number of relatives united under the same set of parents as their next common stock (*Stamm*)." The human body was used by the Helvetians as a metaphor for a *parentela,* so that "husband and wife, united in marriage, belong to the head; the children, born as full brothers and sisters from one man and one wife, to the neck. . .[then] children of full brothers and sisters occupy that place where the shoulders and arms join. These form the first kindred of consanguinity, viz., the children of brother and sister. The others occupy the elbow, the third the hand, etc."

As a general model, Parentela Orders organize kinship relations in the following way:

1. Each *parentela* is headed by an ancestor of Ego, the rank of any *parentela* being a function of the number of generations that this ancestor is removed from Ego. The first *parentela* is headed by Ego and includes all of his descendants; the second *parentela* is headed by Ego's parents and includes all of their descendants apart from those in the first *parentela,* and so on.
2. Within each *parentela*, any relative is located according to the number of generations he is removed from the head of the *parentela*. By determining the *parentela* class into which a relative falls and his *generation* within that *parentela,* one can describe his precise relationship to Ego.

The principles for determining the order of priorities of relatives in the Parentela Orders model are as follows:

1. All members of a lower-ranked parentela have priority over members of a parentela of a higher rank. All of Ego's descendants (i.e., members of the first parentela) have prior rights and obligations over all other relatives. The second class in priority consists of the parents and all of their descendants who are not also Ego's descendants, and so on. In theory, the number of parentelae in an individual's genealogy is infinite.
2. Within each parentela, the head (i.e., a direct-line ancestor of Ego) has priority over all other members and, in turn, each parent has priority over his (or her) children. For example, Ego's children have priority over grandchildren and the grandchildren over great-grandchildren. In the second parentela, Ego's parents have priority in rights and obli-

gations over the brothers and sisters, and the brothers and sisters over the nephews and nieces. In theory, the progression within the parentela continues ad infinitum.

The location of any relative in the Parentela Orders system can be represented symbolically. Let j be the number of generational links between Ego and any ancestor; from Ego to Ego's parent is one link, to the grandparent is two links, and so on. Similarly, let i by the number of generational links between the head of a parentela and his (or her) own descendants; for the third parentela, from the grandparent to the aunt or uncle of Ego is one link and to Ego's first-cousins, two links. Since the progression within parentelae is infinite, the rank ordering of relatives depends upon the entire set of relatives actually considered in a particular instance. Before one goes on to the next parentela, one must exhaust the generational depth (represented by i) of kin in the given parentela. Hence, for a particular set of relatives, the rank order of each relative is influenced by the deepest generational depth (i.e., the largest i) for that set. (The size of the largest i can be represented by m.) The rank order for any relative is then determined by the summation of j (as weighted by $(m + 1)$) plus i. The formula for the rank ordering of relatives in the Parentela Orders system is thus $D = i + (m + 1)j$. The ranking of genealogical distances from Ego is presented in Table 1-1.

Huebner (1968) suggests that the Parentela Orders were derived by the Germans from traditional Jewish law of intestate succession. Morgan (1871), however, believes that Helvetians borrowed the scheme from the Roman system of "numbering collateral or 'transverse' lines of consanguines in which the *first* collateral line consists of the descendants of *parents* (other than Ego himself and his own descendants), while the *second* line consists of the descendants of grandparents of Ego (excluding Ego's parents and their descendants), and so forth" (Atkins, 1974, p. 10). Morgan (1871, p. 35) remarks that "the German [Parentela Orders] is a very perfect system, but its excellence is due to its fidelity to its Roman model." Yet, in the 17th century, John Selden (1636; 1640) presented several well-documented anal-

Table 1-1. Ranking of Distances from Ego According to Parentela Orders Model

Generation within Parentela (in descending order)	Parentela orders (ascending generations)		
	I	II	III
1	Ego (0)[a]	Parents (3)	Grandparents (6)
2	Children (1)	Siblings (4)	Aunts and uncles (7)
3	Grandchildren (2)	Nieces and nephews (5)	First cousins (8)

[a] Ranking of distance from Ego.

yses to support his view that the Roman system had its roots in earlier Hebraic law—both written and oral.

Regardless of origins, the Parentela Orders system survives in modern German law governing intestacy (Model, 1964) as well as in contemporary Israeli and U.S. law. In the *Ordnung Parentelen* of West German laws of succession, those relatives who belong to the second, third, and lower orders (*Ordnungen*) are called to inherit only if at the time of succession *no* relative of an earlier order is capable of being an heir (Model, 1964, p. 11). Heirs of the first order include Ego's children, grandchildren, and other descendants. Heirs of the second order are the decedent's parents and their descendants who are not included in the first *parentela*. The progression goes on endlessly. Similarly, in Israel:

> The deceased's children or their descendants inherit before his parents, his parents before the parents of his parents. . . . The Grandparents will not inherit if there are collateral relatives who are descendants of the parents; that is to say, not only the brothers and sisters of the deceased, and their children, will oust the grandparents from their right to succeed, but also the grandchildren of the brothers and sisters of the deceased (Tedeschi, 1966, pp. 243–244).

Some states, such as Arizona, apply the principles of the Parentela Orders model in a modified form (Wypyski, 1976, p. 65). Arizona intestacy law (1975, 14-2103) provides for the following priorities among kin in the assignment of estates (excluding the spouse's share):

1. To the issue of the decedent.
2. If there is no surviving issue, to the decedent's parent or parents equally.
3. If there is no surviving issue or parent, to the issue of the decedent's parents or issue of either of the parents.
4. If there is no surviving issue, parent or issue of a parent, but the decedent is survived by one or more grandparents or issue of grandparents, half of the estate passes to the paternal grandparent or grandparents equally, or to their issue if both grandparents are deceased; the other half passes to maternal grandparents or their issue in the same manner. If there is no surviving grandparent or issue on either the paternal or maternal side, the entire estate passes to relatives on the other side in the same manner as the half.

Civil Law Model

The Civil Law model for assigning priorities in intestate succession is associated with that body of law developed in ancient Rome and later codified in about the middle of the sixth century as the Institutes of Justinian. The earliest record of this model appears in the Twelve Tables, which had been devised at the time of the founding of the Roman Republic in the fifth century B.C. The Civil Law became highly influential as empires spread throughout Western Europe, and rulers sought a ready-made set of laws to govern with. "The ideological opulence of this Roman Corpus proved irresistible, because it embodied jurisprudential principles which with some adaptation could be utilized for the service of the Western Roman emperors in their function as universal lords (the *domini mundi*)" (Ullmann, 1975, p. 85). As in the days of the ancient Roman empire, the claim was made:

> That Roman law and the governmental themes based on it should become the "common law" (the *ius commune*) of the Western world, its common legal order, so that the old thesis that the Roman *lex* was *omnium generalis* could become a legal reality (Ullmann, 1975, pp. 89–90).

The procedure for computing genealogical distances in the Civil Law is simple. In order to compute the distance between Ego and an ancestor or direct-descendant, one counts the generational links between them. In the ascending line, a parent is one degree of genealogical distance, a grandparent two degrees, and so on; in the descending line, a child is one degree of distance, a grandchild two degrees. For a collateral relative, (a) one counts the number of generational links from Ego to the nearest ancestor who is also an ancestor of Ego's collateral relative; then (b) one determines the number of links between the collateral relative and that ancestor; and finally (c) one takes the sum of these (a and b) as the degree of genealogical distance between Ego and the collateral relative. Symbolically, if j is the number of generational links between Ego and the nearest common ancestor and i is the number of links between the collateral relative and that ancestor, the Civil Law distance between Ego and the collateral relatives is $(i + j)$ degrees. (Designations i and j are taken from Atkins, 1974). For example, for the genealogical distance between Ego and an aunt one starts with finding the nearest common ancestor, who is Ego's grandfather. The number of links j between Ego and the grandfather is 2, and the number of links i between the aunt and the grandfather is 1. The degree of genealogical distance between Ego and the aunt is thus $(i + j)$ or 3. Table 1-2a presents the configuration of close relatives according to Civil Law degrees. Unlike the arrangement of relatives in the Parentela Orders scheme, the mapping by Civil-Law degree permits several kinds of relatives to be equidistant from Ego. For example, although a niece precedes an aunt in the Parentela Order computation, they are of equal degree in the Civil Law procedure.

The Civil Law procedure has been utilized in one form or another in most major legal systems in Western civilization. Max Rheinstein (1955, p. 11)

Table 1-2. Degree of Relationship According to Canon Law, Genetic, and Civil Code Models, by Generation of Relative

A. CIVIL CODE MODEL

Distance from EGO: Degree of relationship

Generation	0	1	2	3	4
2			Grandparents		Great aunts and great uncles
1		Parents		Aunts and uncles	
0	EGO		Siblings		First cousins
−1		Children		Nieces and nephews	
−2			Grandchildren		Grandnieces and grandnephews

(continued)

indicates that, "Although the [Roman] Civil Law was taught in the continental universities from the 13th to the 19th century as a common basis, . . . as such [it] is no longer in force anywhere except, in the form of the so-called Roman-Dutch law, in the Union of South Africa and in Ceylon." Yet, the Civil Law model is widely applied in the computation of genealogical distances worldwide in legislation dealing with intestate succession and often in laws pertaining to the prohibition of incestuous marriage. During the 19th century, the development of the Napoleonic Code, based explicitly on Roman law, and the adoption of that Code in various legal systems (e.g., Austria, Mexico, Louisiana) did much to institutionalize the Civil Law model in modern family law. In the United States, the Civil Law procedure is followed in most state laws governing intestacy and incestuous marriage.

Canon Law Model

The Canon Law computational model of genealogical distances was first introduced into the legal corpus of the Roman Catholic Church; later it was incorporated into English family law. In general, "The diverse sources of the Canon Law were collected from the 13th to the 15th centuries in a compilation which is referred to as the Corpus Juris Canonici. In 1917 it was superceded as the official source of the law of the Roman Catholic Church by the Codex Juris Canonici. . . . At the Reformation the ecclesiastical courts and the Canon Law were continued by the Church of England (Rheinstein, 1955, p. 14)." Since, in England, ecclesiastical courts had jurisdiction over family matters, the Canon Law model was applied particularly in the "elaborate system of marriage law."

Like the Civil Law model for determining genealogical distances, the Canon Law procedure also involves the determination of generational links. For direct descendants and ancestors, the two models are equivalent in assigning priorities; one merely counts the number of generational links (i or j) between Ego and the lineal relative to determine degree of distance. They differ, however, in determining degree of distance of collateral relatives from Ego. As in the Civil Law degree, one counts the links j from Ego to the nearest relative which both Ego and the collateral have in common and then the linkage i from that ancestor to the collateral relative. But, instead of adding i to j, a person applying the Canon Law procedure determines the degree of distance between Ego and the collateral relative to be either i or j, whichever is larger. This scheme of computation yields the configuration of distances in Table 1-2b. Ego's aunt, who was 3 degrees distant according to Civil Law computation, is only 2 degrees distant by Canon Law rules; in Canon-Law degrees, she now shares her locus not only with Ego's nieces and nephews, but also with Ego's grandparents, first-cousins, and grandchildren.

Rheinstein (1955, p. 53) regards current applications of the Canon Law model to the distribution of estates (rather than to incestuous marriages) to be a "consequence of historical misunderstandings." He refers specifically to Georgia law (Code 1933, 113-903) (8)) and to an 1878 Georgia decision which ruled that:

> Under the rules of the Canon Law. . .we must count from the intestate up to the common ancestor one degree for each generation, thence down the collateral line to the contestant; the number of degrees in the longer of these two lines is the degree of kindred between the intestate and the contestant. And by this rule the grandchildren of an aunt are in the third degree, and are heirs at law

Table 1-2 *(continued)*

B. CANON LAW MODEL

Generation	n	\ 1	Distance from Ego: Degree of relationship \ 2	3
2			Grandparents	Great aunts and great uncles
1		Parents	Aunts and uncles	
0	EGO	Siblings	First cousins	Second cousins
−1		Children	Nieces and nephews	
−2			Grandchildren	Grandnieces and grandnephews

(continued)

in preference to the great-grandchildren of a brother, who are in the fourth degree (Rheinstein, 1955, p. 53).

In this instance, according to the Canon Law degree, the aunt's grandchildren inherit ahead of the brother's great-grandchildren; according to the Civil Law scheme, both are 5 degrees distant from the deceased person, and the two would have shared equally; and according to the Parentela Orders procedure, the brother's great-grandchildren would have inherited the estate. Had the Georgia court interpreted the English Statute of Distribution of 1671 to refer to the Civil Law model, as English courts have done, the choice of heirs in Georgia intestacy cases would have been different.

Genetic Model

A fourth approach to kinship distances is described by David M. Schneider in his analysis of American culture. Schneider (1968, p. 23–25) suggests that:

> In the American cultural conception, kinship is defined as biogenetic. This definition says that kinship is whatever the biogenetic relationship is. If science discovers new facts about biogenetic relationships, then that is what kinship is and was all along, although it may not have been known at the time. . . . Two blood relatives are "related" by the fact that they share in some degree the stuff of a particular heredity. . . . Because blood is a "thing" and because it is subdivided with each reproductive step away from a given ancestor, the precise degree to which two persons share a common heredity can be calculated, and "distance" can thus be stated in specific quantitative terms.

If kinship is reduced to genetic ties, then Schneider's position implies that American kinship maps can be drawn in terms of shared chromosomes or "degree of parentage" (Cruz-Coke, 1977). Because of bisexual reproduction among humans, people derive half of their chromosomes from the mother and half from the father; consequently, the degree of shared chromosomes between two relatives is always some factor of one-half. The degree of parentage decreases exponentially with the number of generations between two relatives.

Symbolically, the Genetic model can be represented as follows:

1. Let j be the number of generations linking Ego to an ancestor (as in the Civil Law and Canon Law models).
2. Let i be the number of generations linking Ego to a descendant or linking a common ancestor to a collateral relative of Ego.
3. For lineal relatives of Ego (i.e., ancestors and descendants), the degree

of parentage p is $(½)^{(i,j)}$. For parents, $j = 1$ and $p = ½$; for grand-children, $i = 2$ and $p = ¼$, and so on.

4. For collateral relatives, the degree of parentage p is the product $(½)^j$ $(½)^{i-1}$. For an aunt, $p = (½)^2 (½)^0 = ¼$; for a first-cousin, $p = (½)^2$ $(½)^1 = 1/8$, and so forth. (Where half-siblings are involved, $p = (½)^j$ $(½)^i$.)

The configuration of genealogical distances by degree of shared chromo-somes is presented in Table 1-2c. A comparison between the Genetic model and the Canon Law degree indicates that the two procedures produce similar results for most close relatives and for children of Ego's direct ancestors. For other collateral relatives, however, the genetic proximity seems to re-semble the Civil Law degree in assigning priorities. For example, the brother's great-grandchildren and the aunt's grandchildren (in the Georgia case) both are the same degree of parentage from Ego, $p = 1/16$. The parentage degree thus seems to combine elements of both the Canon Law and Civil Law models.

Cruz-Coke (1977, p. 99) suggests that the Genetic model be applied in laws pertaining to "prohibited marriages, inheritance of property, and even royal succession." Unlike the other models of genealogical priorities, the Genetic model is capable of assigning precise locations on a genealogical map to identical twins and to half-siblings and their descendants. For ex-ample, where Ego is an identical twin, Ego's niece is genetically equivalent to Ego's own child, $p = ½$; where Ego has a half-sibling, the daughter of Ego's half-sibling is genetically equivalent to a granddaughter of Ego's full sibling, $p = 1/8$. Because of growing divorce and remarriage rates in contemporary society, it may be useful to make a distinction between half- and full-sibling ties in future legislation regarding incestuous marriage and intestacy.

Table 1-2. *(continued)*

C. GENETIC MODEL

	Distance from Ego: Fraction of chromosomes shared			
Generation	1	1/2	1/4	1/8
2			Grandparents	Great aunts and great uncles
1		Parents	Aunts and uncles	
0	EGO	Siblings		First cousins
−1		Children	Nieces and nephews	
−2			Grandchildren	Grandnieces and grandnephews

Comparison of Models

The four procedures for determining genealogical priorities involve variations in the application of generational links to relatives (i and j). The Parentela Orders model differs from the others, however, in determining the relative priorities of ascendants as opposed to descendants. For the Canon Law, Civil Law, and Genetic models, i and j are symmetrical, and consequently, their size relative to each other makes no difference in computing the degree of distance. A large i and small j are equivalent in degree of distance to a small i and a large j. For Parentela Orders, however, i and j are not symmetrical. The j is weighted by ($m + 1$), but the i is not. As a result, in the Parentela Orders procedure all descendants have priority over any ancestors.

The models differ primarily in their treatment of collateral relatives of Ego. For collateral relatives, they each deal with the combinations of i and j in a different way:

Parentela Orders: Priority $= i + (m + 1)j$, where m refers to the largest i in the set of relatives considered.

Civil Law: degree of distance $= (i + j)$.

Canon Law: degree of distance $= i$ or j, whichever is larger.

Genetic model: degree of parentage $= (\frac{1}{2})^{i-1} (\frac{1}{2})^{j}$. (For half-siblings, $p = (\frac{1}{2})^{i} (\frac{1}{2})^{j}$).

KINSHIP AND SOCIAL STRUCTURE

Laws governing classifications of relatives in marriage and inheritance have persisted in their general outlines from earlier historical eras to contemporary urban society despite great demographic and technological upheavals. These classification schemes permit both (a) the establishment of boundaries for determining when marriages are considered to be incestuous and (b) the formulation of priorities among relatives in cases of intestacy. Essentially, the same principles that were applied in ancient Israel, Greece, and Rome and in medieval ecclesiastical law still endure in the legal codes governing incestuous marriage and intestacy in the contemporary world. Even newly formed nations follow the rules for classifying relatives drawn from (a) the Parentela Orders model derived from ancient Israel and classical Greece, (b) the Civil Law model from Roman civil law, or (c) the Canon Law model developed in the medieval Church.

The survival of the Canon Law, Civil Code, and Parentela Orders models in modern law suggests that they continue to be relevant to the organization of family and kinship relations in the contemporary world. This relevance can perhaps be clarified by reference to comparisons with nonindustrial societies. The analyses of nonindustrial societies by Eisenstadt (1977), Swanson

(1967; 1969), and Paige (1974) seem to converge in their conclusions regarding the relationship between the mode of political integration in a society and the character of family and kinship institutions.

Implicitly, Eisenstadt, Swanson, and Paige seem to assume that social order is generated, in part, by the need to regulate the distribution of scarce things. There emerges, then, an opposition between a *just* distribution of goods and property for use by the current generation, that acts to equalize life chances for people throughout the society, and a *competitive* distribution of goods and property, that tends to maximize life chances for some people and their descendants more than for others. The motive toward just distribution serves to create an extensive network of families, weaving the society into a cohesive whole. The motive toward competitive distribution serves to establish a hierarchical structure involving congeries of related families, dividing the society into differentiated strata.

As a result of this opposition, two conflicting kinds of kinship structure may develop—one kind supporting the special interests of the congeries of related families and the other kind promoting the common interests that all families in the society share. The different kinds of family and kinship structures expressing special versus common interests in the society have been conceptualized in various ways by different writers.

Generally, writers tend to characterize those family structures that express special interests of a particular group in terms of some sort of corporate reality and those family structures which express communal welfare in terms of personal inclinations and obligations. In each instance, in describing family life that is organized to promote a special interest, the writer endows the kinship group with political, economic and/or religious significance. For example, Jeffrey Paige (1974) shows that in stateless societies, factional political structure is associated with patrilocal (or virilocal) marital residence, which permits related men to act as a cohesive unit in civil affairs. He opposes this form of kinship organization to that found in communal stateless societies, whereby related men (especially brothers) are dispersed, and their ability to mobilize kinship-based groups is limited. Similarly, Guy E. Swanson (1969) has shown that a distinction between associational and social-system emphasis in political regime is related to kinship structure and to religious belief. In one analysis, he has indicated that factional societies that emphasize associational bases for collective action tend to be patrilineal, whereas those societies that stress the common welfare of all members, identifying the political regime as serving the whole social system as a single entity, tend to be matrilineal in kinship organization. (In a second analysis, he has shown a relationship between factional regimes and a propensity for states at the time of the Reformation to become Protestant as opposed to communal states, where the immanence of God is widely believed, to remain Catholic.) A third writer, Shmuel Eisenstadt has dealt with the distinction between patrimonial and imperial regimes. In his conceptualization, patrimonial regimes are characterized by the clustering of kinship groups in ways that impinge upon economic, political, and/or religious institutions of the society, whereas in imperial regimes, kinship structures are relatively independent of other considerations. In addition, Eisenstadt suggests that while imperial regimes are structured in ways which reveal a dominant core and periphery, patrimonial regimes are generally decentralized.

All three conceptualizations—i.e., by Paige, Swanson, and Eisenstadt— share the following characteristics: (a) There is a relationship between the development of kinship structure and the relative emphasis in political structure upon special interests versus general welfare. (b) Societies which have factional (or special-interest) regimes are marked by a strong dependence of political and economic groups upon kinship ties; societies which have communal (or general-interest) regimes are marked by differentiated political and economic structures (i.e., isolated structurally from kinship). (c) In societies with factional regimes, kinship structures are organized to act as the primary vehicles for the continuity of the social order; in societies with communal regimes, kinship structures are organized to permit other corporate groups to act as the primary vehicle for the continuity of the social order.

These statements about the relationship between kinship and social structure are drawn from research on nonindustrial societies. Yet, in principle, they seem appropriate to contemporary societies as well. In his analysis of modern social structure, Edward Shils (1975) applies an approach similar to that of Paige, Swanson, and Eisenstadt. Shils conceptualizes social order in terms of center and periphery, which corresponds in some respects to the distinction between communal and factional structures. "This centrality has, however, nothing to do with geometry and little with geography (Shils, 1975, p. 3)." Rather, for Shils (1975, p. 3):

> The center, or the central zone, is a phenomenon of the realm of values and beliefs. It is the center of the order of symbols, of values and beliefs which govern the society. It is the center because it is the ultimate and irreducible; and it is felt to be such by many who cannot give explicit articulation to its irreducibility. The central zone partakes of the nature of the sacred.

Shils notes that, as compared with earlier eras, modern technological advance has elevated the standard of living and "integrated the population into a more unified economy" and, simultaneously, there has been "more widespread participation in the central value system through education, and in the central institutional system through the franchise and mass communication (Shils, 1975, p. 14)." One effect of this "incorporation of the mass of the population into the central institutional and value systems" is an emphasis upon a concern with the common interests (and consequent equal treatment) of the members of the society.

With an incorporation of the population into this centralized culture, dominant institutions that enable the society to persist as an integrated entity tend to be those of national scope. Major decisions affecting personal destinies are made in large-scale bureaucracies and their supporting agencies. In a centralized culture, the important things in life are those which override parochial interests and local concerns.

However, Shils regards the integration of institutions in modern society as existing in a state of constant tension between the tendencies for the common good and separatist tendencies deriving from special interests. On the one hand, "the common good cannot be realized in a society consisting only of private entities (Shils, 1975, p. 340)." Yet, on the other hand, "even the most integrated society ever known is riddled with cleavages and antagonistic actions (Shils, 1975, p. 85)," and "scarcity, ambition, human contrariness, divergent traditions, conflicting loyalties, and the great unevenness of ecological integration all stand in the way of anything closely approximating a stable, continuous, inclusive, all-embracing cultural and authoritative integration (Shils, 1975, p. 84)."

Shils emphasizes that along side the centralization of culture and its institutional base, there exist collectivities that have been alienated in some manner from the cultural core. These alienated collectivities seek to promote special interests that they perceive to be undermined by the institutional complex supporting incorporation of the mass of the population into the centralized culture. The continual expansion of the core of "public interest" encroaches upon their special domains of religious, ethnic, or economic interest. The threat evoked by this encroachment mobilizes these collectivities to counteract the influence of the "core."

In their reaction to centralization of culture for the "public interest," special-focus collectivities apparently rely not only upon associational means (e.g., religious, welfare, and educational agencies) but also upon communal institutions, such as kinship and family, to sustain an independent identity. Even in a bilateral society, kinship seems able to serve as an effective vehicle for the persistence of (or the enhancement of) the "important things of life." It provides a ready-made base for establishing generational continuity and personal loyalty. Shils (1975, p. 122) suggests that kinship forms a primordial foundation for community.

> The attachment to another member of one's kinship group is not just a function of interaction, as Professor Homans would have it. It is because a certain ineffable significance is attributed to the tie of blood. Even where affection [is] not great, the tangibility of the attachment to the other person, by virtue of our perception of his membership in the kinship group, is clearly in evidence.

The attachment, in order to be effective, however, seems to me to require a central idea around which relatives can rally in mobilizing themselves and their resources. For middleman minorities, this central idea unites kinship with ethnic and economic survival; for religious sects and minority religions, family becomes a vehicle for achieving a set of religious ideals. (Some groups may of course utilize formally-organized associations as an *alternative* to kinship; but when they do, they also presumably disentangle norms pertaining to family and socialization of children from the goals implied in the central idea. By relying only upon formal associations for perpetuating an ideal, these groups must then continually recruit outsiders to participate in their programmatic efforts.) Only by mobilizing family and kinship structures in support of the central idea can factionalist, separatist, or alienated groups create an ensured supply of adherents generation after generation.

The endurance of a central idea that transcends immediate personal need requires particular kinds of norms connecting this idea to kinship structure. It is undoubtedly true that under most circumstances dire need will facilitate the creation of close ties between individual relatives. But lacking a unifying special interest, once personal needs abate, these ties may eventually dissolve, and chances are slim that the succeeding generation, unless it also faces severe problems, will maintain firm kinship bonds. Without a transcendant reason (such as unique community status, minority religion, or ethnicity), there is little initial motivation to concentrate resources among people with close genealogical ties. The presence of a transcendant interest, however, justifies the persistence of kinship structures beyond a single generation without regard to individual privation. Consequently, the transcendental interest not only fosters strong personal commitments, but it also provides a basis for the formation of centripetal kinship norms. By developing norms which sustain a centripetal focus, kinship groups encourage member families to maintain an identifiable structure over generations.

Concentration of kinship resources in modern society over an extended time requires a constant battle with the corporate repositories which constitute the core of control over society. Indeed, the governmental, industrial, and educational bureaucracies in modern society encourage residential and social movement as a means for maximizing utilization of human resources. More and more modern society discourages nonbureaucratic personal commitments (a) by emphasizing personal freedom in non-work affairs and (b) by defining traditional family and kinship institutions as coercive, as ineffective loci of socialization, and as interfering with self-realization in a post-industrial world (e.g., note stress upon the "costs of family life" in Morgan (1975)).

But despite this attempted redefinition of family and kinship structures, there is some evidence to suggest that "primordial" collectivities, based on kinship ties, do persist as viable structures in contemporary society. In his study of urban social structure, Laumann (1973, p. 203) decides that:

> While it would be quite foolish for us. . .to conclude that the American urban scene is a mosaic of highly differentiated, self-contained nationality-religious

groups, it would be equally foolish for us simply to dismiss them as being of little or no importance in accounting for the vitality and heterogeneity of contemporary urban life.

As instruments for mobilizing humans and their resources for attaining special goals—often millenial—family and kinship institutions cannot be considered as obsolete; rather they are seen by some collectivities as being highly relevant to the endurance of group identity over generations. Indeed, in these collectivities, kinship ties are regarded as the very vehicles by which the important things of life endure. Rather, these collectivities consider *individualistic* decisions and adaptations made to meet personal needs as resulting in the long run in a *decrease* in the ability of their families to affect "who gets what, when, where, how, and why"—compared with others.

As noted previously, the analysis by Shils about the tension between the centralization of culture in the "public interest" and the pluralism of "primordial" collectivities somewhat parallels the studies of nonindustrial societies that distinguish between factional and communal regimes (or between patrimonial and imperialistic regimes) (Paige, 1974; Swanson, 1969; Eisenstadt, 1977). The analyses share in (a) their focus upon the relationship between the whole and the parts of the society as a significant aspect of social order; (b) their concern with common interests (or public interests) versus special interests (or private interests) as motivations for generating different social structures; (c) their conclusion that special interests tend to segmentalize societies and break down boundaries between institutions, while common interests tend to sharpen differentiation of boundaries between institutions but destroy boundaries between population segments; and (d) their belief that kinship structure is an important element in determining the character of the social order.

The computational models which form the focus of this study emerged in social orders analogous to the regimes discussed by Eisenstadt, Swanson, and Paige. In the history of Western civilization, (a) the Parentela Orders model of kinship priorities developed in a social setting that fostered an emphasis upon the perpetuation of the "house," along with the development of centripetal kinship norms; (b) the Civil Law model arose in a social setting in which an effort was made to maintain a balance between "family" and civil society; and (c) the Canon Law model was developed in a social setting in which the perpetuation of the "family" was considered as subordinate to the perpetuation of major corporate groups, such as the Church or State.

The stress between centralization and pluralism suggests that contemporary social settings parallel the historical situations from which the kinship models under investigation emerged. The diversity of social settings in a highly complex society may stimulate different emphasis upon the role of kinship in persistence of social order. Thus, the following speculations seem reasonable:

1. Some families exist in settings that reflect their concern for perpetuating special interests. These families are "sectarian" in either a religious or secular sense. These groups may be characterized by a minority religion or they may have a special interest in maintaining a particular socioeconomic position or ethnic identity. These families will appropriate ideas about kinship priorities which follow the Parentela Orders model.

2. Some families exist in settings that reflect concern with the common welfare of the society. Universalistic in outlook, these families affiliate or identify with religious groups that are less sectarian and that may emphasize the ubiquitous immanence of God in everyday life; they emphasize individualism as an expression of equal rights and/or the predominance of general corporate structures (such as government or economy) by which the general well-being of the society is perpetuated. The families would appropriate ideas about priorities that approximate the Canon Law or Genetic models.

3. Some families reach a compromise between the special demands of family continuity and the more general welfare of the civil society. These families appropriate ideas about kinship priorities which approximate the Civil Law model.

Basic to the plan of analysis in this monograph is an assumption that there are only limited modes of organizing family and kinship structures in relation to the larger social structure. These modes are expressed in legal codes pertaining to the continuity of family and kinship "properties," primarily in those laws governing succession and incestuous marriage. In Western society, three general models have been applied to succession and incestuous marriage—the Parentela Orders, the Civil Code, and the Canon Law. I regard these models as markers for popular conceptions about the extent to which family and kinship are considered to be important for transmitting the important things about life from generation to generation. Consequently, the analysis focuses upon the degree to which people in different social contexts (and with different ideas about the family and children) also differ in the extent to which they conform to the configuration of relatives implied in each model.

Putatively, the kinship models express orientations to ways of perpetuating the "important things of life": To the extent that people in "sectarian" settings regard the family as a vehicle by which their way of life will be perpetuated, they will also: (a) have a larger number of children; (b) give greater weight to family obligations than work obligations; (c) give greater importance to maintaining ties with parents and in-laws and with grandparents; (d) regard marriage as a special status rather than as a mere formalization of a man-woman relationship; and (e) consider inducement of self-discipline and instrumental "adultlike" orientation to the world as important aims in socialization.

As significant determinants in organizing family life, the kinship orientations expressed by a model should emerge in specific kinds of social contexts rather than appear as ephemeral concerns which predominate at different stages of the family life cycle or merely as expressions of interpersonal relations.

POPULAR COUNTERPARTS OF LEGAL MODELS

This introductory chapter has discussed legal models for assigning priorities among relatives. Although their applicability to intestacy laws and for defining marital prohibitions may be obvious, their implication with regard to social structure, kinship ties, family interaction, and socialization of children may not be. The remaining chapters of this book will be concerned with an elaboration of these implications. Chapter 2 deals with the historical settings in which these models emerged. Each historical setting seems to have presented a different kind of problem with regard to the role of family and kinship in the persistence of social structure. Chapter 3 turns to modern social settings, and it involves study of ways in which the place of groups in the larger social structure is related to metaphors of social space. The conception of social space is considered to be a function of group boundedness (e.g., independent identity as a faction, sect, or some other social class) in relation to the rest of the society. Chapter 4 presents a new kinship model which emerged through an analysis of cases in the residual category of kinship orientations. This model happens to be widely prevalent among middle-class Protestants. The chapter also describes a componential analysis of the kinship models which reveals their relationship to spatial metaphors. Chapter 5 pertains to diversity in kinship orientation among different segments of the population, and it compares the efficacy of structural variables (such as religion, ethnicity, and socioeconomic status) with that of personal factors in explaining variation in kinship orientation. Chapter 6 deals with the significance of the family of orientation (i.e., the parental family) in determining kinship conceptions, and Chapter 7 with the relationship between kinship orientation and attributes regarding one's family of procreation (i.e., with spouse and children). Chapter 8, based on theories of social exchange, concerns the connection between kinship orientation and actual ties with relatives. Finally, Chapter 9 offers a summary and a set of conclusions drawn from the analysis. As a check on spurious interpretations of the findings, a multivarate analysis was undertaken. The results of this analysis are presented in Appendix A. The methods of data collection are discussed in Appendix B.

Historical Backgrounds of Kinship Models

2

Now I turn to the specific historical contexts in which the kinship models under investigation have emerged. The weight of evidence is that these kinship models were not taken over willy-nilly in the laws where they have been used. Instead, indications are that persons who formulated these laws have found alternative models wanting, and new models were invented to eliminate deficiencies of those then in existence (See Selden, 1636, 1640.). For instance, the Romans dispatched three commissioners to examine the legal systems of the Greek city-states (especially Athens) when the Twelve Tables were derived at the beginning of the Republic (Heitland, 1923, I, 70). Since the Twelve Tables do not follow the Athenian mode of computing kinship distances, presumably the commissioners regarded that procedure as inappropriate.

Similarly, one can consider the invention of the Canon Law scheme for determining genealogical distances as a critique of the Roman system. Originally, "The Christian law took over the Roman system of reckoning relationship as explained by Paulus [and later incorporated into the Justinian Code,] that is, each generation [either ascending or descending] constituted a degree (Smith, 1940, p. 24)." But considerable controversy ensued among those who formulated canon law. Commentators, such as Pope Alexander II, thought that the Justinian mode of counting kinship distances made first cousins appear to be much more distantly related than they considered them to be. "Applied to the church laws of marriage, this method of calculation would have the effect of contracting by half the severity of the canonical prohibitions of marriage among relatives (Smith, 1940, pp. 28–29)." Consequently, the canonists sought a procedure that would more adequately reflect their conceptions about an appropriate definition of extremely close kinship ties.

Significantly, in the past 800 years, legal codes governing incestuous marriage and intestacy have been able to utilize these earlier kinship models without significant revision. Even the recent emergence of the socialist blocs of Eastern Europe has not yet generated new models. (See, for example, Johnson, 1969, p. 188). The only contemporary development in computation procedures pertaining to consanguinity has come from the study of genetics. The

Genetic model was invented in the 20th century to accommodate knowledge about the mechanics of biological kinship through chromosomal reproduction. At least for close relatives, however, the Genetic model generally produces the same configuration of kin as the Canon Law procedure.

The persistence of traditional kinship models in contemporary law suggests that these models still express a meaningful dimension in the life of modern society. The appropriateness of a kinship model apparently does not depend primarily upon degree of industrialization or modernity; rather it seems to rely more upon the place of kinship in the particular cultural context. By examining the historical conditions in which each kinship model has emerged, we should be able to infer the kinds of functions kinship is expected to play wherever that model is applied. The sections below sketch the historical and religious backgrounds out of which Parentela Orders, Civil Law, and Canon Law models were developed.

The description of these historical contexts is not meant to imply a unilineal evolution from one model to another; there may be no necessary evolutionary connection between them. Rather the intention is merely to propose that certain kinds of kinship models have an affinity for particular modes of social structure.

PARENTELA ORDERS MODEL:
JUDAIC AND ATHENIAN BACKGROUNDS

The Parentela Orders model is found both in Judaism and Classical Athens. There are several parallels in Judaic and Athenian social structure that seem to be related to this model. In both societies, (a) kinship units provided the basic political entities; (b) the continuity of social structure depended upon the ability of succeeding generations to carry on familial and religious traditions; (c) the concept of contract underlay the justifications of norms of family and kinship; (d) kinship endogamy was preferred; and so on. Jack Goody suggests that the parallels between Judaic and Athenian marriage norms derive from similar inheritance systems.

> This tendency [towards kinship endogamy] is particularly marked where women are heirs, or even residual heirs, to property of interest to males, for they may be encouraged or obliged to marry within a certain range of kin; this was the case with the daughters of Zelophehad in ancient Israel as well as in the epiclerate of classical Athens (Goody, 1976, p. 14).

Because of this series of similarities between family and kinship norms in ancient Judaism and classical Athens, it may be instructive to review relationships among social structure, the concept of contract, and intestacy law in these two societies.

Judaic Law

Historically, Jewish legal scholars have assigned the family a central role in social organization. To Maimonides (1963, 1967), for example, the family is the basic element in the maintenance of a just social order. In his *Guide of the Perplexed,* Maimonides (1963, pp. 601–602) locates the core of ethical conduct within the family in that:

> Fraternal sentiments and mutual love and mutual help can be found in their perfect form only among those who are related by their ancestry. Accordingly a single tribe that is united through a common ancestor—even if he is remote— because of this, love one another, help one another, and have pity on one another; and the attainment of these things is the greatest purpose of the Law.

A similarity to Classical Greece is noted in Plato (*Laws,* 790b): "When the right regulation of private households within a society is neglected, it is idle to expect the foundations of public law to be secure." Thus both Maimonides and Plato consider the family to be more fundamental than the state in the perpetuation of social order. In both conceptions of society the perpetuation of "tribe" (*mishpokheh*) or "house" (*oikos*) represent special interests that must be attended to if the social order is to persist. The state itself endures only by giving priority to these domestic interests. The political regime itself is not the core of social structure that dominates the individual lives of the members of the society. Rather, its existence is contingent on the fundamental obligations to the family and the "house."

Obligations deriving from the Convenant are basic in Jewish religion and in family continuity. The concept of Covenant appears in Genesis XVII, where God proposes to Abraham that in exchange for an enduring, "wholehearted" commitment by the descendants of Abraham "throughout their generations," God will protect them and give to them "the land of [their] sojourns" (Hertz, 1960, pp. 58–59). A second statement is found in Exodus XIX, 5–6. Here, God tells Moses that by undertaking the mission of bringing other nations "closer to God and Righteousness" by being "a kingdom of priests and a holy nation," they would be his "treasure." The Exodus statement is elaborated in commentary in a way that emphasizes the metaphor of a long-term economic arrangement. According to the commentary:"God asked Israel, 'What sureties have you to give that you will keep My Convenant?' They offered the Patriarchs, the Prophets and their righteous rulers as their guarantors. But all of them were rejected. It was only when they offered their children as sureties for the permanence of the Covenant, that they were accepted (Hertz, 1960, p. 291)."

The symbolism in regarding children as pledged property to ensure the carrying out the terms of a contract has several implications for family and kinship. First, grace or salvation is not a function of an individual's own conduct, but it is instead dependent upon the conduct of descendants and, consequently, one is constrained to emphasize intergenerational obligations: the socialization of children for "righteous" lives and the maintenance of filial piety. Second, there is no closure to the contract: it is "everlasting". Since there is no completion of the terms of the contract, each generation passes on its obligations to the next, like an infinitely-repeating decimal number. As a result, the social structure—in this case, the family and kindred—that sustains these reciprocities endures without ever ending generational obligations. (See Lévi-Strauss, 1969). Hence, kinship continuity is to be realized even at heavy costs—and the concerns of succession are foremost.

The intestacy laws of traditional Judaism place much emphasis upon generational obligations to perpetuate the family. In his *Mishneh Torah,* Maimonides indicates:

> The sages of the Talmud established the following order of legal heirs: 1) sons and their descendants; 2) daughters and their descendants; 3) the father; 4) brothers and their descendants; 5) sisters and their descendants; 6) the father's father; 7) the father's brothers and their descendants; 8) the father's sisters and their descendants; 9) the father's father's father; and so on. To this list, implied in the biblical passages, the sages added another legal heir, the husband, whose right to the inheritance of his wife's possessions was inferred from the biblical expression "nearest relative" (Numbers 27:11). Each son of the deceased receives an equal share of the estate, except the firstborn of the father, who receives a double share. Where there are neither sons nor sons' children, the daughters and their descendants become the rightful heirs. . . .When there are no heirs in the descending line, the property is transmitted to the nearest relative in the ascending line. The father takes priority over the brothers of the deceased in the absence of either sons or daughters (Maimonides, 1967, pp. 292–293).

The priorities in succession described by Maimonides had been established in Judaic law in the *Mishnah,* which was compiled following the destruction of the Temple. Radin (1915, p. 69) suggests that the "creation of houses of prayer demanded local organization, and with local organization gradations of members and the establishment of local magistrates. . . .The organization of the Greek city-state, familiar to the East for many years, became a model for these corporately organized [Jewish] communities" in the Diaspora. Apparently, the necessity for creating a common social order among these autonomous Jewish communities had stimulated the codification of Oral Law in the *Mishnah.*

Although the order of priorities in succession was similar to Greek law, I have not been able to determine the historical sequence. The *Mishnah* justified the ordering on the basis of Biblical references and rabbinical commentary. The priorities are discussed in the Fourth Division of the *Mishnah,* called Nezikin, in the section Baba Bathra, subsections 8 and 9 (Danby, 1933, pp. 376–379). The justifications appearing in *The Babylonian Talmud* (Epstein, 1935, II, pp. 463–478) are founded on the assumption that, "A tribe [must] not be blotted out from Israel" (Judges, XXI, 17). Accordingly, "So shall no inheritance of the children of Israel remove from tribe to tribe (Numbers, XXXVI, 8)" and, "So shall no inheritance remove from one tribe to another tribe (Numbers, XXXVI, 9)." To assure that the continuity of the tribe or family, *The Babylonian Talmud* (Epstein, 1935, II, p. 474) proposes that:

> Once it has been definitely established that none of the line survives, enquiries are instituted in an ascending order, on the paternal side, and are carried on from father (including their heirs, as in the case of the descending line), until the first ancestor of the tribe is reached.

The *Mishnah* then establishes the principle for the order of inheritance in Judaic law:

> This is the general rule: The lineal descendants of any one with a priority to succession take precedence. A father takes precedence over all his descendants (Epstein, 1935, II, p. 478; cf. Danby, 1933, p. 376).

The order of priorities described in the *Mishnah* has been applied in other historical settings as well. Classical Athenian society of the fourth century represents such a setting. The parallels between Jewish communities of the Diaspora and Greek city-states suggest a similar role to be played by family and kinship in maintaining the social structure. The Athenian emphasis on the continuity of the household, the significance of the concept of contract in social relationships, and the importance of intergenerational obligations express these parallels.

Classical Greek Law

The Athenian model of assigning priorities in succession seems to presuppose a society consisting of autonomous segments, co-existing in a common territory, and vying for resources and striving to maintain their individual identities. This conception is consistent with the partitioning of the Greek peninsula into city-states. Ehrenberg (1946, pp. 29–52) suggests that the Greek terrain dictated the structuring of political units into a matrix of city-states rather than an empire with a single major urban center as a core. Given a land "divided into numerous small parts and particles," classical Greece was a quiltwork of autonomous city-states converging on one another and competing for resources and soil. Each city-state tended to develop independent political, economic, and cultural attributes. Yet, they existed "in such a close proximity to one another, that no natural and political boundaries could exclude strife and struggle, while at the same time every State was fully aware of the resources and power of its neighbor (Ehrenberg, 1946, p. 42)." Despite conflicts, no single city-state became the core of an empire. Ehrenberg indicates that, "Even Athens never attained more than a temporary and tyrannical hegemony. The Athenian Confederacy was the rule of Athens over a wide area, but it never became a true empire, because it never became one state (Ehrenberg, 1946, p. 45)." Consequently, for the ancient Greeks, the world was not perceived as an organism with a dominant core extending its influence over a periphery. Rather they thought in terms of the special interests of political entities struggling to survive and prosper vis-a-vis each other (Ehrenberg, 1946, p. 45).

The basic political unit within classical Athens was the *oikos,* that is, the family as a corporate unity, the "house." In fact, Harrison (1968, p. 1) considers the *oikos* to be "the constituent elements of the Athenian city state." One could not be registered as a citizen of Athens without *oikos* membership. Because of this political use of the family, it was imperative to ensure the continuity of the *oikos.* The political significance of the *oikos* was complemented by its religious importance. The continuity of the *oikos* depended, in part, upon the fulfillment of religious obligations in the family cult over successive generations. Indeed, becoming an heir involved an obligation to participate in the sacred rites of the *oikos* (Harrison, 1968, p. 130).

In Athens, the concept of ownership (as power over the disposition of property or persons) was more limited than in Rome. The Athenians placed a greater emphasis upon contractual arrangements, which permitted specified uses of property with the stated limits of the contract—rather than the unlimited domain by paternal power (*patria potestas*) or by the persisting power of "spirits" (*genius*) in Roman society. The limitations of contract seem to have pervaded all relationships within the family, including marriage (Harrison, 1968).

The concept of contract or negotiated reciprocity forms an important aspect of Aristotle's Nicomachean Ethics and consequently of his views regarding family ties. Aristotle (Book V. 5, 1132–1133) notes:

> It is by proportionate requital that the city holds together. Men seek to return either evil for evil. . .or good for good—and if they cannot do so there is no exchange, but it is by exchange that they hold together. . . .If it had not been possible for reciprocity to be. . .effected, there would have been no association of the parties. That demand holds things together as a single unit is shown by the fact that when men do not need one another, i.e., when neither needs the other or one does not need the other, they do not exchange. . . .We do not allow a *man* to rule, but *rational principle,* because a man behaves thus in his own interests and becomes a tyrant [whereas the rule of reciprocity produces stable relationships based on justice.]

Aristotle considers the family as a locus of intensified justice. He regards the *oikos* as ''earlier and more necessary than the city (Book VIII, 12, 1162).'' Identifying family ties as a category of friendship, he indicates that ''the demands of justice. . .seem to increase with the intensity of the friendship (Book VIII, 9, 1160).'' (Compare with Fortes, 1969, pp. 219–249, on axiom of amity in kinship). Not that Aristotle equates friendship with egalitarianism; instead, he views the household as a friendship among persons of unequal status—for the sons, the household constitution is a monarchy; for the wife an aristocracy; and for brothers a timocracy. But above all justice is fundamental to household structure:

> The friendship between a king and his subjects depends on an excess of benefits conferred. . . .Such too is the friendship of a father, though this exceeds the other in the greatness of the benefits conferred; for he is responsible for the existence of his children, which is thought the greatest good, and for their nurture and upbringing. These things are ascribed to ancestors as well. Further, by nature, a father tends to rule over his sons, ancestor over descendants. . . .These friendships imply superiority of one party over the other, which is why ancestors are honored (Aristotle, Book VIII, 11, 1161).

The emphasis upon generational differentiation of obligations in the family, which Aristotle applies in his discussion of just familial relationships, finds expression in the intestacy laws of Athens. These laws follow the same principles as those of the *Mishnah* with regard to priorities.

The order of succession in intestacy laws of classical Athens is as follows:

1. ''First in order of succession came the legitimate sons. . . .Rights of succession of descendants did not. . .run out after the third generation, but the line of heirs continued theoretically *ad infinitum* (Harrison, 1968, pp. 130–131).''

2. ''If a man died leaving behind him no sons but only a daughter or daughters. . . .the daughters became heiresses (Harrison, 1968, p. 132).''

3. ''If a father had a claim upon his son for maintenance in his old age, *a fortiori* he had a claim upon the sons's property if the son died first. . . .A man's heir might be his paternal or even his maternal uncle; and it would seem irrational that these relatives should succeed to the exclusion of his father (Harrison, 1968, pp. 139–141).''

4. ''There were two terms which were used to embrace relatives other than ascendants or descendants. There were *anchisteia* and *syngeneia*. The former of these was the narrower and the more technical. It denoted all those who were related to the deceased, whether on the father's or the mother's side, down to and including sons of cousins (i.e., first cousins once removed), or possibly down to and including second cousins. . . .For the law of succession it determined the limit of relatives of the deceased's father who were entitled before relatives of his mother could come in; a father's first cousin

once removed (possibly a father's second cousin) would take before any relative on the mother's side. The term *syngeneia* on the other hand had no such restrictive use and would apply to relatives beyond this limit. Thus all *anchisteia* were *syngeneia,* but not all *syngeneia* were *anchisteia.*

"Within the *anchisteia* there was a fixed order of relatives entitled to succeed on the father's side, and then, if there was no representative of any of these classes on his side, succession passed to relatives on the mother's side in the same order. Anyone in a nearer group excluded all those more distantly related, while those in the same group shared equally; if one in a group had predeceased the *de cuius* leaving children, those children took his share in equal portions. . . .This is the order: (1) brothers of the deceased by the same father and their descendants without limit; sharing was *per stirpes* [i.e., the share of a deceased heir goes to his children]; (2) sisters of the deceased by the same father and their descendants without limit, also sharing *per stirpes;* (3) paternal uncles, their children, and grandchildren; (4) paternal aunts, their children and grandchildren; there would come next (4a) paternal great-uncles with their children and grandchildren and (4b) paternal great-aunts with their children and grandchildren; (5) brothers of the deceased by the same mother; (6) sisters by the same mother, both with descendants without limit; (7) maternal uncles; (8) maternal aunts, in both cases with their children and grandchildren. . . . This exhaused the *anchisteia.* If there were no relatives within the *anchisteia* the law simply uses for the next entitled the vague phrase 'the nearest on the father's side' (Harrison, 1968, pp. 143–146)."

ROME AND THE CIVIL LAW MODEL

The Civil Law model is rooted in the history of ancient Rome. Before the founding of the Roman Republic, the Patricians, essentially "tribal" heads, provided the governing elite. The Senate itself was a body of these Patricians. Then, as the economic base of Roman society expanded, the power of the Plebian masses increased (Mommsen, 1905, I, p. 342–7). In about 450 B.C., with the creation of the Republic, the Twelve Tables were produced, and the distinction between Patricians and Plebians was reduced. The power of the Plebians was extended, and five years after the issuance of the Twelve Tables, marriages between Plebian and Patrician families could be validly contracted (Mommsen, 1905, I, p. 371; Heitland, 1923, I, p. 95, Sec. 121). The broadening of the body politic weakened those official policies which required strong centripetal kinship ties as a basis for sustaining the social order.

The cultural context of the Roman Republic differed in significant ways from that of the Greeks. Although the Greek gods were regarded as persons, Roman deities were more abstract (Radin, 1915). This difference became especially important with the growth of Roman imperialism. In their conquests, the Romans had to face problems about the domains of the deities in ways far different from those of the Greeks. Since Greek wars involved subjugation of autonomous states, conquest did not demand a change in the jurisdiction of the gods. Roman imperialism, however, necessitated an expansion of the province of the Roman gods—a universalization of authority—and the importation of the gods of the conquered peoples into Rome (Radin, 1915, pp. 44–46). There was thus a close connection between universalistic religious domains of the gods and the imperialism of Roman society.

The universalism in religion and political sphere extended to the Roman family. *Patria potestas* refers not merely to the head of a household, rather it extends to "the children of the sons and more remote descendants through males, without any limit other than that imposed by the span of human life (Jolowicz, 1967, p. 118)." The *paterfamilias*—the oldest male ancestor—had complete control over the private lives of his unemancipated descendants but lacked jurisdiction over their civil (public) lives. Married females were now governed by another *paterfamilias*.

Through its connection with the extensiveness of power, the agnatic group became the significant entity in Roman kinship. "Two people are related agnatically if they are in the *patria potestas* of the same man, or if there is some common ancestor in whose power they would both be if he were alive (Jolowicz, 1967, p. 122)." The relevance of this agnatic group for maintaining collateral ties is suggested by laws governing intestacy in the XII Tables, compiled around 450 B.C. (Jolowicz, 1967, pp. 4–5). The major difference between the Athenian and Roman models for computing kinship distances lies in the degree to which they distinguish between lineal and collateral relatives. The Athenian model regards direct-line relatives as primary links to Ego and considers collateral relatives only as secondary extensions of lineal kin. The Roman model, however, gives equal weight to both lineal and collateral descent. The agnatic group, referring to persons related to each other through males, attaches greater importance to collateral relatives than does the *oikos* of Athens or the "house" of the Jews.

The intestacy laws in the XII Tables provide for the following order of succession:

1. "If a man dies intestate the first people entitled to succeed to his estate are his *sui heredes*, all those in his *patria potestas* or *manus* [i.e., in hand] (Jolowicz, 1967, p. 123)." According to Watson (1971, p. 176), "All *sui*, male or female, who were children of the deceased, and his wife *in manu*, took equal shares." Grandchildren, however, were capable of inheriting only by representation.

2. "Failing *sui heredes* the succession goes to the nearest agnate or agnates, if there are several in the same degree (Jolowicz, 1967, pp. 123–124)."

3. "In default of agnates the succession went to the *gentiles* [i.e., members of the *gens*]. . . .The rights of the *gens* were anterior to those of the agnates. . . .We do not know whether the *gens* took as a corporation or whether, as the use of the word *gentiles* suggests, they took as individuals (Jolowicz, 1967, p. 124. See also Watson, 1971, pp. 178–182)."

Since two individuals are agnatically related to each other to the extent that they derive from a common *paterfamilias*—who may be dead—this fact can be used as the basis for determining the *agnatus proximus*. The generational distance between the person and the common ancestor determines the relative dilution of the ancestor's *potestas* as compared with the power of more immediate ancestors, who have a greater degree of "natural relationship." (See Sandars, 1874, p. 274). The degree of "natural relationship" implies that an ancestor's spirit of *genius* is dissipated at a regular rate for each generation of distance from him. Hence, if one interprets kinship proximity in terms of the mean degree of distance from a *paterfamilias*, the common ancestor, the measurement distance in the XII Tables seem to flow from the concept of *patria potestas*.

The computation of kinship distances found in the XII Tables was, with slight modification, taken over in the Justinian Institutes at about 530 A.D. The major changes introduced by Justinian pertain to the extension of the rights and inheritance to *cognati*, i.e., persons related through female as well as male relatives. By this time, the gens had declined as a viable kinship entity, and with this decline, the agnatic group lessened in significance. The order of succession described in Book 3, Title 6, of the Institutes, "Of The Degrees of Cognation" (*De Gradibus Cognationis*) are the equivalent of those described in the Napoleonic Code and to those followed in subsequent applications of modern civil law.

CANON LAW MODEL: CHURCH AND STATE

Unlike the Parentela Orders and Civil Law models, which emerged through the explication of laws governing succession to property, the Canon Law model was developed to govern marital relationships. Some of the assumptions that guided the canonists in their refinement of the model had been stated earlier in St. Augustine's *City of God* (Book, VX, Ch. 16). Here Augustine described marriage as a basis for expanding the boundaries of group solidarity. Augustine (1966, V. 4, pp. 503–505) wrote:

> For love was accorded its due importance [in choosing marriage partners outside the family] so that men, for whom harmony was useful and honourable, might be bound by ties of various relationships. The underlying purpose [of marrying nonrelatives] was that one man should not comprise many relationships in his one self but that these connections should be severally distributed among individuals and in this way serve to weld social life more securely by covering

in their multiplicity a multiplicity of people. . . .[In the beginning, Eve was compelled to be] both mother-in-law and mother to her children of either sex. But if these relationships had involved two women, one as mother and another as mother-in-law, the bond of social affection would have embraced a wider circle. . . .And thus the social bond would not be restricted to a small circle, but would extend most widely to embrace a greater number of people through the abundant ties of kinship.

Augustine explained consanguineous marriage as resulting from demographic insufficiency, emphasizing the virtues of prohibiting such marriages. Several centuries later, in the 12th century, Gratian formulated a connection between consanguineous marriage and the nature of the community. Specifically, he distinguished between the function of marriage for Jews and for Christians. Gratian indicated that:

God commanded the Hebrews to intermarry [among relatives] because the salvation of man was realized in the pure Jewish race. . . . Christ changed the nature of God's people by spreading the faith beyond the bounds of the Hebrews. Faith, not blood, was to be the criterion for membership in the chosen people. . . . In his discussion of consanguineous marriages, [Gratian] argued that such marriages were no longer permitted because purity of blood no longer served as the foundation of the community (Chodorow, 1972, p. 74).

As Gratian suggested, the conception of community in the 12th century seems to have involved the idea that mechanisms more inclusive than kinship are required to cement relationships in society. Between the ninth and the 13th century, Europe had undergone profound changes. There was a slow shift in the basis for social structure from exchange of personal service to the less personal uses of property and money. This period saw the growth of trade centers and cities as political entities; the dissipation of the vassalage and manorial systems; the emergence of the state "as an entity that was autonomous, independent, self-sufficient and lived on its own norms (Ullmann, 1975, p. 247)"; and the proliferation of universities (Maranda, 1974, pp. 25–41). These movements stimulated efforts toward centralization by both the state and by the Church. Both of them strove to create *una concordia ex diversitate*—concord from diversity (Ullmann, 1975, p. 248). To create this unity, they had to appeal to non-familial motivations for community.

Both the Church and state aimed to unify as large a populace as possible under their jurisdiction, and they were thereby stimulated to standardize and codify laws governing social relations. Following Pauline doctrine, the Church was designated as an organic, concrete union of believers, organized "in accordance with its underlying purpose or aim, its 'finis' or 'telos.'" Canon law was supposed to provide a mechanism for dovetailing the various elements into a coherent *corpus*. In formulating canon law, "The writers were dominated by the concept of the universal Church as constituting an organic entity'' and they applied organic analogies extensively (Ullmann, 1955, pp. 442–443). The Canon Law model emerged in its modern form out of this context.

Unlike old Germanic law, which regarded kinship as analogous to the human body, canon law used the analogy of a tree. The line of descent was considered to be like the trunk of the tree, and distances between two relatives were determined by the number of generations they were removed from a common line of descent. By analogy, they were the branches. This analogy had appeared earlier in different guises. Isidore of Seville "held that the son and daughter were to constitute the trunk, and the grandson and granddaughter were to be the first branch (Smith, 1940, p. 25)." People were to be seen as related when their genealogical connection extended through the sixth degree; in other words, cousinship was the basis for determining kinship distances—Ego's grandchildren (by different children) are first cousins to each other, the great-grandchildren are second cousins, and so on. As John of Orleans later ruled, "Beyond the sixth degree the ties of kinship [are] conceived as being, in a sense, dissipated, to be gathered up again by marriage, whereupon the cycle [is] repeated (Smith, 1940, p. 27)." Isidore's tree analogy was incorporated into later versions of the canon law, including the compilation by Gratian in the 12th century.

During the 12th century, the concept of *cousinage* came into use in France (Maranda, 1974, p. 63) and eventually was extended to include"relatives in general." By the 13th century, the term *genealogie* had already taken on its modern anthropoliogical meaning (Maranda, 1974, p. 67). The degree of cousinship was refined further by Bernard of Pavia in about 1190 in his scheme for computing kinship distance. "Where the lines of descent from a common ancestor were unequal, the longer line was to be considered the determinative factor (Smith, 1940, p. 33)."

Apparently for Bernard, the reasoning was that, given the common ancestor as the core or the trunk in a line of descent, the person farther removed in degree from the ancestor extinguished the relationship to the ancestor and therefore to the other person. For example, let us assume the following situation: one relative A is four degrees removed from an ancestor C (i.e., A is a great-great-grandchild of C). A second relative B is eight degrees removed from this same ancestor C. Since a relationship is considered to be dissipated after the sixth degree, following Isidore of Seville, and the second relative B is eight degrees distance from the common ancestor C, then the relationship between the two "relatives", A and B, should be considered as dissipated. If both A and B had been within the range of "kinship" to the common ancestor, then they would have been kinsmen to one another—having fallen with the cousinship range despite their belonging to different generations. As it is, since one of them is no longer regarded as a kinsman of the common ancestor, the two persons, A and B, cannot be related to each other.

In about 1280, John de Deo completed the model in canon law with his "Tree of Consanguinity," whereby the counting of degrees began with Ego's children rather than grandchildren: children were one degree distant, grandchildren two degrees, and so on. By this time, prohibition of consanguineous marriage had been restricted by the Fourth Lateran Council to relationships within the fourth degree of distance (Smith, 1940, pp. 33–34).

HISTORICAL CONTEXTS COMPARED

The historical settings in which the Civil Law, Parentela Orders, and Canon Law kinship models emerged differ considerably from one another. Despite superficial similarities, the societies in which they developed diverged in religious conceptions, political structure, and kinship organization. The Roman Republic, as a compromise between Patricians and Plebians, emphasized distinction between private (familial) and public (civil) domains. (See Huebner, 1968, V. 4, p. 719). In contrast to Roman society, both in ancient Judaic and classical Athenian societies, family and kinship units themselves constituted the basic entities in the state; there was consequently no sharp separation among Hebrews and Athenians between family, government, and religion: they were all intertwined. Rather, patrimonial segments had to develop strong reciprocities internally in order to maintain their identity as well as to negotiate agreements with other segments for continued coexistence. As for the law of the Church, canon law itself emerged in the late Medieval period as a response to the growth and centralization of the state. The social condition, which favored the development of large corporate entities—with each attempting to carve out an autonomous domain of laws and authority—acted to subdue the power of the family to affect the destiny of its members. Instead, family and kindred were pawns utilized by Church and state to centralize and homogenize their domains. The large corporate entities became the basic mechanisms for continuity of social structure. Church writings often applied organic analogies in describing social reality. Metaphorically, in homogenizing the society, kinship became a tree with spreading branches, its "fruits" supplying the personnel for the larger and more stable corporate entities.

In Athenian and Judaic social structures, kinship provided the mechanism by which patrimonial segments were perpetuated, and the kinship models which were applied in calculating kinship distance emphasized the distinctions between ascending and descending generations. In Rome, the family formed an integral, but subordinate, part in the persistence of civil society, and the model of computing kinship distances stressed the hierarchical distances from a common ancestor. In canon law, the family was socially unimportant as compared with the Church and state in providing for the continuity of institutional structures, and kinship ties were seen only as a branching off from a line of descent. As a metaphor for social structure, kinship was essentially contractual for the ancient Jews and Athenians; it was an expression of hierarchal power relationships for the Romans; and, for the Canonists, it was an organism, a growing tree that spread the branches of the faith. The different models thus imply a range of roles for the family to play in the persistence of society—from social continuity *through* family and kinship extending to the *irrelevance* of corporate family and kinship bonds for the persistence of social structure.

SUMMARY

The depiction of the historical roots of the kinship computational models associated with major religious and civil legal systems suggests that these models vary with the social structures they symbolize. People whose views of kinship approximate the Parentela Orders model have tended to see the continuity of social structure as rooted primarily in corporate aspects of family and kinship. They apparently visualize the glue of society as consisting of a network of contracts (or alliances). The obligations generated in these contracts serve to weld the special interests of the various segments of the society into a stable network of social relations. In history, Jewish law seems to express this conception of kinship.

People who regard family and kinship in ways consistent with the Civil Code model of genealogical distance tend to see society as persisting through two separate spheres—the public and the private. The core of the public sphere is the civil society; the core of the private sphere is family and kinship. The persistence of cohesiveness in society rests upon accommodation between these two spheres of influence and power. Historically, this conception of social structure emerged with the development of the Roman Republic and, as time went on, the Empire.

In the past, people who have shaped family and kinship relations on the basis of the Canon Law model appear to find the basis for the continuity of social structure in overarching institutions, notably the Catholic Church, as coordinating the lives of members of the community. While personal ties among family and kin may be very strong, these are not seen as the roots of continuity of the social order. Instead, organic analogies are applied to express the mechanisms that coordinate actions of the individuals in the society and give form to networks of social relationships.

Kinship Classification and Social Context

3

The review of the historical settings in which the kinship models in legal codes emerged lends support to the view that there are only limited ways of symbolizing kinship structures as they relate to the larger society. In the history of Western civilization, (a) the Parentela Orders model of kinship priorities developed in a social setting that fostered an emphasis upon the perpetuation of the "house," along with the development of centripetal kinship norms; (b) the Civil Law model arose in a social setting in which an effort was made to maintain a balance between "family" and civil society; and (c) the Canon Law model was developed in a social setting in which the perpetuation of the "family" was considered as subordinate to the perpetuation of major corporate groups, such as the Church or State.

But if there is a correspondence between kinship model and historical origins, then it seems plausible to speculate that the underlying dimensions in the models somehow express symbolically the character of the general social structure. If this isomorphism between kinship model and general social structure exists, then it is also reasonable to expect that in contemporary society people who conceptualize genealogical ties according to a particular model are integrated into the larger society in ways which parallel that model.

This chapter presents a general statement regarding kinship orientations as spatial metaphors of social structure. First, it explores previous applications of spatial metaphors. Afterwards, it deals specifically with kinship orientations as spatial metaphors.

METAPHORS OF SOCIAL SPACE

For some time, psychologists have studied the organization of sensory impressions. For example, Gestalt psychologists (such as Köhler, 1947, p. 199) conclude that "sensory organization appears as a primary fact which arises from the elementary dynamics of the nervous system." They also suggest that "the experiences of the various sense modalities are localized in a common space because we have learned in early childhood how they must be spatially correlated'' or because of ''dynamic reasons.'' At any rate, ''All sensory facts do appear in one space, the space in which also the visual objects and the visual self are located (Köhler, 1947, p. 215).''

The organization of sensory facts, however, does not occur in a social vacuum. Names are given to these sensory impressions and their character-istics are defined by others with whom a child interacts. As long as the organization of perceptions pertains to physical things, there is a high prob-ability of accurate communication with regard to objects in the environment. A problem in communication with others (or in thinking about a matter) emerges when the topic is no longer a physical thing but an idea or some other intangible event: How should a hypothetical individual describe to someone else the characteristics of a phenomenon that is not a physical thing in a way which will maximize the probability of accurate communication? Accuracy requires the individual to use words that are understood by the other. Insofar as words describing sensory facts have a high probability of accurate communication, their metaphorical application in the case of intan-gible events (as opposed to physical things) would describe these events in terms readily understood by the other individuals. We would anticipate then that statements which are intended to describe intangible events accurately tend to use many sensory metaphors (especially spatial and visual imagery).

There is agreement that social relationships constitute a significant area of intangible events. This being the case, we expect sensory metaphors to abound in the language used in everyday life and in the social sciences. Just as Kurt Lewin (1936) found the metaphor of psychological space to be valu-able in the study of psychical phenomena, the metaphor of social space has been fruitful in the analysis of social phenomena. The conception that phys-ical and social space are isomorphic leads Lévi-Strauss (1966, p. 168) to suggest that ''space is a society of named places, just as people are landmarks within the group. Places and individuals alike are designated by proper names, which can be substituted for each other in many circumstances com-mon to many societies.'' As subject matter for investigation, folk models of social space may supply vehicles for understanding the development and maintenance of social structures (e.g., alternative procedures for computing kinship distance).

The concept of social distance represents a widespread application of the social space metaphor in the social sciences. There has been, however, dis-agreement over meanings given to the idea of ''distance.'' For Pitirim So-rokin (1959, p. 6), social distance implies that:

Human beings, who are members of the same social groups and who within each of these groups have the same function, are in an identical social position. Men who differ in these respects from each other have different social positions. The greater the resemblence of the positions of the different men, the nearer they are toward each other in social space. The greater and more numerous are their differences in these respects, the greater is the social distance between them.

For Emory S. Bogardus (1959), however, the expression *social distance* grows out of common-sense usage and draws upon such terms as intimate relations, feeling distant, feeling near, or feeling far away. Bogardus (1959, p. 7) defines social distance as "the degree of sympathetic understanding that functions between person and person, between person and group, and between group and group. Sympathy refers to feeling reactions of a favorably responsive type, and understanding involves that knowledge of a person which also leads to favorably responsive behavior."

McFarland (1973) refers to Sorokin's conception of social distance as embodying the notion of categorical similarity, whereby individuals or groups who are similar in attributes designating social position are "close"; in contrast, McFarland refers to Bogardus' conception as relying upon degree of probability of sympathetic interaction. The conceptual distinction between categorical similarity and degree of probability has important consequences for the analysis of social relations. The measurement of social distance according to the Sorokin conception involves the classification of individuals or groups in such nominal categories as occupation, income, education, ethnicity, and so on. However, the measurement of social distances, according to the Bogardus conception, involves a gradient of interactions according to implied "sympathetic understanding"—intermarriage, commensalism, degrees of residential propinquity, gradations of doing business together, and the like. The difference in meaning of social distance between Sorokin and Bogardus thus leads to divergent understandings about how social relationships evolve. For Sorokin, similar social positions generate similar economic, political, and social interests, and therefore in a highly diverse society social nearness promotes the development of factions with special interests. For Bogardus, sympathetic understanding transcends group boundaries, and social nearness promotes the establishment of a cohesive order and good will across population segments.

The distinction between categorical and gradient representations of social space is not restricted to the measurement of social distance. A similar distinction extends through a wide range of social phenomena and, in each case, leads to opposing conceptions about the character of social existence. For example, in describing the growth patterns of cities, the Burgess concentric-circle hypothesis and the Hoyt sector hypothesis lead to different interpretations of the process of urban development (Burgess, 1973; Hoyt, 1933). Like the Bogardus conception of social distance, the Burgess concentric-circle hypothesis seems to fall into a class of spatial metaphors involving a gradient; like the Sorokin conception, the Hoyt sector hypothesis falls into a class of metaphors that emphasize differing values for diverse bounded regions and yield a series of nominal categories. I will describe these two classes of spatial metaphors in greater detail below.

The first class of spatial metaphors, like Burgess' concentric-circle model, rests on a dimension of core versus periphery, intimacy versus remoteness, or some other characterization of a gradient. The use of gradients for describing social relationships has had a long tradition in sociology. In their analysis of primitive classification, Durkheim and Mauss (in Parsons et al., 1961) indicate that primitive societies based their systems of classification upon such gradations:

> The first classes of things were classes of men, into which these things were integrated . . . phrateries were the first genera; the clans, the first species. Things were supposed to be integral parts of the society, and it was their place in society that determined their place in nature. . . . It is a fact of common observation that the things included in genera are generally imagined as located in a sort of ideal milieu, the space dimensions of which are more or less clearly defined. It is certainly not without reason that concepts and their relationships have so often been represented by circles—concentric or excentric, outside or inside one another, etc. (Durkheim and Mauss, in Parsons et al., 1961, p. 1066).

The assumptions made by Edward Shils (1975) about the nature of society constitute a coherent statement about the existence of a gradient, extending from core to periphery, as expressing a basic dimension in social life. For Shils, it is the length of the gradient that describes the degree of integration of the society: the longer the gradient, the greater is that chance that new centers will emerge, which will, in turn, act to increase the size of the gradient further. According to Shils' exposition:

1. "All human collectivities have a tendency toward closure into self-containment. They seek through their authorities to establish and maintain a certain identity, to define their boundaries, and to protect their integrity (Shils, 1975, p. 45)."

2. "The main factors which establish and maintain a society are a central authority, consensus, and territorial boundedness. . . . Every society, seen macrosociologically, may be interpreted as a center and a periphery. The center consists of those institutions (and roles) which exercise authority—whether it be economic, governmental, political, military—and of those which create and diffuse cultural symbols—religious, literary, etc.—through churches, schools, publishing houses, etc. The periphery consists of those strata or sectors of the society which are the recipients of commands and of beliefs which they do not themselves create or cause to be diffused, and of those who are lower in the distribution or allocation of rewards, dignities, facilities, etc. (Shils, 1975, p. 37 and 39)."

3. "The existence of a central value system rests, in a fundamental way, on the need which human beings have for incorporation into something which transcends and transfigures their concrete individual existence. They have a need to be in contact with symbols of an order which is larger in its dimensions than their own bodies and more central in the 'ultimate' structure of reality than is their routine everyday life (Shils, 1975, p. 7)." Moreover, "This central value system is the central zone of the society. It is central because of its intimate connection with what the society holds to be sacred; it is central because it is espoused by the ruling authorities of the society (Shils, 1975, p. 4)."

4. "All territorially extensive societies tend to have a spatial center as well, which is, or is thought to be, the seat of the central institutional and cultural systems (Shils, 1975, p. 39)."

5. "Integrated societies in which the authoritative institutional and cultural systems are well established can become civil societies with a wide diffusion of the virtues required for the effective practice of citizenship. They become so where closure around the center is accompanied by the approximation of center and periphery. This is the path which has been followed over the past century and a half in Western Europe, the United States, and Australia, and to a lesser extent by Japan and Canada. In these countries, the mutual exchange between center and periphery, and the heightened sense of affinity which attends this interchange, have brought larger proportions of the population into the center and obliterated to some extent the boundary which has in the past separated center from periphery (Shils, 1975, pp. 46–47)."

The second class of metaphors of social space, like Hoyt's sector model in urban growth, refers to qualitative differences in the structure of social relationships. Like the gradient metaphor, the second metaphor of social space has had a long history of application in the social sciences. It too appears in the analysis by Durkheim and Mauss of primitive classification schemes. They write (in Parsons et al., 1961, p. 1067):

What is here conceived as perfectly homogeneous is represented elsewhere as essentially heterogeneous. For us, space is formed of identical parts, interchangeable one with the other. We have seen, however, that for many peoples space is profoundly differentiated, depending upon the region considered. This is because each region has its own affective value. Under the influence of various sentiments, a particular region of space is referred back to a specific religious principle; in consequence, it is endowed with virtues *sui generis*, which distinguish it from any other region.

The distinction between the gradient and categorical metaphors of social space appears in Lévi-Strauss' discussion of dual kinship organization. Dual kinship organization is generally characterized by the presence of moieties that divide a society into two major kin groups. Lévi-Strauss (1963, pp. 132–

163) shows a correspondence between the spatial layout of villages and the organization of moieties. In societies with moieties, villages tend to be laid out so that they are divided physically along an axis into two parts, which Lévi-Strauss designates as diametric dualism. Sometimes these villages also display (in common with other societies which are not divided into moieties) a layout of concentric circles, usually with a core and a periphery differentiated according to function or residential use. Lévi-Strauss emphasizes the interplay of these layouts in structuring social relationships; however, it may be equally important to stress their distinctiveness as illustrating the two metaphors of social space.

In concentric patterning, the core of the village, according to Lévi-Strauss, is ordinarily reserved for communal functions such as ceremonial activities, dancing, burial, or the living quarters for chiefs or unmarried men. The periphery holds the individual clans, the homes of married couples, and the work areas. On the other hand, diametric structures signify categorical distinctions in social relationships and responsibilities. Lévi-Strauss suggests that frequently "the opposition between moieties expresses a more subtle dialectic" in function. Dualistic structure appears to present not merely a dichotomy in social categories but also an opposition: warfare and policing versus the arts of peace and arbitration, continuity versus discontinuity. In this manner, the diametric structure of dual kinship appears to express the barriers, the boundaries, and the conflicting valences described in topological psychology. The diametric structure seems to represent another instance of the categorical metaphor of social space, in which a line of demarcation acts as a basis for partitioning the space.

In contrast to users of gradient models, those scholars who apply a categorical conception of social space take as a starting point an initial state of conflict among collectivities—a battle of group against group. In his work on kinship, for example, Lévi-Strauss begins with an original state of hordes in conflict and proposes that social structures greater than the nuclear family emerged as a result of the incest taboo and of the reciprocities developed and elaborated between groups through marital exchange. From the beginning, according to the structural position, community life was based on political alliances of groups realizing their special interests in reciprocities established with other groups. In the categorical conception of social space, thus, one assumes as a starting point the predominance of special interests of different groups.

The nominal-category metaphor of social space thus implies that relationships in the family emerge as an entity only insofar as obligations—reciprocities—within the family coalesce. The categorical representation suggests that the family affects the collective destiny of its members in competition with similar collectivities for wealth, power, means of grace, or other scarce goods.

It may be advisable to summarize at this point. The previous discussion of social space metaphors and their apparent implications for the analysis of social relationships may be stated as follows:

1. Social space metaphors derive their utility from the greater effectiveness of words pertaining directly to sensory impressions (especially visual imagery) than of more abstract terms to communicate accurately the description of social relationships.

2. The application of spatial metaphors suggests an isomorphism between physical and social space, which may exist as explicit "translations" in classification schemes of social space.

3. Two kinds of spatial metaphors appear to be applied generally; a gradient conception of social space and a nominal-category conception of social space.

4. The gradient conception of social relationships implies a social space consisting of a core and periphery, with concentric circles denoting degrees of remoteness; the categorical conception of social relationships implies a social space consisting of a set of regions (defined as categories of bounded areas), with a line of demarcation (rather than a single point) as a basis for generating the model.

5. These social space metaphors seem to apply to a large variety of social phenomena and, as Durkheim, Mauss, Lévi-Strauss, and others have suggested, to express some basic elements in ways societies (or social groups) are organized.

6. The two metaphors further imply a difference in the way social relationships develop: the gradient-metaphor rests upon the assumption of tendencies toward consensus or common concern as the basis for social structure; the categorical metaphor assumes that factionalism or group conflict over special interests is at the root of social structure.

7. Given the differences in assumptions about the development of social relationships, the two metaphors presuppose opposing resolutions to disorder in society. The gradient representation presupposes a strengthening of consensus with regard to the common welfare; the categorical model presupposes an accommodation by the opposing factions.

KINSHIP MODELS AS METAPHORS OF SOCIAL STRUCTURE

Kinship models seem to symbolize the relationship between the social whole and its parts in terms of space. In discussing kinship ties, people often refer to "the proximity of relatives," "distantly related persons," "intimate kin," or "cousins who are far removed." David Schneider (1968, pp. 72–73) proposes that there are three different meanings of distance in American kinship: physical distance, socio-emotional distance, and genealogical distance. While these three meanings are not necessarily related, they seem to be correlated. The connection between kinship and the concept of distance suggests that the kinship models in legal codes can indeed be regarded as spatial metaphors of social structure.

Ever since Lewis Henry Morgan's seminal work, conceptions of genealogical structure have been regarded as synonymous with patterns of kinship nomenclature. Using a linguistic model, anthropologists seek to determine semantic domains, which are supposed to yield a system of social classification based on roles, statuses, and group membership. Analysis of kinship terms has indeed produced numerous insights pertaining to family and kinship structure, particularly in nonindustrial societies. These insights refer primarily to the semantic dimensions underlying a table of organization of kinship relationships. The tables of organization vary in the ways they partition relatives according to consanguinity versus affinity, lineality versus collaterality, the distinction between ascending and descending generations, bifurcation versus merger by relative's gender, and so on (Murdock, 1949). Anthropologists have uncovered numerous correlations between kinship terminology and table of organization.

In modern society, the relatively high degree of social stratification, occupational differentiation, religious and ethnic diversity, frequent contact with foreigners, and variations in domestic life styles all interact to sustain a broad spectrum of kinship tables of organization. Still, despite the heterogeneity of kinship tables of organization and their supporting ideologies, virtually everyone in the society learns a common set of kin terms (of the dominant language spoken). Consequently, even with a common kinship terminology, people often do not agree about what constitutes an appropriate table of kinship organization. For instance, some people include in-laws and distant cousins in their "kin universe," while others do not (Schneider and Cottrell, 1975).

This lack of association between table of kinship organization and terms for designating relatives suggests that in contemporary society a supplementary criterion is needed to handle the tasks which terminology ordinarily accomplishes in nonindustrial societies. While people may differ in tables of organization, they still need a vocabulary to describe priorities of duties and rights with respect to their "kin universe." Since contemporary societies do not generally have formally-organized descent groups in which membership would define these priorities, another means must be devised to serve this purpose.

Schneider and Cottrell (1975, p. 92) propose that "one of the fundamental features" of the structure of the American kin universe is the division of relatives "into those who are 'close' and those are are 'distant.' " In fact, "the greater the genealogical distance, the more important nongenealogical and nonkinship considerations become, the more choice Ego has over whether to include or exclude [the relative] from his kin universe and whether to transmit [the relative] to his children (Schneider and Cottrell, 1975, p. 96)." Sheila Klatzky (n.d., p. 84) also has found that genealogical distance is associated with the structure of kinship relations—in that "there is a greater element of choice in contacts with genealogically more distant relatives." Likewise, Litwak (1960a) has shown that the closer the genealogical tie, the less apt is geographical distance to diminish contact, mutual aid, or sentimental bond. (See also Rosenberg and Anspach, 1973; Adams, 1968.)

The tie between social structure and conception of genealogical space presupposes that the societies in which the kinship models in legal codes were first developed exhibited many of the complexities found in modern society. Jewish social structure, classical Greece, and the Roman Republic all show these complexities. Indeed, the presence of laws of succession presumes an elaborate system of property institutions, whereby individuals (or individual families) can accumulate wealth and resources. Each of these societies held urban centers, with a high degree of social stratification and with foreign residents interspersed among the population. In each society, there was also considerable contact with various other ethnic and/or religious groups. Canon law itself was explicitly established to create a unity out of the diversity of European customs and traditions. So there was much heterogeneity in these societies with respect to social and economic hierarchy, diversity of family norms, range of citizenship rights, and so on. The broad ranges of population characteristics in these societies perhaps encouraged the metaphorical use of the concept of social distance (especially in the sense in which Sorokin used the term) to describe similarities in property interest by various groupings. Since property interests were generally connected with the family or kin group, it apparently was reasonable to apply the concept of distance to the measurement of genealogical relatedness.

Despite their considerable complexity, the societies in which the legal models originated in no way even approximate the size and heterogeneity of modern society. These older societies were still homogeneous enough for the particular kinship models implied in legal codes to serve their special needs for social continuity. The heightened complexity of modern, urban society (as suggested by the discussion in the introductory chapter), however, is capable of accommodating the full range of conceptions of genealogical space found in the legal codes of the Hebrews, ancient Athens, the Roman Twelve Tables, and Catholic canon law. The variations in conception of genealogical distance found in the studies reviewed above, associated as they are with social characteristics, may well be expressions of the models which appear in legal codes—Parentela Orders, Civil Law, Genetic, and Canon Law.

The discussion of metaphors of social space leads to the speculation that the kinship models applied in legal codes fall on a continuum. At one extreme is the Canon Law model, which expresses the concentric-circle conception of space, implying consensus or common concern as a basis for social structure. At the other extreme is the Parentela Orders model, which yields a set of bounded classes, implying that an accommodation by special interests lies at the root of social order. Specific implications of this symbolization are that:

1. People who conceptualize kinship ties in accordance with the Parentela Orders model regard their participation in segmental groups (perhaps deriving from religious, ethnic, or some other special interest) as more significant for social continuity than their involvement in universalistic associations and movements in the civil society.

2. People who conceptualize kinship ties in accordance with the Civil Law model regard social continuity as deriving most effectively from a balance of participation in segmental, special interest groups and in universalistic associations and movements in civil society.

3. People who conceptualize kinship ties in accordance with the Genetic (or shared chromosome) model or the Canon Law model regard social continuity as deriving more effectively from participation in universalistic associations, institutions, and movements in civil society than from segmental groups.

Two investigations have been undertaken in which adherence to a particular kinship model is related to place in the community. In part, both studies dealt with the extent to which participation in a segmental, religious community—that is, Judaism and Christian sectarianism—is associated with conception of genealogical space in terms of the priorities of the Parentela Orders model. In the first study, based on a sample of 248 students at Arizona State University, Jews and Christian sectarians showed the greatest conformity to the Parentela Orders model; denominational Protestants were next; and Catholics and atheists exhibited least conformity to this model (Farber, 1977). In the second study, based on 182 Jews living in the Kansas City metropolitan area, persons indicating a high degree of conformity to the Parentela Orders model had the following characteristics: (a) most often Orthodox in upbringing, next Conservative, and least often Reform; (b) born in rather than migrated to Kansas City; (c) live in areas of Kansas City with a relatively high concentration of Jewish population; (d) more active than their own parents in Jewish activities; and (e) disapprove of intermarriage with non-Jews (Farber, 1979). The findings of both studies are hence consistent with the previous discussion regarding the relationship between organization of genealogical space as expressing an ideology regarding the role of the family in social continuity, whereby a segmental community—in this case, religious—translates its concerns about continuity into a system of priorities in genealogical space. For example, the centripetal family ideology of Judaism expresses this concern about continuity through the vehicle of the Parentela Orders model, and among Jews, it is those who are most involved in Jewish communal life who organize their kin universe in terms of this model.

Since the two past studies are based on atypical populations (university students and Jews in Kansas City), the question may be asked: To what extent does the relationship between social structure and kinship orientation appear in data generated from a more representative sample? The analysis that follows is addressed to this question.

Cognitive Kinship Maps: A Serendipitous Finding

4

Briefly, the previous chapters in this monograph proposed that the computational measures for determining priorities in intestacy and for defining certain kinds of consanguineous marriages as "incestuous" in law produce orderings of consanguines that can be regarded metaphorically as cognitive kinship maps. Historical analysis indicates that the kind of measure adopted in law is related to the character of the social structure. In his rigorous analysis of such measures, John Atkins (1974) described in particular the Canon Law and Civil Law computational models and their homologues. He indicates that, although the homologues may be "historically distinguishable" from these measures, they "create exactly the same ordering of consanguines (Atkins, 1974, p. 13)." Unexpectedly, this study has unveiled an ordering of consanguines that has not appeared among any of the previous measures (including those described by Atkins (1974)), and the analysis in this chapter will focus upon this serendipitous finding.

FORMAL AND POPULAR CONCEPTS OF KINSHIP

Although an analysis of the formal measures of genealogical proximities may provide numerous insights into the character of kinship in different societies, the question recurs: Do these formal models of genealogical proximities represent in any way the kinds of kinship maps that people carry around in their own minds? If these models do represent distillations of popular conceptions of kinship, then in a population one should be able to find some degree of association between cognitive conformity to a model and various social and cultural characteristics. Pilot studies (Farber, 1977; 1979) on limited populations have indicated that there is indeed a relationship between conformity to kinship models and predictable characteristics in religion, fertility, migration, and education.

The widespread presence of a previously unknown model in the Phoenix population has important implications for the understanding of middle-class kinship structure. Consequently, the chapter also includes the results of a componential analysis that uncovers the cognitive dimensions shaping the new model—as well as the other models under investigation. This type of analysis clarifies the interrelationships among the various models (Atkins, 1974) and it should expedite interpretations of the Phoenix study findings in the chapters that follow.

In the Phoenix study, individuals were classified by kinship mapping orientation on the basis of their responses to questions pertaining to priorities in intestacy law. The technique was as follows:

1. The respondents were presented with a series of paired comparisons of relatives for whom the four models—Parentela Orders, Civil Code, Genetics, and Canon Law—differ in genealogical remoteness.

2. The instructions to the respondents were:

   Next, we have a few questions about inheritance laws.

   When someone dies without leaving a will, the laws says that the estate goes to the nearest relatives. The law then tries to follow what *most* people look upon as their nearest relatives.

   Suppose you had to write a law for Arizona to decide which relatives should have a greater claim to the estate when a person dies without leaving a will.

   Categories of relatives are listed on this form.

   These pairs were chosen because they stand for different ways of figuring which relatives are closer.

   For each pair of relatives, please check the kind of relative who should have a greater claim to the estate—when there is no will.

3. The respondents were then asked to assign priorities in nine pairs of consanguineous relatives. The list included parents, children, brothers and sisters, grandchildren, first cousins, aunts and uncles, nieces and nephews, grandnieces and grandnephews, and grandparents. For each pair, the respondents were given three choices. For example:

   Comparing *brothers and sisters* with *grandchildren:*

   ( ) *Brothers and sisters* should have a greater claim.

   ( ) Both should have an *equal* claim.

   ( ) *Grandchildren* should have a greater claim.

   In the comparison between *brothers and sisters* and *grandchildren*, the choice of *brothers and sisters* would be appropriate for the Canon Law and Genetic models; "equal claim" would be appropriate for the Civil Law model; and *grandchildren* would be the appropriate response for the Parentela Orders model.

TABLE 4-1. Patterns of Answers to Intestacy Questions Used to Classify Respondents by Kinship Model

Kin types compared in intestacy question	Parentela orders	Civil law	Genetic model	Canon law
Grandparents versus aunts and uncles	Grandparents	Grandparents	Equal claim	Equal claim
Aunts and uncles versus nieces and nephews	Nieces and nephews	Equal claim	Equal claim	Equal claim
Nieces and nephews versus grandparents	Nieces and nephews	Grandparents	Equal claim	Equal claim
First cousins versus nieces and nephews	Nieces and nephews	Nieces and nephews	Nieces and nephews	Equal claim
First cousins versus grandnieces and grandnephews	Grandnieces and grandnephews	Equal claim	Equal claim	First cousins
First cousins versus aunts and uncles	Aunts and uncles	Aunts and Uncles	Aunts and uncles	Equal claim
Brothers and sisters versus grandchildren	Grandchildren	Equal claim	Brothers and sisters	Brothers and sisters
Brothers and sisters versus parents	Parents	Parents	Equal claim	Equal claim
Parents versus children	Children	Equal claim	Equal claim	Equal claim

4. Each respondent was then classified according to the kinship model to which a majority of answers corresponded. The response patterns used to classify each person by kinship mapping orientation are shown in Table 4-1. When there was no majority for any one model, the person was assigned to a residual category. (See Farber, 1977 and 1979.)

AN AMERICAN STRATEGY

In an ideal world, all participants in a social survey would provide responses consistent with the investigators' expectations. In a study of kinship models by which people organize priorities among relatives, all respondents would dutifully provide answers that would permit classification in one of the pre-determined categories of kinship orientation. Specifically, each respondent would produce a pattern of responses that could be classified unambiguously as conforming to an identifiable model—Parentela Orders, Civil Law, Genetics, or Canon Law. But, the world is not totally predictable—and not all respondents conduct themselves as if they were using the investigator's research design as a script. In this study, responding to the questions on preferred priorities in intestacy law, 17 percent of the sample produced patterns of answers that fell into a residual category.

The large number of cases that did not correspond to any of the kinship models under examination evokes the questions: Do sizeable segments of the population conceptualize priorities among relatives in an idiosyncratic fashion? Or has the investigation omitted a widely-applied kinship model from consideration? Supporting the interpretation of residual category cases as idiosyncratic is my experience that many persons say that, in responding to the questions, they are drawing from their own personal experiences with kin. This argument, however, is specious since most people, even when they conform closely to an existing model, are unaware of their rationale.

A Serendipitous Model

In order to determine whether many of the residual-category cases actually conform to a coherent pattern, I examined the modal responses to the individual questions on priorities in intestacy law. The pattern of modal responses in the residual category appears in Table 4-2. A clue to the organizing principle of this pattern is suggested by the fact that, with one exception (that of cousins versus nieces and nephews), the kin types in the modal categories are always in an older generation than are the types with which they are compared. That is, grandparents are given priority over aunts and uncles, parents over children, and so on.

The next step in the analysis of the residual cateogry is to find a compu-

TABLE 4-2. Modal Responses to Intestacy Questions for Cases Falling into Residual Category of Kinship Classifications

Kin types compared in intestacy question	Modal kin type	Percentage of cases falling into modal category[a]
Grandparents versus aunts and uncles	Grandparents	53.8
Aunts and uncles versus nieces and nephews	Aunts and uncles	78.8
Nieces and nephews versus grandparents	Grandparents	78.8
First cousins versus nieces and nephews	Nieces and nephews	41.7
First cousins versus grandnieces and grandnephews	First cousins	75.8
First cousins versus aunts and uncles	Aunts and uncles	56.1
Brothers and sisters versus grandchildren	Brothers and sisters	60.6
Brothers and sisters versus parents	Parents	52.3
Parents versus children	Parents	49.2

[a] Number of cases classified as Residual = 132.

tational formula that yields the pattern of priorities suggested by the modal responses. The computational model that fits the pattern is: $D = (n + 1)i + j$, where D refers to priority rank; j as before is the number of generations between EGO and the nearest ancestor in common with a collateral relative; n is the number of generations between EGO and the most remote ancestor (i.e., the largest j) to be considered in a set of the computations; and i is the number of generations between the nearest common ancestor and the collateral relative. In computations involving lineal rather than collateral relatives, j alone is used for EGO's direct ancestors, and $(n + 1)i$ by itself is used for EGO's descendants. This computational model produces the configuration of kin types in Table 4-3.

Comparison with Parentela Orders Model

There is some similarity between Parentela Orders and the serendipitous model yielded by the residual-category analysis. Both models depend upon differentiating ancestral lines from lines of descent, and both models provide for unique rankings of distance for each kin type. Differences, however, appear when the pattern of priorities in Table 4-3 is compared with that yielded by the Parentela Orders model. As noted earlier, while the computational formula for the serendipitous model is $D = (n + 1)i + j$, the formula

50

TABLE 4-3. Ranking of Distances from Ego According to Model Based on Modal Responses in Residual Category (Standard American Kinship Model)[a]

Order in line of descent (*i*)	Order in ascending generations (*j*)		
	0	1	2
0	Ego (0)[b]	Parents (1)	Grandparents (2)
1	Children (3)	Brothers and sisters (4)	Aunts and uncles (5)
2	Grandchildren (6)	Nieces and nephews (7)	First cousins (8)
3	Great-grandchildren (9)	Grandnieces and grandnephews (10)	

[a] Computational formula is $(3i + j)$.

[b] Ranking of distance from Ego.

Note: For these kin types, the appropriate formula for the Parentela Orders model is: $(i + 4j)$. Ranking of distances in the Parentela Orders model is as follows:

(1) Children
(2) Grandchildren
(3) Great-grandchildren
(4) Parents
(5) Brothers and sisters
(6) Nieces and nephews
(7) Grandnieces and grandnephews
(8) Grandparents
(9) Aunts and uncles
(10) First cousins

for the Parentela model is $D = i + (m + 1)j$, where m in this case refers to the most remote descendant (instead of ancestor), i.e., the largest i to be condsidered in a set of computations. Whereas the serendipitous measure stretches distances of descendants of common ancestors, the Parentela Orders measure elongates the distances of the ancestors themselves. The serendipitous model thereby emphasizes the closeness of *ancestry* and the importance of the line of ascent; the Parentela Orders model stresses the proximity of *descendants* and the significance of the descent line. Symbolically, the serendipitous model sees kinship from the perspective of family history, while the Parentela Orders model views kinship from the standpoint of family destiny.

The Standard American Kinship Model

One interpretation of the finding is that the serendipitous model is merely a version of another, more traditional kinship orientation. However, a more plausible alternative interpretation is that this new model represents a conception of kinship that predominates in contemporary, postindustrial society. There is some empirical support for this position.

All 723 cases in the Phoenix probability sample were examined to determine the extent to which they conformed to the pattern of modal responses in the residual category. The findings were: (a) responses for almost half the sample fit this pattern; (b) most cases for which there had been a tie between Parentela Orders and Civil Law scores had an even higher score for this model (47 out of 85); (c) large numbers of cases which had previously fallen into the Parentela Orders and Civil Law categories were reclassified as conforming to this new model; (d) the size of the residual category was reduced considerably (from 17.3 percent to 7.0 percent). In short, the introduction of this new model into the analysis has greatly modified the distribution of cases by kinship classification.

Persons conforming to this model seem to be similar to those exhibiting ''standard'' American characteristics in general—language patterns, values, life style, and so on. Table 4-4 shows the extent to which certain social characteristics are overrepresented in persons who conform to this model. Although the overall percentage of cases in this classification was 43.5 percent, higher percentages appeared for Protestants in denominations originating in the Reformation era, non-minorities, persons in professional or technical occupations, those who have a family income $25,000 or over, and/or people whose fathers are native-born. Conversely, low percentages appeared for Jews, blacks, and American Indians, semi-skilled and unskilled workers, those with a family income of under $10,000, those persons who did not graduate from high school, and individuals with foreign-born fathers. In general, the Standard American kinship model seems to be most prevalent among middle-class, non-minority Protestants, whose parents are native-born.

The extensiveness of the serendipitous mapping in the sample, along with the social characteristics of persons conforming to it, suggest that it is not merely a version of another measure in the series examined. Rather, the findings support the view that the serendipitous mapping represents a kinship orientation *sui generis*. Consequently, pending further analysis, I am naming this orientation the Standard American kinship model.

Both religion and socioeconomic status appear to influence the distribution of the Standard American model. Table 4-5 compares the percentages of persons in the Standard American category when respondents are classified by their religion and by the occupation of the male co-head of the household. (The Jewish respondents in the supplementary sample are included here and because of their general occupational homogeneity, all of them are placed in the column headed Professional, Managerial, or Administrative.) A comparison among religious groups reveals that, in the Professional, Managerial, or Administrative category, Jews (43 percent) are somewhat less likely to hold the Standard American model than are Protestants (54 percent), Catholics (52 percent), or persons expressing no religious preference (54 percent)—there being little distinction among the latter three groups. In Blue Collar families, however, Protestants (44 percent) are clearly more predominant in the Standard American rubric than Catholics (28 percent) or those without

TABLE 4-4. Social Characteristics of Respondents as Overrepresented or Underrepresented in Standard-American Category

Social characteristics	N	Percentage of cases falling into Standard american category (k)	Extent of over- or under- representation (k/43.5)
Total Sample (N=723)		43.5	—
Religion[a]			
Protestant (no denomination)	54	50.0	1.15
Reformation Era Protestant denomination	100	49.0	1.13
No religious preference	82	46.3	1.06
Pietistic Protestant denomination	139	46.0	1.06
Neo-fundamentalist sect	47	40.5	.93
Catholic	205	40.5	.93
Latter Day Saint (Mormon)	43	39.5	.91
Jewish	10	30.0	.69
Minority Status			
Non-Minority (i.e., not Black, Oriental, Mexican American, American Indian, etc)	582	45.3	1.04
Mexican American	90	38.9	.95
Black, American Indian, Oriental[b]	50	30.0	.69
Birthplace of Father			
United States	619	45.2	1.04
Latin America[c]	51	37.3	.86
Europe	36	27.8	.64

(continued)

[a] Reformation era Protestant denominations include: Lutheran, Congregational, Presbyterian, Evangelical, Reformed, United Church of Christ, and Episcopalian. Pietistic denominations include: Methodist, Baptist (not Primitive or Southern), and Disciples of Christ. Neo-fundamentalist sects and denominations include: Church of God, Nazarene, Pentecostal, Church of Christ, Primitive Baptist, Seventh Day Adventist, and Southern Baptist. Other denominations held too few members in the sample to collect into a meaningful category.

[b] In this category are 31 Blacks, 14 American Indians, 4 Orientals, and 1 Black and Mexican American

[c] Includes one person born in Canada.

a religious preference (36 percent). As for occupational differences, all religious groups show that the Professional, Managerial, Administrative category contributes the highest percentages of persons with a Standard American orientation and the Blue Collar category the lowest. Thus, the data in Table 4-5 testify that neither socioeconomic status nor religion can be discounted as factors in conformity to the Standard American model.

TABLE 4-4 *(continued)*

Social characteristics	N	Percentage of cases falling into Standard american category (k)	Extent of over- or under-representation (k/43.5)
Occupational Status			
Professionals, managers, and administrators	250	49.6	1.14
Sales, clerical, craftsmen	223	41.3	.95
Blue collar workers (i.e., operative, service, laborer)	151	35.1	.81
Family Income			
$25,000 or over	177	45.8	1.05
$10,000 to $24,999	405	43.7	1.01
Under $10,000	124	38.7	.89
Educational Status			
Some graduate work	53	45.3	1.04
Some college	290	48.3	1.11
High school graduate	259	45.2	1.04
Not a high school graduate	121	27.3	.63

TABLE 4-5. Religion, Occupation of the Male Co-Head of the Household, and Percentages of Persons in the Standard American Category

Religion	Occupation of male co-head of household		
	Professional, managerial, or administrative	Clerical, sales, or craft	Blue collar
Jewish (%)	43.4[a]	—	—
N	53[b]		
Protestant (%)	54.0	44.3	43.9
N	139	115	82
Catholic (%)	51.7	43.9	27.5
N	60	66	40
No religious preference (%)	53.6	44.4	35.7
N	28	18	14

[a] Includes a few persons from other occupations.

[b] Includes respondents from both the probability sample and the supplement.

Standard American Kinship: A Speculation about its Sources

The unexpected discovery of a new measure of collaterality stimulates queries about the sources out of which it has arisen. The tendency for the Standard American model to be characteristic of middle-class Protestants in denominations founded during the Reformation era leads to a speculation that this model may have emerged as family capitalism (and Protestantism) took hold in Western Europe and in American society. With the rise of the bourgeoisie, relationships with kin seem to have been affected markedly both on the European continent and in England. Maranda (1974) documents changes in French kinship terminology with the decline of the *freresche* and the expansion of commerce. He finds that "the lineal dimension of the French system became accentuated through time by segregative terminological refinements and by an increasing stability (p. 137)" and that "the system of jural norms emphasizes the rights of the lineal nucleus and minimizes those of collaterals and affines (p. 136)." In England, the transformation of ties between kin followed a similar pattern. Stone (1975) notes that by the English revolution of the 1640s, cousinage had become "hopelessly fragmented." As trade increased in importance, the state became stronger, and its functions encroached more and more upon the kinship domain. Simultaneously, geographical mobility "among the lower, lower-middle and middle-class groups . . . was remarkably high (Stone, 1975, p. 22)." Yet, "The growth of paternalism was deliberately encouraged by the new Renaissance state (Stone, 1975, p. 54)." Indeed, "The State was as supportive of the patriarchal nuclear family as it was hostile to the kin-oriented family; one was the buttress and the other a threat to its own increasing power (Stone, 1975, p. 55)." It is this form of family organization that is identified with the Protestant reformation (and the emergence of capitalism) and that seems to have provided the basis for contemporary domestic life styles in Western Europe and the United States.

The American family has had deep roots in the New England tradition that emerged out of Puritanism. Even in the years following the Revolution, the institutional life of such communities as Salem, Massachusetts, resembled that of the earlier Puritans in various ways. For example, the old Puritan conception of an elitist ruling class of merchants still lingered in Salem community organization (Farber, 1972). Today, the middle-class descendants of these early American families still "associate themselves with events that are of historical significance for the community" through memberships in hereditary associations (such as the Daughters of the American Revolution) "and pass these memberships, and their concomitant status, to others in the family (Rosenfeld, 1974, p. 407)." In a highly industralized society, these hereditary associations "are enclaves of ascribed status for mobile families, and [they] perpetuate the symbolic value of family biographies (Rosenfeld, 1974, p. 408)."

In an analysis of elite American families, Saveth (1963) has indicated that the historical background of the family affects "life style" of individuals; family connections provide a basis for power; and through the individual's identification with ancestors or involvement in the management of resources, the family defines one's status in society. More specifically, Beale has suggested that a family tradition of public service and *noblesse oblige* led Theodore Roosevelt into public life and induced him into a "lifetime concern over public questions (Beale, 1964, p. 166)." But not all kin are equally important in establishing a style of life, status, and power. As Saveth (1963, p. 259) proposes, "It is the achieving individuals within the achieving family who become family history." The biographies and genealogical location of such kinsmen become part of the symbolic property of the modern American family.

In discussing his own family history, Stewart Alsop (1968, p. 40) explicates the role of a symbolic estate in establishing one's personal identity and place in a society which emphasizes achieved status over ascribed status:

> Knowing something about his ancestors . . . gives a man a satisfying sense of being part of a continuum, of a process of birth, death, and rebirth that started long before he was born, and will continue long after he is dead. And as a man's age increases, this sense of being part of the endless human parade through history is an oddly comforting sense.
>
> It is reassuring, somehow, to know that all sorts of people—poets and eccentric ladies and rum importers and reactionaries and politicians and murderers and wisemen and fools—have gone before, In such times as these, it is also comforting to know that, barring some final act of human idiocy, all sorts of people are still to come after.

For individual family histories to persist as oral traditions, there must be some interest and communication among family members. Indeed, Firth (1956, p. 28) reports that in London kinship information does not appear to be the property of an individual only. Instead, this information "tends to be drawn from and contributed to a household pool." Moreover, "The contemporary family has a special archival function as a repository of [mementos serving as] identity symbols which compose a biographical museum or even a [familial] hall of fame (Weigert and Hastings, 1977, p. 1174)."

The impulse to communicate information about kin seems to be strongest in the middle class. By way of contrast, the shallowness of knowledge about kin and friends among low socioeconomic individuals has been indicated in various contexts. In Mexico, Oscar Lewis (1967, p. 12) reports that "in some villages, peasants can live out their lives without any deep knowledge or understanding of the people whom they 'know' in face-to-face relationships." Similarly, Liebow (1967, pp. 205–206) remarks in his study of street corner men that "a man may have detailed knowledge of his friend's present circumstances and relationships, but little else." There is the assumption that "there's a skeleton in every closet (Farber, 1971, p. 111)." Studies of kinship among lower-class socioeconomic status individuals evoke such statements as, "I don't know much about my grandfather and I don't much care" or, "All I know is that grandma died when mama was little, and she doesn't tell me much about her life. She keeps it pretty much a secret (Farber, 1971, pp. 112–114)." Despite an occasional hero, there seems to be little pooling of biographical information in lower-class families in America. This lack of pooled kinship information would inhibit the development of a comprehensive family history by individuals outside the middle class.

In keeping with the middle-class Protestant emphasis upon achievement, however, the Standard American model may emphasize "roots" in one's own family history. It is plausible that, in a society that is more interested in promoting notions of self-actualization and achievement, people remain oriented toward kinship as personal history. Instead of viewing kinship in terms of its implications for the future, people with a Standard American kinship orientation, may regard their kin (living and dead) primarily as an orienting mechanism, one pertaining to their own social placement and achievement—and only secondarily as a determinant of the life chances of their descendants from one generation to the next in an ever-changing world.

THE STANDARD AMERICAN MODEL AND THE DISTRIBUTION OF KINSHIP MAPS

I have reported in this chapter the serendipitous finding of the existence of a Standard American map of collaterality. If its prevalence is compared with that of other maps, one can draw implications about the ability of current laws that pertain to the family, particularly intestacy law, to represent the views of most people.

Table 4-6 describes the distribution of cognitive kinship maps in a probability sample of 723 Phoenix residents. As the methodological appendix indicates, this sample is restricted to persons, aged 18–45, who are currently married or who had been divorced, separated, or widowed. (The table does not include the Jewish supplementary sample.)

The percentages in Table 4-6 clearly demonstrate the predominance of the Standard American orientation over other conceptions. In contrast to the 44

TABLE 4-6. Kinship Orientations of Respondents in Phoenix Probability Sample[a]

Kinship orientation	N	Percentage
Parentela orders	116	16.0
Standard american	314	43.5
Civil law	110	15.3
Genetic	56	7.7
Canon law	76	10.5
Residual category	51	7.0
Total	723	100.0

[a] Ties in the respondent's conformity to categories of kinship orientation generally occur between measures which, in Table 1, are adjacent in degree of collateral removal of first cousins (e.g., Parentela Orders and Standard American or Civil Law; not Parentela Orders and Genetic or Canon Law measures). Where such ties occur, cases are classified in the category with a smaller degree of collateral removal of first cousins. For any category, ties represent a minority of cases (e.g., one percent of cases in Standard American; 10 percent in Canon Law).

percent of the cases falling into the Standard American category, Parentela Orders holds only 16 percent, Civil Law 15 percent, Canon Law 11 percent, and the Genetic orientation only 8 percent. Because of the small number of persons with a Genetic or Canon Law perspective, these two categories will be combined in the analyses described in the succeeding chapters. The patterns of collaterality are similar in both Genetic and Canon Law maps among those relatives included in the questions on intestacy law used to classify respondents; for these kin the two maps differ only with regard to distance of first cousins. (See Table 1-2 in Chapter 1.)

The finding that the Standard American model is predominant in popular conceptions of kinship also has serious legal implications. It raises a doubt about the appropriateness of the Canon Law, Civil Law, and Parentela Orders models, now in general use in American law, to express the will of the people regarding priorities in case of intestacy. Specifically, this finding has relevance for the priority given to children as opposed to spouse in intestacy law. Generally, intestacy laws now in force provide for a sharing of the estate by children and spouse. Table 4-7 describes the answers of the Phoenix respondents to the question whether, in case of intestacy, one's children or one's spouse should have prior claim to the estate. Support for current intestacy law is found only among persons with Genetic and Canon Law orientations (52.5 percent); individuals holding other orientations favor the spouse. Persons in the Standard American category are the most inclined of all to give the spouse priority over the children.

This finding on priority of the spouse is consistent with investigations on

TABLE 4-7. Children Versus Spouse in Priority of Claim to Estate, by Kinship Orientation[a]

	Kinship orientation				
Priority in claim to estate	Parentela orders	Standard american	Civil law	Genetic model or canon law	Total
Children should have prior					
claim (%)	10.3	5.7	6.0	11.3	7.7
Ratio to total	1.34	.74	.78	1.47	
Children and spouse should					
have equal claim (%)	19.8	20.7	30.2	52.5	28.3
Ratio to total	.70	.73	1.07	1.86	
Spouse should have prior					
claim (%)	69.8	73.7	63.8	36.2	64.0
Ratio to total	1.09	1.15	1.00	.57	
N	132	362	83	141	718

[a] Includes cases in supplementary sample. Chi square = 67.516; d.f. = 6; $p < .001$

choice of heirs in wills. These studies show that, overwhelmingly, people leave their estates to their spouse, with the eventual disposition of the property at the spouse's discretion (Sussman et al., 1970; Simon et al., 1980, Gluckman, 1976). Hence, at least with regard to the choice between children and spouse as heirs, persons with a Standard American orientation seem to be closer than those with other kinship maps in conforming to current inheritance norms. Given the prevalence of the Standard American orientation (shown in Table 4-6), this finding may have practical implications. If additional research supports the tendency for testation to follow the Standard American map of priorities, then legislators should take this fact into account in future revisions of intestacy law.

COMPONENTIAL ANALYSIS AND STANDARD AMERICAN KINSHIP

The partitioning of terms applied in American kinship into various components has in the past contributed to our understanding of the cognitive dimensions that organize this terminology into a coherent semantic pattern.

(See Buchler and Selby, 1968, pp. 181–190.) An application of componential analysis to measures of collaterality may yield significant insights into the dimensions structuring the Standard American model.

In their componential analysis, Romney and D'Andrade (1964) have identified three cognitive dimensions underlying the classification of kin terms in American society. These dimensions are: (a) reciprocity (i.e., complementary terms used by two relatives to refer to each other—such as aunts and nieces or grandparents and grandchildren); (b) generational distinctions between relatives (i.e., the number of generations between Ego and a relative in a superior or inferior generation); and (c) degree of collateral removal (i.e., lateral distance from Ego's line of descent in any given generation— brother versus cousin, father versus uncle, son versus nephew, and so on). The results of the Romney and D'Andrade analysis have been verified by Wexler and Romney (1972). Insofar as there is an isomorphism between terminological usage and models of collaterality, one would expect these models to reveal comparable dimensions.

John Atkins (1974) has demonstrated that the i and j dimensions applied in collaterality measures can be transposed into dimensions derived from componential analysis. Specifically, he has translated i and j into dimensions of generational differences and degree of collateral removal. Generational difference (G) between Ego and a relative can be expressed as $(j - i)$, while degree of collateral removal (R) is given by i or j, whichever is smaller. These transformations permit the presentation of an orthogonal kinship grid based on G and R instead of i and j. Table 4-8 presents a grid of kinship relations based on the dimensions of generational differentiation (G) and collateral removal (R). In its essential features the grid appears to correspond to diagrammatic representations of American kinship terminology yielded by componential analyses (Wallace and Atkins, 1960; Romney and D'Andrade, 1964; Wexler and Romney, 1972). Presumably, like these analyses, measures of collaterality also vary with differential weights assigned to G and R and with the introduction of additional dimensions.

For those models in which i and j play symmetrical roles, the transformations from i and j into the dimensions of generational difference (G) and collateral removal (R) are described by Atkins (1974, pp. 18–21) as follows:

Canon Law model $= G + R$;

Genetic model $= G + 2R - f$ (where $f = 0$ for lineal kin or half siblings, and $f = 1$ for all other kin) (This model is designated as the Murdock degree by Atkins.)

Civil Law model $= G + 2R$.

TABLE 4-8. **Grid of Kinship Relationships Based on the Dimensions of**
Generational Differetiation (G) and Collateral Removal (R)

Generational differentiation (G)	Collateral removal (R)		
	Direct line descent	First step of collateral removal	Second step of collateral removal
+2	Grandparents	Great aunts and great uncles	Grandparents' first cousins
+1	Parents	Aunts and uncles	Parents' first cousin
0	Ego	Siblings	First cousins
−1	Children	Nieces and Nephews	First cousins' children
−2	Grandchildren	Grandnieces and grandnephews	First cousins' grandchildren

The diversity of semantic dimensions found through componential analysis suggests that in discriminating among degrees of relationship, the various measures of collaterality combine the G and R components in different ways. An examination of the above measures of collaterality indicates that:

1. The *Canon Law* model treats G and R as equivalent; partitioning of kin is based on gradient distances from Ego, through the nuclear family, and then outward from there. Thus, immediately outside the nuclear family, no distinction is made among grandparents, aunts and uncles, first cousins, nieces and nephews, and grandchildren; all of them are two degrees distant from Ego. The next ring of relatives around the nuclear family is three degrees distant, and so on.

2. The *Genetic* model apportions to collateral removal (R) twice the weight of generational differences (G) in assigning degree of distance between Ego and a relative, but then it weakens this weight by f. For close kin (i.e., where i or j = 0 or 1) the degree of relationship computed with the Genetic measure is equivalent to that obtained with the Canon Law measure. But the larger that i and j become, the closer is the Genetic degree of relationship to that of the Civil Law model. Hence, the Genetic model apparently stands between the Canon Law and Civil Law models in extent of stress on collateral removal and generational differentiation.

3. Assigning a double weight to R as compared with G in the *Civil Law* model enhances the role of collateral removal in partitioning kin by degree of relationship. The allocation of weights in the Civil Law component seems to offer a compromise between the nuclear family emphasis of the Canon

Law model and the stress on line of descent in the Parentela Orders and Standard American models. The core of the Civil Law component consists of Ego's *lineal* links in his family of orientation and family of procreation. These direct links place both parents and children immediately adjacent to Ego in distance (G = 1 and R = 0). Those kin just outside this abbreviated lineal core are then located one unit away; thus, Ego's siblings (G = 0; R = 1) are equivalent to Ego's grandparents and grandchildren (G = 2; R = 0) in being two degrees distant from Ego. Next in remoteness from this core are the great grandparents, aunts and uncles, nieces, and nephews, and great-grandchildren, and these are still an additional step away from the abbreviated descent line (or three degrees from Ego). In general, the degree of remoteness of any class of kin from the abbreviated descent line is defined by this component.

The transformation of the Standard American and Parentela Orders models into the generational-collateral (G-R) grid is complicated by the fact that in these models i and j are asymmetrical. Since j represents ascent from Ego and i descent, the translation into generational differentiation $(j - i)$ and collateral removal (i or j, which ever is smaller) depends specifically upon whether a particular relative is in a superior generation as opposed to a subordinate generation in relation to Ego. The transformation of these models into G-R terms requires a special weighting for this disparity.

In the translation of the Parentela Orders model, three special symbols must be introduced, S, A, and m. Let S refer to the comparative generation of Ego and kin. If the relative is in an ascending generation, then $(j>i)$; if the relative is in a descending generation, then $(i>j)$. If j is greater, then let S = 1; if i is greater, let S = −1; and if $i = j$, then S = 0. Furthermore, let the quantity $(1 + S)/2 = A$.[1] In the transformation, as in the formula [$i + (m + 1)j$], let m refer to the largest i in the set of relatives for whom the computations are being performed. The derived formula for Parentela Orders is a modification of the Civil Law transformation (G + 2R):

$$G(Am + 1) + R(m + 2), \text{ or}$$
$$GAm + G + Rm + 2R, \text{ or}$$
$$(G + 2R) + m(GA + R).$$

The transformation of the Parentela Orders formula into the orthoganal generational-collateral form hence produces a second component [m(GA + R] in addition to the dimensions in the Civil Law scheme (G + 2R). The major element in this second component (apart from m) is the incorporation of generational ascendance versus descendancy vis-a-vis Ego into the model (i.e., A for ascending generations = 1; A for descending generations = 0).

The transformation of the Standard American formula $[(n + 1) i + j]$ is comparable to that of Parentela Orders. The only difference pertains to the symbols A and m. For the Standard American translation, let the quantity $(1 - S)/2 = D$. Then D will $= 1$ when i is larger than j, and D will $= 0$ when i is smaller; in addition, let n refer to the largest j in the set of relatives for whom the computations are being performed. The transformed version of the Standard American model is as follows:

$$(G + 2R) + n(GD + R).$$

The components for the Standard American model thereby resemble those for the Parentela Orders model. Both consist of the Civil Law component and a unique factor. Distinctions refer primarily to the reversal in treatment of ascending and descending generations in the formulae.

The impact of the unique components in the Standard American and Parentela Orders models upon classification of kin is indicated in Table 4-9. This table separates the contributions of the Civil Law component and the unique Parentela Orders and Standard American components in producing priority rankings. The Parentela Orders components are discussed first, and afterwards those for the Standard American model.

A review of the components of the Parentela Orders priority scores in Table 4-9 discloses that, with the effect of the Civil Law degree removed, the remaining component derives directly from a hierarchy of Parentela Orders (P). The latter component, $m(AG + R)$, can also be expressed in terms of j. Since R is zero for a direct ancestor, and since $A = 1$ in ascending generations, any parentela class can be identified by $(G + 1)$. But inasmuch as $[R = 0, G = j]$ refers to a direct ancestor, a parentela class can also be identified by $(j + 1)$. As the verbal description in introductory chapter attests, the ordering of any parentela P thereby depends upon the generations of Ego's direct ancestor, who is then "head" of that particular descent line. In the table, the unique component scores for a descent line are the same as that for its "head." Within a parentela class, only the Civil Law component varies.

A few illustrations from Table 4-9 may clarify the relationship between the Civil Law and Parentela Orders components. For great-great grandparents, $G = 4$ and $R = 0$. The Civil Law component, $G + 2R$, produces a score of 4, and (since here $m = 3$) the Parentela Orders component, $m(AG + R)$, yields a score of 12. The total priority ranking is $(4 + 12)$ or 16. Removing the effect of m, we find that $12/3 = 4$, and $(AG + 1) = 5$, which tells us that the great-great grandparents are at the head of the fifth parentela set. Looking down the unique-component column, we find that, like the great-

TABLE 4-9. Priority Rankings for Various Relatives Yielded by Parentela Orders and Standard American Models, with Scores Decomposed into Civil Law and Unique Components

Relatives	Generation $(G*)^a$ (1)	Collateral removal (R) (2)	Civil law component $(G + 2R)$ (3)	Parentela orders		Standard american	
				Unique component $(m(AG + R))^b$ (4)	Total priority ranking $(3)+(4)=(5)$	Unique component $(n(DG + R))^c$ (6)	Total priority ranking $(3)+(6)=(7)$
Great-great-grandparents	4	0	4	12	16	0	4
Great-grandparents	3	0	3	9	12	0	3
Grandparents	2	0	2	6	8	0	2
Parents	1	0	1	3	4	0	1
Children	−1	0	1	0	1	4	5
Grandchildren	−2	0	2	0	2	8	10
Great-grandchildren	−3	0	3	0	3	12	15
Great-great-aunt	3	1	5	12	17	14	9
Great aunt	2	1	4	9	13	4	8
Aunt	1	1	3	6	9	4	7
Sibling	0	1	2	3	5	4	6
Niece	−1	1	3	3	6	8	11
Grand niece	−2	1	4	3	7	12	16
First cousin	0	2	4	6	10	8	12
First cousin's child	−1	2	5	6	11	12	17

a (G*) differs from (G) in that (G) is an absolute number whereas (G*) = (SG), in which S = +1 for ascending generations, S = 0 for collateral generations, and S = −1 for descending generations.

b Because the largest i = 3 (Great-grandchildren), m = 3.

c Because the largest j = 4 (Great-great-grandparents), n = 4.

great grandparents, the great-great aunt also has a component score of 12. Her Parentela Orders component score (12) is obtained by the figures [3(3 + 1)], where $m = 3$, $A = 1$, $G = 3$, and $R = 1$. Since the great-great aunt is a descendant from the great-great grandparents, she is indeed a member of the fifth parentela and differs from the grandparents only in the Civil Law component of her priority score, 5 instead of 4.

In Table 4-9, members of the second parentela, with the parents as "heads," include siblings, nieces, and grandnieces—all of whom have a 3 in the Parentela Orders component column. For the parents, $(AG + 1) = 2$, and for the remaining members of this set, $(AG + R + 1) = 2$. Note that for relatives in descending generations $(R + 1)$ is equivalent to parentela membership, 2. Again, variations among total priority rankings within a given parentela class issue only from the Civil Law component.

The Parentela Order component thus explicitly classifies kin according to the descent lines from Ego and his ancestors: (a) Ego's own line of descendants, (b) Ego's parents' line of descendants (except for Ego's own line), (c) Ego's grandparents line of descendants (except for Ego's parents' line), (d) and so on. As noted earlier, these classes are based on j, the remoteness of direct-line ancestors from Ego.

The Standard American component has a somewhat different effect upon the establishment of classes of kin in the measurement of collaterality. This component categorizes kin on the basis of i, the remoteness of descendants from Ego and Ego's ancestral line. For example, in Table 4-9, the unique-component weight for all of Ego's direct ancestors is *zero*; the weight for the children of Ego and each ancestor is 4 (since $n = 4$), and this category includes Ego's great-grandparents' child (i.e., Ego's great aunt), his grandparents' child (who is his aunt), his parents' children (i.e., Ego's own siblings), and Ego's own children. For grandchildren of Ego's ancestral line, the weight in Table 4-9 is 8, and the line's great-grandchildren are assigned a 12. Hence, the Standard American component is defined by the number of generations between Ego's line af antecedants and categories of progeny—children, grandchildren, great-grandchildren—classified with reference to that line. As in Parentela Orders, the differences in total Standard American priority rankings among the various relatives within each group accrue from their scores on the Civil Law component.

The existence of unique components in the Parentela Orders and Standard American models implies that the differences in kin statuses in Civil Law are complemented in these models by categories derived from the distinction between ascending and descending generations (i.e., S in the componential analysis). For Parentela Orders, this distinction results in the partitioning of classes of ancestors and their individual lines of descendants. In the Parentela Orders component, the distance between Ego and any collateral kin is defined therefore specifically in terms of how remote their nearest common ancestor is from Ego. For the Standard American model, the separation between ascending and descending generations has a different set of consequences. The unique Standard American component organizes kin solely on the basis of distance from Ego's ancestral line, and it defines degree of kinship by remoteness from this line. At some point of removal from the ancestral line, presumably kinship is extinguished. In this respect the Standard American model differs from Parentela Orders, which defines lines of descent as theoretically infinite.

In summary, the componential analysis of the models yields three cumulative components in cognitive kinship mapping:

1. A component of gradient distance of individual relatives from Ego and the nuclear family. This component is further decomposable into the dimensions of (a) generational difference between Ego and a relative and (b) collateral removal between a relative and Ego's line of descent. It is symbolized in the Canon Law model.
2. A component modifying the distance component by doubling the weight of collateral removal in kinship mapping. This modification places Ego's immediate lineal ties (to parents and children) at the core of kinship. This component is symbolized in the Civil Law model.
3. A component identifying classes of kin by their relationship to Ego's line of descent. This component is analyzable into two subcomponents. One subcomponent groups kin on the basis of their removal from Ego's ancestors, and it is symbolized in the Standard American model. The other subcomponent groups kin on the basis of their descent from Ego or from specific ancestors of Ego, and it is symbolized in the Parentela Orders model.

The three components in the kinship models represent a series in conception of social space. (See Chapter 3.) The first component organizes this space into gradients of social distance emanating from a core—Ego. The second component modifies the first one somewhat by stressing degree of collateral removal. The third component carries this progression further by dividing social space into categories based on the relationships of kin to Ego's ancestral line. In the third component, Ego is significant only insofar as he too is an ancestor. The three components therefore represent differences in conceptions of social space—from Egocentric gradients to corporate categories. The proposition of the Phoenix study is that the various components of social space symbolized in the kinship models are isomorphic with kinds of religious, ethnic, and socioeconomic settings in the social structure—communal versus segmental settings—and that each model is associated with a particular kinship ideology consistent with its setting.

STANDARD AMERICAN KINSHIP: A SUMMARY

This chapter has reported an unanticipated finding, the presence of a widespread kinship orientation that has not been previously identified. This orientation is particularly prevalent among Protestants, but it is also widespread among others at high educational and income levels. It is underrepresented especially among racial minority groups, Jewish respondents, persons with foreign-born fathers, and poorly-educated persons at poverty levels. Both religion and socioeconomic status seem important in determining its distribution. Because of the social characteristics associated with the popularity of this orientation, I have called it the Standard American model. This model emphasizes the social closeness of relatives in ascending generations, and it appears to have emerged during the Protestant Reformation. Family and kinship attributes associated with the Standard American model are described in succeeding chapters.

The cognitive structure of the Standard American model is suggested by an analysis of its components. Like the Parentela Order model, it can be decomposed into two parts: the Civil Law contribution and a unique component. The analysis then indicated that the Civil Law component serves to distinguish among kin *within* categories defined by the unique component. In addition, the unique component derives its qualities from the fact that, like Parentela Orders, the Standard American model makes a distinction between relatives in generations above Ego and those in inferior generations. Because of this distinction, the unique component in the Standard American model stresses classes of relatives according to descent from Ego's own ancestral line. Accordingly, the children of Ego's great-grandparents, those of his grandparents, the offspring of his parents, as well as Ego's own progeny all constitute one class; the grandchildren of each of these ancestors make up another class; and so on. This accentuation of closeness to Ego's ancestral line is consistent with the characterization of the Standard American model as stressing family history. While the Parentela measure also exhibits a unique component that relies upon a principle of descent, its cognitive structure is different from that in the Standard American model. In Parentela Orders, the descent-line component refers not to removal of kin classes from Ego's ancestral line but to lines of descendants from Ego and Ego's own line of ancestors. Unlike the Canon Law, Genetic, and Civil Law components, which generate gradients from Ego in spatial representations, the Standard American and Parentela Orders components organize genealogical space into categorical schemes based upon ancestral lines. The cognitive components of the kinship models thus appear to be symbolic referents for the spatial metaphors described in Chapter 3, and these attributes should be borne in mind when the findings on family and kinship ties are presented in the chapters that follow.

NOTE

[1] This application of the S factor in the componential analysis was suggested by John R. Atkins (personal communication).

Variations in Kinship Distances: Fundamental or Superficial?

5

There is consensus among social scientists that collaterality is associated with priorities in kinship relations. Still, the concept of genealogical closeness is not systematically applied either by researchers or, for that matter, by the people studied. For example, the pattern of Klatsky's (n.d.) data conforms generally to the Civil Law model for computing kinship proximities but departs considerably from the Canon Law or Genetic models. Yet Klatsky (n.d., p. 84) writes that "elasticities [in contact] differ systematically by genealogical distance." Similarly, Schneider and Cottrell (1975, p. 94) report that, "With each genealogical step away from Ego, less and less substance [i.e., "blood"] is shared; yet, they are "careful not to provide any definition of [close and distant relatives] in terms of generation-collateral removal cells or in such terms as 'uncle-aunt' or 'first cousin' (Schneider and Cottrell, 1975, p. 97)." The reason for avoiding a precise definition "is simply that the definition varies not only for various populations but also from informant to informant within [their] sample."

In spite of the ambiguity of the concept of genealogical distance in the studies cited, findings indicate that variations in its application are not randomly distributed. Schneider and Cottrell (1975, p. 97) find that a series of social variables, "such as age, sex, class, occupation, ethnicity, religion, income etc. . . tend to influence the inclusion or exclusion decisions of different kinds of Egos about different kinds of [relatives]—particularly distant ones." Excluding a relative from one's "kin universe" obviously implies that Ego conceives of that relative as being extremely distant. But even within the kin universe, Schneider and Cottrell (1975, p. 98) have found considerable variation—"for some informants, the uncle-aunt category is close; for others, it is distant." Other studies support their conclusions. For example, religion seems to play a particularly important role in conceptions of genealogical structure. Klatsky's (n.d.) data show that Catholicism is related to kinship contact mainly because the Catholics in her sample tended to live close by; Winch (1974, p. 158), however, has concluded that Chicago-area "Jews were not more familistic [in ties with relatives] because they were less migratory, but that they were less migratory because they were more familistic than the Christians.'' The various investigators thus show how configurations of genealogical distance vary in predictable ways in American kinship.

Although social scientists agree that there is considerable variation in kinship ties in different segments of the American population, they disagree over the significance of this variation. For some, this variation represents a series of deviant expressions of the same basic kinship structure, in which differing modes of expression derive from the particular social conditions under which people operate. For others, these modes themselves convey diverse principles of kinship structure fundamentally distinct from one another. In this chapter I shall examine the issue of kinship variation and present data relevant to its resolution.

The position of Schneider and Smith (1973) is that the American kinship is essentially unitary, with variations accruing with conditions under which relatives play their roles as persons. Their view is as follows:

1. ''At the level of pure cultural conceptions in the domain of kinship, . . . Americans of all classes share the same conceptions about the manner in which 'blood' is transmitted and the imperishable bonds it creates between people . . . . At this level, each person in his capacity as a relative or kinsman is equal to each other relative, and undifferentiated from him. (Schneider and Smith, 1973, p. 103).''

2. ''At this cultural level we may also say that Americans share a conception of 'the nuclear family' as the basic configuration of kinship elements out of which the whole domain of kinship is defined and differentiated (Schneider and Smith, 1973, p. 104).''

3. Variations which occur in family and kinship relationships issue from the fact that people conduct themselves in a number of distinct social domains—occupational role, family role, associational membership—and participation in these domains molds kinship ties. ''We argue that normative role structures for family members vary precisely because they are conglomerate structures of this kind, and the most important dimension of variation is in the class differences in sex-role (Schneider and Smith, 1973, p. 105).''

4. ''Over and above these variations in the sex-role component of familial norms is . . . a feature of middle-class normative structure that the nuclear family itself, as a unit, is singled out for special emphasis (Schneider and Smith, 1973, p. 105).'' Indeed Schneider and Smith (1973, p. 107) point out, ''One of the most important sets of forces affecting familial behavior is the relationship of individuals and families to the economic system.''

The position opposed to that of Schneider and Smith is that variations in kinship ties can be traced to ideological factors that often fit the socioeconomic realities but which at times override economic considerations. In *Kinship and Class* (1971), I described these ideologies as American Biblical and Western American kinship. In the American Biblical scheme, norms with a

Biblical source have been adopted to justify middle-class family life, and Western American norms fit economic and ecological contingencies often faced in the lower class. However, this earlier formulation is too simplistic. Indeed, the analysis of kinship maps in the Phoenix study is intended to supplement that statement about sources of kinship conceptions.

We can interpret maps of collaterality as expressing sets of assumptions about the nature of the connection between domestic institutions and general social structure. The character of these assumptions is suggested by the social structure in which each map has crystallized historically. The previous chapters have proposed the following:

1. The Parentela Orders orientation appears to have emerged in pluralistic settings (e.g., Biblical Hebrews, classical Greece). The ideology upon which this orientation rests is that kinship is aimed at the perpetuation of the special political and/or religious interests embodied in the *mischpokheh*, the house, or the *oikos*.

2. Indications are that Standard American kinship principles were formulated as Protestantism blossomed and the merchant class dominated economic and political life in Western society. The Standard American orientation appears to be associated with high achievement motivation and therefore with the perpetuation of special socioeconomic interests.

3. The Civil Law map represents a compromise in the Twelve Tables between the pluralism of the Patricians and the universalism of the Plebes at the founding of the Roman Republic. Its principles thus seem to express a middle ground in the pluralism-universalism continuum.

4. The Canon Law measure was devised in the 12th century to express the aims of the Church toward universalism in spreading the faith over vast domains—with centralized authority and a common body of law. The main vehicles for the perpetuation of society were organized to promote the common interests of the entire social organism.

Resolution of the issue whether American kinship rests upon a single cultural base or upon multiple sources depends, in the final reckoning, upon three kinds of data:

1. The first kind of data refers to religious and philosophical ideologies that reveal the structure of group values and their fundamental assumptions about the nature of society. If it can be shown that variations in religious belief are associated with conceptions about collaterality, such findings would lend support to the multiple-source position regarding American kinship.

2. The second kind of data pertains to the predominance of the "nuclear family" as a unit singled out for special emphasis among middle-class populations. If the middle-class chooses a set of priorities among kin that emphasizes the unity of the nuclear family, the data would support Schneider and Smith; however, if they tend to give priority to lineal relatives outside the nuclear family (e.g., grandparents or grandchildren) over brothers and

sisters, then the unitary conception of American kinship would be called into question. It would be difficult to justify the view that the nuclear family constitutes "the basic configuration of kinship elements out of which the whole domain of kinship is defined" when the putative major protagonist of this position—the American middle class—deviates from it.

3. The third kind of data bears upon familiarity with specific relatives as compared with religious identity as factors in kinship mapping. In particular, grandparents are ranked as especially close in the Standard American model, and it would be of interest to determine whether familiarity with grandparents is more effective than religion or ethnic origin in explaining conformity of individuals to the Standard American model.

The materials which follow fall into four parts: (a) religious identity and kinship orientation; (b) occupational status and kinship orientation; (c) income and minority-group status; and (d) assimilation and the Standard American model.

RELIGIOUS IDENTITY AND KINSHIP ORIENTATION

Religious belief can be regarded as a way of symbolizing the structure of society (Durkheim, 1915; Swanson, 1960). Briefly, religious beliefs seem to "arise as symbols of men's experiences with the basic purposes and decision-making procedures of society and of enduring and independent groups within societies" (Swanson, 1967, p. viii). In preliterate societies, people who aim at the unification of the society tend to promote the existence of a "high" god, that is, a god who transcends all special interests of groups and who welds the divergent factions in ths society into a unified, coherent whole. Societies with multi-dieties, however, remain factionalized, with each group alienated from the central state or other competing collectivities. In modern societies, where tradition dictates the existence of a single diety, different groups may fix upon the special characteristics of this diety. In effect, these differences in definition of the nature of the overall diety are equivalent to the worship of special gods. Consequently, modern society itself may be said to be governed by specialized gods while it voices monotheism. God as defined by the Jews differs from that of the Christians; the god of the Reformation Protestants differs from that of the Neo-fundamentalists or the Pietistic Protestants; and the god of the Protestants differs from that of the Catholics—not in all ways, of course, but sufficiently to generate sentiments for perpetuating distinctions among the more divergent views.

By stressing theological distinctiveness, religious tracts ordinarily promote the perpetuation of a unique identity of religious minorities and sects. This literature also stresses the importance of the family in maintaining ties and creating boundaries for the religious group. (See, for example, Schlesinger, 1974.) Schneider and Cottrell (1975, p. 67) suggest that "religious affiliation tends to be treated as a badge or a mark of identity of the entire family, [and] . . . within the Jewish and Catholic traditions, there is a tendency to 'drop' and not count members who marry 'outside the faith' '' Insofar as family identity operates as a vehicle for maintaining boundaries of distinct religious communities, kinship orientations that emphasize centripetal tendencies would facilitate their perpetuation. Hence, one would anticipate that the kinship orientations of Jews and Protestant sectarians would differ from that of denominational Protestants and that these, in turn, would be dissimilar from Catholics.

Kinship and Religion: Findings

In the analysis of data, the religious identity reported by the respondent was cross-tabulated with his (or her) type of kinship orientation. It was anticipated that separatist religious groups would be overrepresented in the Parentela Orders category, while groups favoring universalism would tend to dominate the Genetic and Canon Law categories. It was also expected that intermediate religions, which aim for a moderate separatism through associational obligations (rather than communal ties), are overrepresented in the Standard American and Civil Law categories. Whether one uses current religious identity or religion in which the respondent was raised, the results with regard to kinship orientation are similar; current identity is chosen arbitrarily for the analysis.

Parentela Orders. As Table 5-1 shows, Jews and Neofundamentalist Protestants tend to fall into the Parentela Orders category disproportionately. The ratio of the percentage for Jews to the percentage of the total sample in the Parentela Orders category is 1.47, and in the case of the Neo-fundamentalists, the ratio of 1.59. The Catholics are the only others with a ratio greater than *one* in the Parentela Orders category. All three of these religious groups rely to a considerable extent upon communal ties (as opposed to associational elements) for their coherence as collectivites. Especially the Jews and sectarians strive to persist as autonomous religious "communities"—setting themselves apart in identity. Variations among the Jews, Mormons, and Catholics will be discussed in succeeding paragraphs.

Among Jews, differences in kinship orientations are found among the Orthodox, Conservative, and Reform branches. As Table 5-2 indicates, persons raised in Orthodox homes show a far greater proclivity to the Parentela Orders model than do individuals from Conservative and Reform families. This finding appears for both the respondents in the current Phoenix study and in the previous Kansas City analysis (Farber, 1979). In contrast, persons brought up in Reform Judaism are most likely to develop Genetic or Canon Law kinship orientations. With the decline of Orthodox Judaism in the United

TABLE 5-1. Current Religion of Respondent and Kinship Orientation

	Kinship orientation				
Current religion	Parentela orders	Standard american	Civil law	Genetic model or canon law	N
Jewish (%)	25.9	42.6	14.8	16.7	54
Ratio to total	1.47	.91	.91	.85	
Neofundamentalist					
Protestant (%)	27.9	44.2	20.9	7.0	43
Ratio to total	1.59	.95	1.29	.36	
Pietistic Protestant (%)	14.9	47.8	17.9	19.4	134
Ratio to total	.85	1.03	1.11	.98	
Reformation Protestant					
(%)	13.7	51.6	17.9	16.8	95
Ratio to total	.78	1.11	1.11	.85	
General Protestant (%)	17.0	50.9	13.2	18.9	53
Ratio to total	.97	1.09	.81	.96	
Roman Catholic (%)	19.6	43.9	14.3	22.2	189
Ratio to total	1.14	.94	.88	1.13	
Mormon (LDS) (%)	10.3	43.6	28.2	17.9	39
Ratio to total	.59	.94	1.74	.91	
No Religious Preference					
(%)	16.0	50.7	13.3	20.0	75
Ratio to total	.91	1.09	.82	1.02	
Total	17.6	46.6	16.2	19.7	717[a]

[a] Excludes all religious categories with fewer than 30 respondents.

States, current Jewish identification tends to be restricted to Conservative and Reform branches. But whether current affiliation or branch of upbringing is examined, the results are similar; the more traditional and separatist branches of Judaism tend toward the Parentela Orders orientation and Reform Judaism shows a greater concentration in Genetic and Canon-Law models.

Although, as a group, Mormons do not exhibit a Parentela Orders kinship orientation, the conception of "celestial marriage" in Mormon theology seems conducive to that perspective. Like Orthodoxy in Judaism, the Mormons who are most conformist in their beliefs are expected to lead a family life in accordance with religious law. In order to qualify for a temple wedding, Mormons must not only be members in good standing and believe in the charismatic authority of the church, but they must also be obedient to church law. Because of the rigorous demands on the "orthodox" Mormon life style, only a minority of the Mormons have their marriages sealed in the church (Campbell and Campbell, 1976).

Having one's marriage sealed in the temple represents a major step in achieving celestial marriage throughout eternity. In Mormon theology there is an isomorphism between earthly and heavenly family structure: "The or-

TABLE 5-2. Branch of Judaism and Kinship Orientation

Kinship orientation	Branch of Judaism		
	Orthodox	Conservative	Reform
Branch during upbringing			
Parentela orders (%)	37.5	21.1	25.0
Standard american (%)	37.5	52.6	41.7
Civil law (%)	25.0	15.8	—
Genetic or canon law (%)	—	10.5	33.3
N	8	19	12
Current religious identity			
Parentela orders (%)		31.3	23.1
Standard american (%)		43.8	42.3
Civil law (%)		25.0	3.8
Genetic or canon law (%)		—	30.8
N		16	26

Note: Because of an error in instructions to an interviewer, information on branch of Judaism was not obtained for the remaining cases.

ganizational structure of heaven is the extended family-kinship network (Campbell and Campbell, 1976, p. 386).'' According to the Mormon conception, ''a man must enter into the 'new and everlasting covenant of marriage' by which he and his wife or wives will be married for all eternity and will have the privilege and duty of procreating spirit children throughout eternity even as God procreated us (Campbell and Campbell, 1976, p. 385).'' Consequently, it is incumbent upon the devout Mormons to have a temple marriage, ''which is sealed by the Holy Spirit of promise (Church Educational System, 1976, p. 198).''

If one interprets Mormon doctrine as an attempt to justify a distinctive identity of Latter Day Saints, then one would anticipate that conceptions of kinship would be affected. Specifically, devoutness among Mormons, like Orthodoxy among Jews, would be associated with an emphasis upon line of descent in views on kinship organization. This anticipation is borne out in Table 5-3. Although 20 percent of those persons whose marriages had been sealed in the temple fall into the Parentela Orders category, only 7 percent of the other Mormons are in that class. Conversely, none of the persons with sealed marriages conforms to the Genetic or Canon Law models in responses, but fully 24 percent of the others do. Hence, despite the small number of cases involved, the findings lend additional support to the putative relationship between religious sectarianism and emphasis upon line of descent in conceptions of kinship.

Standard American Model. Table 5-1 shows no marked tendency by any major religious group to be concentrated in the Standard American category.

TABLE 5-3. Kinship Orientation and Sealing of Mormon Marriage in Temple for Time and Eternity (Mormon Respondents)

Kinship orientation	Marriage sealed in temple	Marriage not sealed in temple
Parentela orders (%)	20.0	6.9
Standard american (%)	40.0	44.8
Civil law (%)	40.0	24.1
Genetic or canon law (%)	—	24.1
N	10	29

Only denominational Protestants and those with no religious preference reveal any special proclivity at all for the Standard American pattern. Presumably, conformity to this pattern depends also upon a range of other variables.

Civil Law Model. Religious groups that have strong associational components for establishing cohesiveness in promoting their special interests are overrepresented in the Civil Law category of kinship orientation. (See Farber, 1979.) As Table 5-1 shows, these include many (but perhaps not the most devout) Mormons (with a ratio of 1.74 over the expected percentage) and Neofundamentalists (here by a factor of 1.29 over the expected percentage). Among Neofundamentalists, data (not reported here) indicate that members of Pentacostal sects tend to fall into this category (as opposed to Southern Baptists, who generally hold a Parentela Orders orientation). Inasmuch as many Mormons and Pentacostal sectarians seem to minimize ethnicity as factors in their lives, the church itself may become the focal point of their activities and their commitments. To a lesser extent, denominational Protestants organize their existence around the church and, consequently, one finds a small overrepresentation of Pietistic and Reformation-Era Protestants (both with ratios of 1.11) in this category.

Genetic and Canon Law Models. In Table 5-1, only the Roman Catholics are overrepresented in the Genetic and Canon Law categories (but by only a 1.13 ratio). The Roman Catholic Church has always aimed at becoming the universal church and, in recent years, has promoted ecumenical movements. The overrepresentation of Catholics both in Parentela Orders and in the Genetic and Canon Law classifications suggests that there are diverse ethnic and socioeconomic factors that seem to confound kinship orientation of Catholics.

A supplementary comparison of Catholics in the Parentela Orders category with those in the Genetic and Canon Law class (not presented in tabular form) reveals significant differences in ethnicity. Of the 49 Catholics in the Parentela Orders category, 33.3 percent are Mexican-Americans, whereas for the 41 Catholics falling into the Genetic and Canon Law class, fully 48.7 percent are Mexican American. Thus, the Genetic and Canon Law category seems heavily loaded with Mexican Americans. For the non-Mexican-American Catholics especially, the nativity of the grandparents seems to be an important variable in determining kinship orientation. Over 80 percent of the grandparents of the non-Mexican-American Catholics with a Parentela Orders orientation are European born, while only 69 percent of the grandparents of those with a Genetic or Canon Law perspective have been born outside the United States. The difference is especially great for paternal grandparents. Among these non-Mexican-Americans, only 46 percent of the respondents with a Parentela Orders orientation are descended from grandparents who were both American born, in contrast to 71 percent for those persons in the Genetic and Canon Law categories. Hence, Catholics with a Parentela Orders kinship orientation appear to be closer to their European roots than are those with a Genetic or Canon Law perspective.

Kinship and Religion: Summary

The findings pertaining to religious identification and kinship orientation indicate quite clearly a relationship between separatist, communal tendencies in religious groups and the attractiveness of the Parentela Orders model in kinship orientation. Jews and Neo-fundamentalists (particularly Southern Baptists) are far overrepresented in the Parentela Orders category. Within Judaism, the more separatist and traditional branches, especially Orthodoxy, are associated with the Parentela Orders model, and the least traditional, Reform Judaism, is tied more often to the Genetic and Canon Law perspective. Although as a group Mormons do not hold a Parentela Orders orientation, devout Mormons whose marriages had been sealed in the temple do emphasize Parentela Orders and de-emphasize Genetic and Canon Law conceptions of kinship. By way of contrast, the Standard American model seems to pervade all religious groups; only the Reformation era and non-denominational Protestants and those persons with no religious preference are to some extent overrepresented. Religious groups that seem to have strong associational components, however, seem to dominate the Civil Law category of kinship orientation. These groups, especially the ordinary (as contrasted with very devout) Mormons and the Pentacostal sectarians, seem to play down ethnicity as a factor in their lives, and apparently the church becomes the focal point of all activities and commitments. Finally, religious groups that aim at creating unity out of diversity tend to maintain Genetic and Canon Law orientations. Those Roman Catholics without strong European ethnic ties are overrepresented in this category. Thus, viewed as a whole, the findings on religious identity support the contention that religious pluralism as an ideology is associated with type of kinship orientation.

FAMILY INCOME AND MINORITY-GROUP STATUS

One issue in an analysis of conceptions that people hold about kinship is the comparative influence of minority-group status and financial resources on their views. Schneider and Smith (1973, p. 39) take the position that "much 'ethnic life-style' is of rural, traditional, lower status origin" and that "becoming a middle-class American necessarily involves abandonment of much of the class orientation of ethnic life ways." Moreover, they propose that, "The very traditionalism, rural origin, and adjustive functions of these subunits provides a certain structural uniformity which coincides with and reinforces the general lower-class orientation derived from similar positions in the occupational, power and prestige hierarchy of American society." The opposing position, as expressed by Staples (1971) in his discussion of the black family, is that the common experience of oppression and discrimination that pervades all phases of life in a minority group is more penetrating than socioeconomic factors in affecting family and kinship. "One trait that black families usually share is a history of racial oppression, whether under colonialism or slavery, [with the result that] no white family has faced the historical subjugation and contemporary racism that black families have encountered and continue to encounter even within the same socioeconomic stratum (Staples, 1971, p. 3)."

The issue of ethnicity versus socioeconomic factors is thus not whether one excludes the other as an influence upon kinship; rather the issue is one of comparative weighting of importance (Farber, 1971, p. 117). The data reported in this section first refer to family income generally and then to minority-group status.

Family Income and Kinship Orientation

Findings on the impact of family income upon kinship orientation are presented in Table 5-4. Unlike other indicators of socioeconomic status, family income takes account of multiple breadwinners and the existence of investments. Because of the influence of religious identity upon kinship orientation, the data are shown for Jewish, Protestant, and Catholic respondents separately. Unfortunately, since there are few cases in minority Protestant denominations and sects, all Protestant groups must be handled together.

As a whole, Table 5-4 can be interpreted as follows:

1. The religious groups vary in their concentration of cases in the Parentela Orders category by family income. Only the Protestants produce an overrepresentation of Parentela Orders responses among high income families. Consonant with this finding, however, Catholics with a low family income are underrepresented in the Parentela Orders orientation. Neither Jews nor those without a religious preference reveal much variation in concentration in the Parentela Orders category by income level.

TABLE 5-4. **Family Income and Kinship Orientation, with Religion Held Constant**

	Family income in 1977			
Kinship orientation	Under $10,000	$10,000 to $24,999	$25,000 or over	Total
Jewish[a]				
Parentela orders (%)	—[b]	26.7	23.7	24.5
Ratio of total		1.09	.97	
Standard american (%)	—	40.0	44.7	43.4
Ratio of total		.92	1.03	
Civil law (%)	—	13.3	15.8	15.1
Ratio of total		.88	1.05	
Genetic or canon law (%)	—	20.0	15.8	17.0
Ratio of total		1.18	.93	
N	—	15	38	
Protestant[c]				
Parentela orders (%)	18.3	12.6	21.6	15.9
Ratio of total	1.15	.79	1.36	
Standard american (%)	36.7	50.2	48.0	47.5
Ratio of total	.77	1.06	1.01	
Civil law (%)	15.0	18.1	20.6	18.3
Ratio of total	.82	.99	1.13	
Genetic or canon law (%)	30.0	19.1	9.8	18.3
Ratio of total	1.64	1.04	.54	
N	60	215	102	

[a] For Jewish respondents, Chi square not statistically significant.

[b] No cases in this category.

[c] For Protestant respondents, Chi square = 14.967; d.f. = 6; p = .05.

(continued)

2. There are inconsistencies among religious groups on the extent to which low income families are underrepresented in the Standard American and Civil Law categories. Family income alone seems insufficient to explain variation in conformity to Standard American and Civil Law conceptions of kinship.

3. Generally, the relationship between family-income and kinship orientation is strongest in the Genetic and Canon Law category. For Protestants, Catholics, and "no preference" respondents alike, persons with a family income of $25,000 or over are underrepresented in this category, while those with a family income under $10,000 are overrepresented. In this kinship category, family-income level seems to outweigh religious identity as a factor in orientation. With a dirth of financial resources, families at low income levels would have to rely upon kin—perhaps on a daily basis—to provide the economic assistance and personal services required to avoid disaster and to overcome crises as they arise. As a result, their conceptions of the character of kinship would undoubtedly be affected. (An alternative interpretation

TABLE 5-4 *(continued)*

Kinship orientation	Family income in 1977			
	Under $10,000	$10,000 to $24,999	$25,000 or over	Total
Catholic[d]				
Parentela orders (%)	6.3	22.7	20.5	19.4
Ratio of total	.32	1.17	1.06	
Standard american (%)	50.0	39.1	50.0	43.5
Ratio of total	1.15	.90	1.15	
Civil law (%)	9.4	15.5	15.9	14.5
Ratio of total	.65	1.07	1.10	
Genetic or canon law (%)	34.4	22.7	13.6	22.6
Ratio of total	1.52	1.00	.60	
N	32	110	44	
No religious preference[e]				
Parentela orders (%)	17.6	16.7	14.3	16.4
Ratio of total	1.07	1.02	.87	
Standard american (%)	41.2	52.4	57.1	50.7
Ratio of total	.81	1.03	1.13	
Civil law (%)	11.8	14.3	14.3	13.7
Ratio of total	.86	1.04	1.04	
Genetic or canon law (%)	29.4	16.7	14.3	19.2
Ratio of toal	1.53	.87	.74	
N	17	42	14	

[d] For Catholic respondents, Chi square not statistically significant.

[e] For respondents without a religious preference, Chi square not statistically significant.

would be that this orientation toward kinship tends to keep them at low income levels.)

4. Among Jews in particular the data indicate that family income has little influence on kinship orientation; there is little overrepresentation or underrepresentation of respondents from different income levels in the various categories of kinship orientation. This finding is consistent with those of other studies, which suggest that socioeconomic distinctions within the Jewish population are blunted by at least two factors. First, there is a growing homogeneity in financial status among Jews as the children and grandchildren of immigrants are absorbed into the American occupational, educational, and economic systems. Second, the distinctions in family and kinship "style of life" among Jews are determined more by religious orthodoxy and "Jewishness" (*Yiddishkeit*) of identity than by economic variables, and consequently those persons who are most assimilated into the Standard American culture simply leave the fold (Sherman, 1964). Hence, for Jews, socioeconomic homogeneity and the persistence as a "people"—religious and ethnic—seem to overshadow family income as an influence upon kinship orientation.

TABLE 5-5. **Minority-Group Status and Kinship Orientation, with Religion Held Constant**

Kinship orientation	Nonminority[a]	Mexican american	Other minoritites	Total
Protestant[b]				
Parentela orders (%)	15.2	—	24.2	16.0
Ratio of total	.95		1.51	
Standard american (%)	49.6	—	24.2	47.3
Ratio of total	1.05		.51	
Civil law (%)	19.6	—	3.0	18.2
Ratio of total	1.08		.16	
Genetic or canon law (%)	15.5	—	48.5	18.4
Ratio of total	.84		2.63	
N	341	12	33	
Catholic[c]				
Parentela orders (%)	20.5	18.8	—	19.9
Ratio of total	1.03	.91		
Standard american (%)	45.1	40.6	—	43.5
Ratio of total	1.04	.93		
Civil law (%)	17.2	9.4	—	14.5
Ratio of total	1.19	.65		
Genetic or canon law (%)	17.2	31.3	—	22.0
Ratio of total	.78	1.42		
N	122	64	3	

[a] There are no Jewish respondents in minority-group categories. Of the 75 residents with no religious preference, only 9 are in minority groups. On the other hand, minority groups are prone to adopt religions in non-Protestant and non-Catholic categories (e.g., Black Muslim, Traditional American Indian, Buddhist).

[b] For Protestant respondents, Chi square = 27.764; d.f.= 3; $p<.001$.

[c] For Catholic respondents, Chi square not significant.

Racial Minority-Group Status and Kinship Orientation

Table 5-5 displays the cross-tabulations for racial minority-group status and kinship orientation, by religion. In the table, "Other Minorities" consist mainly of Blacks. The total sample includes 46 persons in this category—29 blacks, 12 American Indians, 4 Orientals, and 1 black and Mexican American. Of the 10 minority persons who are neither Protestant nor Catholic, most adhere to American Indian, Oriental, or other non-Christian religions; these are excluded from the analysis.

The data for Protestant minorities are presented in the upper part of Table 5-5. (The 12 Mexican-American Protestants are not included.) Among Protestants, minority-group respondents are concentrated in Parentela Orders (ratio = 1.51) and in the Genetic and Canon Law category (ratio = 2.63); they are sparse in the Standard American and Civil Law orientations (ratio = 0.51 and 0.16, respectively).

The data for Catholics appear in the lower part of Table 5-5. (Since only three minority-group Catholics are not Mexican American, these cases are dropped from this analysis.) The Mexican Americans are overrepresented in the Genetic and Canon Law category (ratio = 1.42), and they are underrepresented in the Civil Law classification (ratio = 0.65). In contrast, nonminority group Catholics are underrepresented in the Genetic and Canon Law category (ratio = 0.78). However, Mexican-American Catholics are similar to Anglo Catholics in the percentages falling into the Parentela Orders and Standard American categories.

The high concentration of racial minority-group respondents in the Genetic and Canon Law classification suggests that family income may play an important role in organizing their kinship orientation. An analysis was undertaken of the relationship between family income and kinship orientation for persons in the minority-group category. The findings of this analysis are presented in Table 5-6. The various minorities are grouped together in Table 5-6 on the assumption that each "racial" or ethnic minority—whether black, Mexican American, or American Indian—has in some way had a history of subjugation and oppression which has given them all a similar kind of experience

The data in Table 5-6 signify that some variation in kinship orientation can indeed be attributed to differences in family income. The strongest trends of the data on minority-group income are: (a) the upward skewing of cases in the Parentela Orders category toward the high-income levels (with a ratio of 2.48 when income is $25,000 or over) and (b) the downward skewing of cases in the Civil Law and in the Genetic and Canon Law classifications toward low income levels.

But the role of income in determining kinship orientation is, however, limited. A multivariate analysis in Appendix A shows that, when a long series of

TABLE 5-6. Family Income and Kinship Orientation in Minority Groups

| Kinship orientation | Family income in 1977[a] | | | |
	Under $10,000	$10,000 to $24,999	$25,000 or over	Total
Parentela orders (%)	13.2	10.8	38.9	15.7
Ratio of total	.84	.69	2.48	
Standard american (%)	34.2	46.1	38.9	41.3
Ratio of total	.69	1.16	.94	
Civil law (%)	10.5	7.7	—	7.4
Ratio of total	1.42	1.04	—	
Genetic or canon law (%)	42.1	35.4	22.2	35.5
Ratio of total	1.19	1.00	.63	
N	38	65	18	121

[a] Chi square = 9.914; d.f. = 6; p = .10.

social background and family organization variables are taken into account, the direct effect of family income on kinship orientation is dissipated. As in Table 5-5 above, racial minority-group status then re-emerges as an important influence on kinship orientation. The minority groups tend to be overrepresented in the Genetic and Canon Law categories and underrepresented in the Parentela Orders and Civil Law classifications (where religious factors predominate). Hence, despite the apparent association between income and kinship orientation (when minority status is held constant in Table 5-6), the multivariate analysis reveals that it is racial status which molds conceptions of kinship.

The data on racial minority groups thus clarify the basis for the contradictory views held by Schneider and Smith (1973) and by Staples (1971). When the interaction of minority-group status and family income are examined in isolation from other background and family variables, the Schneider and Smith (1973) interpretation is supported, namely, that the economic factor is primary in determining kinship perspective. But, when other competing influences are considered, the impact of income is washed away, and the Staples (1971) conclusion survives, namely, that the oppression of minority groups transcends economics in structuring ideas about kinship.

Summary: Kinship, Income, and Minority-Group Status

The relationships among kinship orientation, religion, family income, and minority-group status are somewhat complex. The configuration of results for religious and racial minorities suggests that ethnicity outweighs income in influencing kinship orientation. Among Jewish respondents, family income is generally inconsequential for kinship orientation, while, among the racial minorities, family income (considered in isolation from other variables) is of substantial importance. But Jewish identity is tightly bound up with an ideology associated with Judaic law, and even secular Jews have not abandoned this ideology altogether. This ideology tends to overwhelm effects of family income on "life style." Similarly, the analysis of religious sects in the previous section has indicated that Protestant sectarians, despite their low income and blue collar occupations, tend to hold a Parentela Orders perspective and to veer away from Genetic and Canon Law views. But as people lose their identity as Jews and sectarians, the guiding family ideology which had previously overpowered socioeconomic considerations then weakens.

Mere membership in a racial minority, however, is independent of ideology. Racial identity is only raw material for social relations. One is identified as a Mexican American, American Indian, black, or Oriental by physical features and linguistic characteristics—that is, by overt biological and social signs. Consequently, the ideological overtones which emerge in interaction provide direction for the development of kinship orientations in these minorities. Oppression of racial minorities tends to drive persons toward Ego-centered kin orientations, which imply a communalistic (rather than factional) conception of the way society ought to be.

OCCUPATIONAL STATUS AND KINSHIP ORIENTATION

Most analyses of kinship ties in modern societies deal with extensiveness of interaction with discrete "relatives" rather than with the gestalt of priorities among kin. Consequently, statements about kinship generally refer to variations in extendedness as related to social stratification. As a result, much concern about modern kinship has been bound up with the nuclear-family household and its relationship to the economic structure of society. For example, economic and technological development of societies has been associated with "the ideology of the conjugal family (Goode, 1963, p. 369)," and Adams (1970, p. 577) suggests that "this ideology is buttressed by the personal freedom promised in the urban-industrial economy." Similarly, Smelser (1976, p. 153) proposes that if the family has to move about through the labor market, it cannot transport all its relatives with it or maintain close ties with them. It would thus be the economically unsuccessful, immobile families who deviate from this norm. Accordingly, "the working classes . . . express a stronger kin orientation, live closer to their kin, and interact with them more regularly than the middle classes (Adams, 1970, p. 585)."

Yet one problem with studies of extensiveness of ties with relatives is that they do not take into account the separate effects of migration (Klatzky, n.d.) and fertility patterns (Gordon, 1977). Since fertility and migration themselves affect extensiveness of kinship ties, socioeconomic interpretations may be misleading. As a result, such studies have limited value in providing insight into the role of kinship in modern social structure. The issue remains as to whether certain kinds of orientation toward kin are more conducive than others toward the maintenance and/or achievement of high socio-economic levels. (See Litwak, 1960a; Burr, 1973, p. 156.) It is this topic that is the focus of analysis in this section. The discussion below is presented in three parts: (a) occupational status of male co-head of household, (b) couples with the same occupational status, and (c) social mobility.

Occupational Status of Male Co-Head of Household.

Data relevant to the relationship between occupational status and kinship orientation are presented in Table 5-7. Occupation is used here as a way of labeling socioeconomic status of the family. Inasmuch as both husband and wife are regarded as co-heads of the household, the term male co-head (rather than head) is used in the table. In the case of male respondents, the male co-head's occupation refers to the respondent's own occupation; in the case of female respondents, the male co-head's occupation refers to her husband's occupation. Occupations were classified according to the 1970 U.S. Census classification index. Although the findings by co-head are alightly less conclusive than those for male respondents themselves in describing the influence of occupational status on kinship orientation, the inclusion of husbands permits a more extensive analysis. (In the table, religion is that of the respondent (male or female) rather than the religion of the male co-head.

The impact of occupational status upon kinship orientation depends in part upon religion of the respondent. The results, therefore, are presented by religious groups separately. (Since virtually all Jewish male co-heads are professionals, managers, or administrators, an occupational analysis is not feasible, and Jewish respondents are dropped from the table.) Table 5-7 reveals the following:

Protestants. Because of the small number of cases in the various denominations, all Protestants are grouped together in the table, and the findings are presented by occupational group:

1. Professional and managerial occupations are underrepresented in the Genetic and Canon Law category (ratio = 0.79).
2. Persons in clerical, sales, and craft occupational status do not show any marked tendency to occupy any given kinship orientation.
3. Blue-collar Protestants, however, are sparse in the Parentela Orders class (ratio = 0.67), and they tend to concentrate in the Genetic and Canon Law category (ratio = 1.41).

Catholics. Occupational status seems to play a different role in kinship ties of Catholics than in those of Protestants. As a result, Catholic families reveal patterns of kinship orientation which contrast with those of Protestants:

1. Unlike Protestants, professional-and-managerial-status Catholics are underrepresented in the Parentela Orders category (ratio = 0.75); but they are overrepresented in the Standard American orientation (ratio = 1.21).
2. Catholics in families where the husband is in a clerical, sales, or craft occupation also show a slight concentration in the Civil Law category (ratio = 1.20).
3. Finally, blue-collar Catholics are disproportionately represented in the Parentela Orders and the Genetic and Canon Law categories (ratio = 1.38 and 1.41, respectively) but underrepresented in Standard American kinship (ratio = 0.64).

TABLE 5-7. Occupation of Male Co-Head of Household and Respondent's Kinship Orientation, by Religion of Respondent[a]

	Male co-head's occupation			
Respondent's kinship orientation	Professional, managerial, or administrative	Clerical, sales, craft	Blue collar	Total
Protestant				
Parentela orders (%)	17.3	19.1	11.0	16.4
Ratio to total	1.05	1.16	.67	
Standard american (%)	54.0	44.3	43.9	48.2
Ratio to total	1.12	.92	.91	
Civil law (%)	15.1	20.0	20.7	18.2
Ratio to total	.83	1.10	1.14	
Genetic or canon Law (%)	13.7	16.5	24.4	17.3
Ratio to total	.79	.95	1.41	
N	139	115	82	336
Catholic				
Parentela orders (%)	15.0	19.7	27.5	19.9
Ratio to total	.75	.99	1.38	
Standard american (%)	51.7	43.9	27.5	42.8
Ratio to total	1.21	1.03	.64	
Civil law (%)	11.7	16.7	12.5	13.9
Ratio to total	.84	1.20	.90	
Genetic or canon law (%)	21.7	19.7	32.5	24.1
Ratio to total	.90	.82	1.35	
N	60	66	40	166
No religious preference				
Parentela orders (%)	25.0	16.7	14.3	20.0
Ratio to total	1.25	.84	.72	
Standard american (%)	53.6	44.4	35.7	46.7
Ratio to total	1.15	.95	.76	
Civil law (%)	14.3	22.2	14.3	16.7
Ratio to total	.86	1.33	.86	
Genetic or canon law (%)	7.1	16.7	35.7	16.7
Ratio to total	.43	1.00	2.14	
N	28	18	14	60

[a] For Jewish respondents, the number of cases in Clerical and Blue Collar categories was too small for meaningful crosstabulation. Chi square for all cases, regardless of religious affiliation (including Jewish) = 15.00; d.f. = 6; p = .02.

No Religious Preference. The distribution for men in families where the respondent has no religious preference embodies patterns found in both Protestant and Catholic families:

1. Like Protestants, "no preference" people in the professional and managerial occupational class tend to concentrate in the Parentela Orders

orientation, (ratio = 1.25) as opposed to a Genetic or Canon Law perspective (ratio = 0.43).

2. Like Catholics in the clerical, sales, and craft occupations, these individuals are abundant in the Civil Law category (ratio = 1.33).

3. Uniquely, "no preference" blue-collar families are underrepresented in both Parentela Orders and Standard American classes (ratio = 0.72 and 0.76, respectively) and overrepresented in the Genetic and Canon Law category (ratio = 2.14).

As a whole, the data in Table 5-7 indicate that occupational status of the male breadwinner seems to provide a strong influence on kinship orientation somewhat independently of religious identity. Apart from the singular exception of Catholics with a Parentela Orders orientation, persons in families marked by high occupational status (i.e., professional and managerial) tend to hold Parentela Orders and Standard American kinship orientations, while those with low socioeconomic status (i.e., blue collar) tend toward a Genetic or Canon Law kinship orientation. The middle occupational group (i.e., clerical, sales, and craft) clusters in the middle-ground Civil Law category.

Couples in Same Occupational Status

Probably, influence of occupational status on kinship orientation is most clearly identified when both husband and wife are in the same occupational category. Otherwise, comparisons might involve (a) households in which both husband and wife are working as well as households in which only one is employed or (b) households in which there are diverse occupational statuses within the family. Table 5-8 reports on the kinship orientations of persons in families in which the husband and wife are in the same occupational status.

Except for respondents in the Parentela Orders category, the results in Table 5-8 are similar to those in the previous section on male co-heads of households. In Standard American kinship, there is a skewing of percentages away from blue collar status; persons in clerical, sales, and craft occupations tend to concentrate in the Civil Law category (ratio = 1.23); in the Genetic and Canon Law class, the percentages are skewed away from professional and managerial families toward the blue-collar group. As with co-heads, the findings in the Parentela Orders category are likely confounded by the differences between Catholics and Protestants, inasmuch as high-status Protestants (but not Catholics) are overrepresented in that category. Hence, occupational status—whether classified by male co-head's occupation, by male respondent's occupation, or (in this case) by joint occupational status of husband and wife—yields a stable series of findings: Standard American kinship is associated with professional and managerial status, and Genetic

TABLE 5-8. Kinship Orientation of Respondents in Families in Which Husband and Wife Are in Same Occupational Status

Kinship orientation	Professional, managerial, or administrative occupation	Clerical, sales, or craft occupation	Blue collar occupation	Total
Parentela orders (%)	23.1	18.6	19.4	20.4
Ratio to total	1.13	.91	.95	
Standard american (%)	50.8	45.7	32.3	45.1
Ratio to total	1.13	1.01	.72	
Civil law (%)	13.8	20.0	12.9	16.3
Ratio to total	.85	1.23	.79	
Genetic or canon law (%)	12.3	15.7	35.5	18.1
Ratio to total	.68	.87	1.96	
N	65	70	31	

(Header spanning the three occupation columns: Couples in occupational status)

and Canon Law perspectives are generally found in blue-collar families. As the results on religion have indicated, however, in the case of Parentela Orders, socioeconomic influences interact with religious variables in a complex manner.

Social Mobility

Past research on kinship and social mobility has indicated little connection between occupational mobility and such variables as orientation toward kin, extent of interaction, mutual aid, and sharing of households (Adams, 1970). The only distinction of note is that sibling relations are sometimes affected. Differential achievement between brothers "usually means affectional distance and non-identification," but mutual upward or downward occupational mobility apparently results in mutual support and strengthened bonds (Adams, 1968, p. 172). The focus upon individual ties among relatives, however, leaves unanswered the question of the association between social mobility and general kinship orientation.

Table 5-9 displays data relevant to intergenerational social mobility. The extent of upward and downward social mobility of the respondents is examined separately for each level of father's occupation. The socioeconomic status of the respondent is classified by the occupation of the male co-head of the household (i.e., by the male respondents' own occupation and the female respondents' husband's occupation).

The first segment of Table 5-9 describes the downward social mobility of persons whose fathers are classified in professional and managerial occupa-

TABLE 5-9. Kinship Orientation and Intergenerational Social Mobility: Respondent's Father's Occupation as Compared with Male Co-Head's Occupation[a]

	Father's occupation								
	Professional or managerial[b]			Clerical, sales, craft[c]			Blue collar[d]		
	Downward mobility of child		Ratio of mild to extreme downward mobility	Upward mobility of child; To professional or managerial	Downward mobility of child: To blue collar	Ratio of upward to downward mobility	Upward mobility of child		Ratio of extreme To mild upward mobility
Kinship orientation	Mild: To clerical sales, crafts	Extreme to blue collar					Extreme: To professional or managerial	Mild: To clerical, sales, crafts	
Parentela orders	19.7%	12.1%	1.63	20.5%	6.4%	3.20	12.5%	16.4%	.76
Standard american	46.1%	27.3%	1.69	53.0%	46.8%	1.13	58.3%	42.5%	1.37
Civil law	28.9%	30.3%	.95	13.3%	17.0%	.78	12.5%	17.8%	.70
Genetic or canon law	5.3%	30.3%	.18	13.3%	29.8%	.45	16.7%	23.3%	.72
N	76	33		83	47		48	73	

[a] For male respondents, "Male Co-Head's Occupation" is occupation of respondent; for female respondents, "Male Co-Head's Occupation" is spouse's occupation.

[b] Chi square = 14.239; d.f. = 3; p = .01.

[c] Chi square = 8.681; d.f. = 3; p = .05.

[d] Not statistically significant.

tions. There is generally more mild downward mobility (to the clerical, sales, and crafts category) than extreme downward movement (to the blue-collar category). However, as the ratios of mild to extreme downward mobility indicate, considerable differences exist among the various kinship orientations. There is relatively less extreme downward mobility among persons in the Parentela Orders and Standard American categories than in the Civil Law and the Genetic and Cannon Law groupings. In fact, the chance of extreme downward mobility in the Genetic and Canon Law category tends to be high (ratio = 0.18).

The middle segment of Table 5-9 refers to the intergenerational social mobility of children whose fathers are classified as clerical, sales, or craft occupations. As a whole, there is more upward mobility of the children (to professional and managerial status) than there is downward mobility (to blue-collar occupations). But the differences among kinship orientations are profound. As before, persons with Parentela Orders and Standard American perspectives exhibit less downward mobility than do those in the Civil Law and Genetic and Canon Law categories. Persons with a Parentela Orders orientation are particularly more prone to upward than to downward mobility (ratio = 3.20), and those individuals with a Genetic or Canon Law orientation are especially more often downwardly mobile (ratio = 0.45).

The third segment of Table 5-9 deals with the upward social mobility of children whose fathers are (or had been) blue-collar workers. As expected, the Standard American orientation is found more often among respondents with extreme upward mobility (to professional and managerial status) than among persons with mild upward movement (to clerical, sales, or craft status) (ratio = 1.37). All other orientations, however, are associated with mild upward mobility from a blue-collar status of the father. Since this finding is contrary to expectations regarding the Parentela Orders orientation, one suspects that other influences—such as sectarianism, Catholicism, or minority group status—may have confounded the findings.

In general, Table 5-9 suggests that Parentela Orders and Standard American kinship orientations seem to signify the existence of some sort of brake on downward social mobility in certain families and indeed the probable presence of pressures toward upward mobility. In contrast, a Genetic or a Canon Law orientation appears to express the absence of such a brake.

ASSIMILATION AND THE STANDARD AMERICAN PATTERN

The findings in Chapter 4 on on the social characteristics of persons conforming to the Standard American model suggest that adoption of this model can be applied as an index of assimilation into middle-class American culture. Simultaneously, the study of assimilation seems to provide an opportunity to investigate the comparative influence on conceptions of collaterality deriving from ideological factors as opposed to viewing relatives as persons. This section compares religious factors and familiarity with grandparents as they each impinge upon conformity to the Standard American model. Because the vast majority of grandparents of respondents are no longer alive, this analysis focuses upon familiarity with them at the time when the respondent was growing up.

According to the position that, above all, variations in collaterality depend upon personal relationships rather than ideology, one would expect that an individual would assign a higher priority to those kinds of relatives he knows well than to those he does not know. For example, if an individual has known a grandparent well, under the principle of relatives-as-persons, he would probably think of "grandparents" as close, whereas if he has never known any of his grandparents, he would likely consider grandparents to be somewhat distant relatives. Moreover, if during childhood, the person has known his grandparents well, chances are high that he also is quite familiar with aunts or uncles.

Compared with the various kinship models under investigation, the Standard American pattern gives a higher priority to grandparents (and others in ascending generations) over other relatives. In this pattern, grandparents (followed by uncles and aunts) are placed second only to parents in priority. By way of contrast, in Parentela Orders, the grandparents come after all descendants of Ego and Ego's parents. In Civil Law, the grandparents follow both parents and children, and they are equal in closeness to Ego's grandchildren and siblings. In Genetic and Canon Law models, all nuclear family members are given priority over grandparents, and grandparents are on a par with aunts and uncles, grandchildren, and nieces and nephews (and, in Canon Law, with first cousins as well). Hence, with grandparents as reference point, an analysis of conformity to the Standard American model seems appropriate for determining whether acquaintanceship with a grandparent is associated with assignment of a high priority to grandparents in conceptions of collaterality.

One of the findings in Chapter 4 is that those respondents with a European-born father are far less likely than children of an American-father to conform to the Standard American model. Obviously, fewer American-born persons with a foreign-born father would know their grandparents and aunts and uncles than would those whose father had been born in the United States. This contingency evokes the question: Is a person with European born grandparents less apt to conform to the Standard American model because he has not known them or is it because of a difference in more general conceptions of kinship ties? The remainder of this section is concerned with the resolution of this issue.

Religion and Familiarity with Grandparents

Table 5-10 displays the percentages of persons with a Standard American orientation, sorted by their own religion and the birthplace of their grandparents. The table also indicates, for each religious group and grandparental birthplace, the percentage of persons who had known their grandparents well prior to adulthood. (In order to incorporate the findings for Jewish respon-

TABLE 5-10. Percentage of Persons in Standard American Category and the Respondent's Familiarity with Grandparents Prior to Adulthood, by Respondent's Religion and Birthplace of Grandparents

Specific grandparent, by respondent's religion	Grandparent born in Europe[a]			Grandparent born in United States[b]		
	Percent in standard american category	Percent familiar with grandparents[c]	N	Percent in standard american category	Percent familiar with grandparents[c]	N
Father's father						
Jewish	41.9	41.9	43	50.0	60.0	8
Protestant	42.2	23.4	45	52.2	49.8	230
Catholic	48.8	42.9	41	35.1	38.2	57
Father's mother						
Jewish	39.0	56.1	41	60.0	80.0	10
Protestant	40.9	37.8	44	52.1	61.8	236
Catholic	38.9	47.4	36	40.0	54.0	55
Mother's father						
Jewish	48.8	56.1	41	42.9	85.7	7
Protestant	40.8	40.1	49	52.5	61.0	236
Catholic	47.2	38.5	36	40.9	56.8	66
Mother's Mother						
Jewish	42.9	66.7	42	62.5	100.0	8
Protestant	37.2	53.5	43	52.4	71.0	248
Catholic	41.9	57.6	31	42.1	69.1	76
Means for all grandparents						
Jewish	43.2	55.2		53.9	81.4	
Protestant	40.3	38.7		52.3	60.9	
Catholic	44.2	46.6		39.5	54.5	

[a] For persons with European-born grandparents, *Rho* between percent in Standard American category and percent familiar with grandparent is 0.02.

[b] For persons with American-born grandparents, *Rho* between percent in Standard American category and percent familiar with grandparent is 0.62.

[c] Based on responses to question, "When you were growing up, how well did you know these relatives?—Your father's father (Grandfather on your father's side," and so on. "Familiar" includes response categories: *very well* and *fairly well*. "Unfamiliar" response categories are: *not so well, I did not know him (her)*, and *He (She) was not alive*.

dents, I had to compute percentages with bases less than 10; but even this small group shows much consistency with others in the analysis.)

In the interview, the respondents were asked, "When you were growing up, how well did you know these relatives?" The four grandparents were included in a list of consanguines: your father's father (grandfather on your father's side), and so on. In the analysis, respondents are classified in two groups—familiar and unfamiliar. Being *familiar* with the grandparent includes the response categories; (a) knew him very well and (b) knew him fairly well. Being *unfamiliar* with the grandparent refers to the categories: (a) not so well; (b) I did not know him; and (c) he was not alive.

Presumably, if the relative-as-a-person hypothesis is operative, there should be a linear relationship between percentages of persons knowing their grandparents well and percentages of persons with a Standard American orientation. Persons who have known their grandparents well should conform to the Standard American pattern of collaterality—regardless of religious category. However, if the ideological hypothesis is true, differences in percentages of persons in the Standard American category should vary according to the religious characteristics found in Chapter 4—rather than by familiarity with grandparents.

In order to test the relative-as-a-person hypothesis, Spearman rank correlation coefficients were computed to determine whether the percentage of persons who are familiar with grandparents varies directly with the percentage in the Standard American category (over all religious groups and all four grandparents together). For persons whose grandparents were born in Europe the correlation coefficient, *rho,* is *zero* ($r_s = .02$; $N=12$), which indicates that there is no relationship between familiarity with grandparents and Standard American kinship orientation. For persons whose grandparents were born in the United States, however, the results are ambiguous. Although the *rho* is high ($r_s = .62$; $N=12$), an inspection of the data casts doubt on its meaningfulness. First, among individuals with American-born grandparents, there is a constant percentage of Protestants in the Standard American category (about 52 percent despite a considerable variation in familiarity with different grandparents (50 to 71 percent)). Second, within religious groups there is little relationship between percent in the Standard American category and familiarity with grandparents. Third, Jews and Protestants both tend to adopt the Standard American orientation and to know grandparents more often than do Catholics. The *rho* is thus strongly influenced by religious factors.

Further comparisons among Jews, Protestants, and Catholics reinforce (rather than dispel) doubts about the relative-as-a-person hypothesis. When comparison is made between persons whose grandparents have been born in Europe and those whose grandparents are American-born, there is considerable diversity among religious groups in familiarity with grandparents. For Jews, the average difference in familiarity with grandparents, by birthplace of the grandparents, is 26.2 percent (or 55.2% versus 81.4%); for Protestants, the average difference is 22.2 percent (or 38.7% versus 60.9%); and for Catholics the difference is only 7.9 percent (or 46.6% versus 54.5%). These figures suggest that the amount of contact between the respondent's parents and his grandparents during the respondent's childhood is itself, in part, a function of religion. Insofar as contact with grandparents is influenced by religious community, the data imply that religious ideologies themselves differ in the salience they attach to relationships with grandparents—with a higher salience among Jews and Protestants than among Catholics.

Familiarity with grandparents itself seems unimportant in holding a Standard American orientation. Rather, the extent of assimilation into American culture appears to be a key element. Assimilation, in turn, seems to depend upon religious codes. When comparison is made simply between persons whose grandparents are European and those whose grandparents are American-born, religious groups vary systematically in conformity to the Standard American model. As Table 5-10 indicates:

1. For Jews, the average difference between persons with European as contrasted with American-born grandparents is 11 percent (or 43% versus 54%). But among Jewish respondents, the nativity of grandmothers seems to be of particular importance—much greater than that of grandfathers—in inducing assimilation into the Standard American system. In traditional Jewish law, it is the task of males to maintain ties with ascending generations and of females to care for children (and grandchildren). Sixty-one percent of Jewish persons with a American-born grandmother ($N = 18$) are in the Standard American category as compared with only 41 percent of those with European-born grandmothers ($N = 83$). This finding of a 20 percent difference implies that the respondents with American-born grandmothers have parents who themselves have been integrated into American middle-class culture.

2. Among Protestants, consistently 10 to 15 percent more respondents with American-born grandparents hold a Standard American orientation than do those whose grandparents were born in Europe (with an average difference of 12.0 percent).

3. Catholics, however, are least affected by birthplace of grandparents in their conformity to the Standard American pattern. If anything, having an American-born grandfather *decreases* the probability of their being in the Standard American category (an average difference of −4.7 percent). In general, over generations Catholics seem to be less assimilated than Jews or Protestants into the Standard American system.

American and European Grandparents: Summary

This section has dealt with an issue regarding the basis for differences in conformity to the Standard American model between persons whose recent ancestors were born in Europe and those whose close antecedants were born in the United States. Ultimately, the issue rests upon the kinds of factors which influence kinship orientation generally.

One position is that, since the Standard American model gives a high priority to grandparents, aunts, and uncles, people who are quite familiar with their relatives in ascending generations will tend to conform to this pattern. (Presumably, those individuals who in childhood had known their grandparents well also were familiar with aunts and uncles.) From this perspective, which depends upon considering relatives as persons, differences between respondents with European-born grandparents and those with American-born grandparents in conforming to the Standard American model stem directly from the fact that fewer individuals with European grandparents would have known them (and/or aunts and uncles).

The other position is that ideological factors provide a more powerful influence than personal ties in the organization of collaterality. The ideological position is that certain religious norms and justifications facilitate acceptance of the Standard American model and encourage close ties with grandparents. Hence, from this perspective, distinctions between persons with European-born and American-born grandparents in conforming to the Standard American model are greater among different religions than by degree of familiarity.

In brief, the findings on assimilation of European families indicate that (a) knowing a grandparent well per se seems to play only a minimal role in determining kinship orientation, (b) by the third American generation, the effects of foreign origins (like those of minority-group status) are sustained mainly through the intervention of religious or other ideological factors; and (c) at least in an American social context, the various religions seem to differ in the salience they attach to relationships with grandparents—with Jews and Protestants assigning a greater importance to them than do Catholics. (This proclivity apparently provides Jewish and denominational Protestant ideologies with a good "fit" with the Standard American kinship model.)

At first glance, the finding that Jewish respondents with American-born grandmothers have an affinity to the Standard American model seems to contradict the data in Table 5-1 that show that Jews are underrepresented in that model. But two other facts are also relevant, namely, that orthodoxy is associated with the Parentela Orders model, and other investigations have revealed that the number of generations in the U.S. is associated with a languishing of orthodoxy (Farber et al., 1977). Loss of orthodoxy decreases the traditional emphasis upon lines of descendants and apparently permits the high salience of ties with grandparents to become manifest. Consequently, the connection between having an American-born grandmother and holding a Standard American kinship orientation is actually not inconsistent with previous findings. Rather it confirms them in describing assimilation to the American middle class from a kinship perspective. (These conclusions are supported by the multivariate analysis in Appendix A.)

SUMMARY: VARIATIONS IN COLLATERALITY

The opening section of this chapter posed the question: Are variations in collateralty in American kinship merely an elaboration of themes on a single cultural model, or do these variations reflect a diversity of ideological sources of kinship norms? In that section, it was proposed that three kinds of data might shed light on the resolution of this issue: data on religion, data on specific socioeconomic variations in kinship mapping, and data on familiarity with specific relatives. The information gathered in the Phoenix survey was analyzed to determine how religion, socioeconomic factors, and familiarity are related to kinship mapping.

Religion

With regard to religion, the findings are that (a) persons leaning toward orthodoxy in sectarian-like religious groups—neofundamentalist Protestants, Mormons, and Jews—tend to hold a Parentela Orders kinship orientation to a greater extent than others do; (b) Protestants in the traditional denominations are overrepresented in the Standard American category; and (c) persons with religious orientations espousing universalism—Catholics and those with no religious preference—are overrepresented in the Genetic and Canon Law classification. These findings are generally similar to those of other studies involving university students (Farber, 1977) or a Jewish community (Farber, 1979). My interpretation is that the findings do confirm the proposition that degree of pluralism in religious ideology is associated with type of kinship orientation.

It might be argued that it is the religious label, rather than ideology, that is responsible for these variations. However, such an argument fails to deal with the fact that Jews tend to be overrepresented in the pattern of collaterality found in Jewish sources (e.g., the *Mishnah*) and Catholics appear more often than do other religionists in the mode of collaterality described in the Canon Law of the Church. Nor does this argument consider the detail that Western religions in general are explicit in their judgments regarding family life and that, in particular, sectarian-like groups (such as the Mormons) organize appropriate family relationships in terms of the model appearing in the Pentateuch. Hence, although these findings may not convince those persons who are skeptical about the influence of religious ideology on kinship mapping, neither would they sway anyone from the conclusion that ideological content has an effect on these maps.

Religion appears to be augmented by minority-group status in structuring kinship maps. The analysis indicates that, when other variables are taken into account, income is less powerful than minority-group status (as Mexican-American, black, or American Indian) in the patterning of kinship orientations. This finding suggests that membership in a racial minority group carries with it experiences of oppression which may generate a communalist position—and a Genetic or Canon Law kinship perspective.

Socioeconomic Status

As for socioeconomic characteristics themselves, the pattern of overrepresentation in the findings is that (a) there is a tendency for persons in professional and managerial families to fall into the Standard American classification; (b) persons in the middle socioeconomic category (i.e., clerical, sales, and craft occupations) are more often found in the Civil Law grouping; and (c) those in blue-collar families cluster more than anticipated in the Genetic and Canon Law pattern. The results on the Parentela Orders pattern show the confounding influence of religion and ethnicity. (When the respondents are classified by family income or by educational level, the results are similar to those based on occupation.)

This configuration of findings for socioeconomic characteristics contradicts the expectation in the Schneider and Smith (1973) formulation, namely, that the middle class emphasizes the unity of the nuclear family to a greater extent than does the lower class. Instead, the middle-class respondents—professionals, managers, and administrators—stress line of descent at the expense of nuclear family ties, particularly the ancestral line in the Standard American model. It is clearly the blue-collar respondents who, in holding Genetic or Canon Law perspectives, give priority to nuclear family members over other kin.

One might argue that the blue-collar respondents place much value on the coherence of the nuclear family because of the fragility of such ties in the lower class. However, other findings in this study, such as those pertaining to the Srole index of anomia (Srole, 1956; Miller, 1977, pp. 375–377), fail to support this argument.[1] Apparently aside from economic adversity, people who regard social ties as fragile also display other attributes of an alienated *Weltanschauung*—a sense of powerlessness, pessimism about the future state of society, and a lack of trust in others. These elements are tapped in the Srole index. As Table 5-11 indicates, the anomia attributes are more prevalent among people in lower than at higher socioeconomic levels, minority groups, low educational level, income less than $10,000, and persons in blue-collar families. The findings on socioeconomic characteristics of persons with high anomia scores support the Schneider position; but other findings seem even more important for the resolution of the issue. Table 5-11 also shows that (except for persons with a graduate school education, with no religious preference, and with incomes over $25,000) people with Genetic and Canon Law mappings have a higher than average score on the anomia index regardless of religion, minority-group status, educational level, family income, or occupation of the male co-head of the household. Indeed, for all social characteristics (with the few exceptions noted above), the mean anomia score in the Genetic and Canon Law category is actually the highest of any of the kinship orientations. It is the consistent tendency for persons with a Canon Law or Genetic orientation to have a high score on the Srole scale, regardless of social characteristics, that seems to be significant in the interpretation of the findings.

Both the Srole Anomia Scale and the Canon Law (or Genetic) orientation imply that (a) the principal vehicles for social continuity are the major economic, political, and religious corporate structures in the society rather than

TABLE 5-11. Mean Scores on Srole "Anomia" Scale for Respondents in Genetic and Canon Law Category of Kinship Orientation, by Social Characteristics[a]

	Mean scores on srole "anomia" scale		
Social characteristics	Persons in genetic and canon law category	Total sample	N
Religion			
Jewish	2.11	1.30	54
Protestant	2.30	1.75	387
Catholic	2.02	1.77	189
No religious preference	1.60	1.63	75
Minority-group status			
Nonminority	1.69	1.49	590
Mexican Americans	3.00	2.64	80
Other (Black, American Indian, and			
Oriental)	3.00	2.89	46
Educational level			
Not a high school graduate	3.18	2.64	104
High School graduate	2.09	1.92	245
Some College	1.73	1.25	303
Some graduate work	0.56	1.08	65
Family income in 1977			
Under $10,000	2.61	2.25	114
$10,000 to $24,999	2.08	1.82	387
$25,000 or over	1.16	1.16	200
Occupational status of male co-head of household			
Professional, managerial, and			
administrative	1.44	1.25	268
Clerical, sales, and crafts	2.05	1.87	213
Blue collar	2.89	2.34	139

[a] A high score denotes a high degree of "anomia."

family and kinship and (b) everyone ought to have ample chance to participate in these structures. An individual with a high score has a view of the world such that (a) life chances generally are diminishing; (b) the dimness of the future suggests that one should not bring additional children into the world; (c) the larger social forces are so overwhelming that one cannot plan ahead effectively; (d) one cannot place trust in others; and (e) government will not be forthcoming with realistic solutions. By implication, though, one *ought* to be able to do these things; the larger forces and the major corporate structures ought to facilitate life chances, provide an optimistic setting for a fulfilling family life, and be truly adaptive in the face of social problems and crises. The perception of failure by the larger social structure to deal effectively with problems permeating the society leaves high scorer on the "anomia" index with only a fragile institution to deal with—one's nuclear family.

Social Mobility

The connection between kinship orientation and striving for achievement is revealed in the analysis pertaining to intergenerational social mobility. These findings indicate that Parentela Orders and, in particular, the Standard American model are associated with upward mobility and restraint on downward movement. At this point in the analysis, one cannot determine whether the kinship pattern resulted from the intergenerational mobility or whether something in the individual's family of orientation was responsible for this movement. The premise that kinship mappings represent more extensive ideologies, that may be transmitted from one generation to the next, leads me to the latter interpretation.

The significance of the Standard American model for upward social mobility and restraint on downward mobility suggests a tantilizing interpretation of the relationship between kinship orientation and achievement motivation. Since the Standard American map emphasizes a sense of closeness to relatives in ascending generations, one can interpret this finding (in a fanciful way) to mean that achieving individuals regard their place in society as reflecting the "inherent" worthiness of their family line—surely their ancestors and hopefully their progeny. Such an orientation would also lead people who are currently of low socioeconomic status to "prove" the worthiness of their line by inducing a high degree of achievement motivation in their children. Carrying this interpretation further, one might even consider the Standard American model as a "survival" of the Puritan doctrine of the predestined Elect, whose Earthly success signaled their fated Eternal Salvation and set them apart from the mass of the society. But, of course, such an interpretation cannot be tested empirically.

Grandparents and Kinship Mapping

The findings on grandparents confirm the conclusion that European heritage (but only in conjunction with religion) has a bearing on kinship mapping. Distance from European roots seems to have most affected assimilation of Jews into the Standard American system and touched Catholics least. Still, Catholics with European grandparents tend to provide Parentela Orders mappings, while those with non-European grandparents are more concentrated in the Genetic and Canon-Law category (and not in the Standard American pattern). Together these findings make a strong case for regarding European tradition, functioning together with religion and minority-group status, as an element which shapes kinship orientation.

Viewed collectively, the findings on familiarity with grandparents and conformity to the Standard American model do not support the hypothesis that kinship mapping derives primarily from factors pertaining to relatives-as-persons. Rather, the findings indicate that birthplace and childhood familiarity with grandparents are dependent upon ideological factors to determine the ways they affect kinship mapping.

Variations: Fundamental or Superficial?

The thrust of the findings is that variations in patterns of collaterality in American kinship appear to represent ideological differences associated with position in the social structure rather than superficial elaborations of differences in personal attributes. But, the issue is *not* whether the configurations of attributes that define relatives as persons are alone important in influencing interaction between kin. Certainly, interaction with specific kin is influenced by personal characteristics apart from relatedness—gender, age, common interests, personal resources, religious labels, pleasantness, and so on. But a formulation that emphasizes these attributes as the primary basis for collaterality does not explain why individuals whose relatives have similar configurations of attributes exhibit different patterns of collaterality (or vice versa). Rather the issue is whether patterns of collaterality imply, in addition to personal proclivities, a series of ideologies that serves to organize relationships with family and kin. True, one's perceptions of relatives as persons may incorporate whatever else these relatives are (apart from their being biologically related), but the grounds for these perceptions, it seems, depend upon the kinds of assumptions about the nature of kinship and its relationship to the general social structure. My view is that these grounds are expressed in terms of kinship models that have emerged in the historical process.

Schneider and I reach different conclusions with regard to the significance of variations in collaterality. Why? Schneider's position is that these variations are superficial manifestations stemming primarily from the fact that people in modern societies participate in several social domains, while my position is that these variations in collaterality themselves involve fundamental ideological distinctions. Perhaps a major source of this difference lies in the methods we use to analyze kinship distances.

Schneider relies heavily upon the genealogical method of collecting data on kinship ties. Because of the huge financial investment, laboriousness, and time expenditure required to construct reliable and "complete" genealogies, Schneider's analyses are necessarily restricted to a relatively small number of genealogies. Much of Schneider's work is based upon 43 genealogies gathered in 1961-1963, supplemented by extensive interviews with 47 couples, several women, and 99 children and their mothers (Schneider, 1968; Schneider and Cottrell, 1975). In addition, the analysis of lower-class kinship by Schneider and Smith (1973) is based on "59 Afro-American, Southern White, and Spanish-American families living in Chicago (of which 40 provided relatively full information)." The interviews covered a wide range of topics dealing with kinship, occupation, and status domains, but in addition they included a range of factual information of a genealogical nature. The amount of detailed information in these interviews and genealogies is immense.

The richness of materials in Schneider's studies must reveal an extensive amount of variation (within the same genealogy) in the perception of social distance among relatives of equal genetic relatedness. The extent of this variation within genealogies undoubtedly has evoked questions by Schneider regarding the reasons why an individual would make these distinctions. A reasonable response to these questions (which Schneider provides) is that the individual perceives relatives as persons, whose genetic relatedness is but one facet of their configuration of personal and social attributes. From this point, it is only a short step to conclude that, since social relationships are reciprocal, individual respondents differ (i.e., variations *between* genealogies occur) because of the diversity of individuals' own role configurations. For Schneider, the respondent too is a person whose non-kinship attributes influence his interaction with relatives. Thus, Schneider's conceptions regarding the character of collaterality in American society seems to be tied to a particular mode of data collection which permits ample observation of within-case variations, but which is limited in the extent to which it allows the observation of regularities between groups in a highly heterogeneous society.

My own method is intended to discount variations within individual genealogies and to focus instead upon general patterns of collaterality in a large diverse population. For example, my technique for classifying respondents by kinship orientation requires only that a majority of responses correspond to a given pattern. The procedure thereby rests on the assumption that variations within genealogies are irrelevant in assessing an overall pattern for an individual. Consequently, by ignoring details of genealogies, I can determine whether regularities occur in a differentiated population, and I then ascribe these regularities to ideological factors. Whereas the focus of Schneider's analysis is upon "the relative" (or, to use his term, Alter), the focus of my analysis is upon the individual (i.e., Ego) and the *organization* of ties with relatives.

The difference between Schneider's and my conception of collaterality in American kinship appears to be analogous to a controversy occuring in the field of linguistics. Some linguists believe that the various regional, socio-economic, and ethnic variations in the use of English represent dialectal deviations from Standard English; others regard some of this diversity as representing distinct systems, each with its own rationale and set of usage rules, so that Standard English is but one of several such systems. In looking at collaterality, Schneider seems to take the "dialect" position, while I hold the "systems" position.

NOTE

[1]Carr (1971) reports a study showing that the Srole index is affected by tendencies of blacks of low socioeconomic status to acquiesce to any statement in an interview. Carr's criticism, however, is not applicable in this investigation.

1. First, unlike his sample, Phoenix respondents of lower occupation, education, and income levels do not overwhelmingly tend to agree with the Srole items. In the Carr sample, the ratio of responses in the high categories (4,5) as compared with those in the low categories (0,1) is 19.3 for blacks at the lower end of socioeconomic scale. The Phoenix investigation, however, shows little such skewness in responses toward acquiescence. In the Phoenix study, the ratio of high to low scores for persons with less than four years of high school is 1.04; the ratio for persons with family incomes under $10,000 is .67; and the ratio of respondents from blue-collar families is 0.81. Blacks and Mexican Americans indicate a slight skewness toward agreement. (For blacks, the ratio is 1.79 and for Mexican Americans 1.25.) But this degree of skewness cannot be interpreted as indicating that the Srole index measures acquiescence rather than a form of disillusionment with society.

2. A second reason for rejecting the acquiescence view is that the findings on the relationship between anomia and kinship orientation persist even when such variables as religion, minority-group status, educational level, family income, or occupational status are held constant statistically. Similarly, when Lenski and Leggett (1960) remove effects of acquiescence from their sample, the rank order of percentages of persons in various socioeconomic categories who agree with a Srole item remains unchanged.

3. A third basis for rejecting the acquiescence position is that in a later chapter (Table 7-4) the association between anomia and kinship orientation is sustained when the respondent's own score on anomia is compared with his estimate of his spouse's answers to the Srole questions. This comparison is made by the individual, and many distinctions between self and spouse occur at all socioeconomic levels. It thus appears that individuals in the Phoenix study have little difficulty in discriminating between anomic reactions of self and other.

In summary, three reasons for rejecting the Carr position have been put forth: (a) the lack of skewness toward acquiscence among low socioeconomic status respondents; (b) the persistence of statistical relationships even when socioeconomic variables are held constant; and (c) ability of individuals at all socioeconomic levels to distinguish between anomia in one's self as compared to spouse. The findings pertaining to the Srole index thereby argue against the Carr interpretation that it represents an acquiescence scale rather than a sense of disillusionment or anomia.

Family of Orientation

6

The findings in the previous chapter indicate that kinship orientations are associated with religious tenets and socioeconomic status. Insofar as conceptions of kinship represent ideological positions, one would anticipate that they tend to be transmitted from one generation to the next in family lines, from parents to children. Accordingly, families of persons with different kinds of kinship orientation should differ in important ways from one another. Diverse kinship orientations should thus reveal particular characteristics not only about the respondents themselves but also about their parents and siblings.

Here I shall discuss the relationship between kinship orientation and attributes of the respondents' parental family. The first section sets forth a series of basic propositions regarding this relationship; it refers to the ideological aspects of factionalism and communalism. Succeeding sections deal with findings pertaining to respondents' parents and siblings, and they involve such characteristics as prevalence of divorce, religious endogamy, age at marriage, maternal employment, and fertility patterns.

IDEOLOGICAL ASPECTS OF FACTIONALISM AND COMMUNALISM

As the earlier chapters have proposed, characteristics associated with kinship orientations seem to be derived from the social positions of population segments and, ultimately, from the general social structure itself. This section deals with the ideological content of factionalist versus communal structures in society, particularly as this content refers to marriage and family ties.

Earlier chapters distinguish between social structures giving priority to special interests of a single group—factionalism—and those giving priority to common interests of all groups in a society—communalism. Factionalism implies a situation in which special interest groups are vying for superiority over other groups for economic, political, or religious "goods"—that is, access to wealth, to power, or to eternal or secular salvation. Since factionalist polity refers to organization aimed at procuring or maintaining superiority, its presence may be regarded as a mechanism for stratifying a society.

Factions are, after all, a means for the gathering of forces and of mobilizing members for conflict or competition. Insofar as factionalism in kinship organization involves this pulling inward and engaging the obligation and/or loyalty of members, it seem appropriate to call this type of kinship organization *centripetal*.

Communalism, on the other hand, implies a situation in which special interests are subordinated to common concerns. In stateless societies these common concerns may well emerge from economic interdependence or the presence of a common enemy. In societies with more highly developed governmental institutions, other common interests may exist as well—the presence of a universal religion (as opposed to sects and denominations), nationalism (as opposed to subnational "ethnic" identities), centralized political bureaucracy (Weber, 1961, p. 51), values of political, social and economic equality, and so on. For example, Max Weber reports that in medieval Europe, the Church "strove to abolish the rights of the clan in inheritance so that it might retain land willed to it." The common concerns would best be served if members of kin groups were to be dispersed throughout the society. In this manner, the maximum number of social networks would be created to scatter the loyalties and obligations of any individual as widely as possible. Under the conditions of communalism, major forces would exist to minimize property-based familial ties and to expel family members outward; it thus seems appropriate to regard this kind of kinship associated with communalism as *centrifugal*.

As a consequence, those kinship systems that are oriented toward the dispersal of human property throughout the society (as a matter of common interest to all kinship units) stimulate the homogenization of society and bolster the development of communal regimes. Because of an orientation toward status maintenance in an indefinite future, kinship systems that tend to emphasize saving (i.e., centripetal systems) involve long-range perspectives, establishment of mechanisms for stabilizing obligations, and a redundancy of family roles. However, because of an orientation toward immediate psychological and physical comfort of the mass of the population, other systems which stress distribution of people and their property throughout the society (i.e., centrifugal systems) involve short-range perspectives, use of mechanisms for maximizing cross-pressures, and a minimum of jural kinship obligations.

Many observers have noted the "fit" between the decline of the significance of the extended family and the rise of modern urbanized industrial society. This fit is attributed to ease of mobility and the reduction of obligations which might impede individual destiny (Goode, 1963: Burgess, Locke, and Thomes, 1963). Still, even in societies that ideologically uphold communal norms in family organization, there may be strong motivations among those groups vying for power to adopt centripetal norms. Although competing elites in the United States around 1800 were not constituted as formal corporate entities, they organized themselves into collections of families, forming political factions, pooling resources, intermarrying with one another, and creating almost separate social worlds (Farber, 1972). Indeed, in the absence of constraints on familial accumulation of resources, one would anticipate that rival elites would favor centripetal norms of kinship for themselves (but perhaps not for others).

Centripetal and centrifugal tendencies in kinship seem to generate kinship norms that are related to the kinship models under investigation. In the case of centripetal kinship this relationship appears to occur in the following way:

1. When members of a special-interest group, at some time in its history, reach a consensus that its continued existence (or position in society) as an identifiable entity (or as ''successful'') is threatened by the incursion of other groups—who would ''raid'' its members or ''reduce'' its position in society—the members will resort to the strategy of mobilizing the group to resist this incursion.

2. If the threat persists, this mobilization stimulates the group to organize itself in a centripetal manner, that is, to create sharply defined boundaries between it and other groups and to draw its members inward.

3. The mobilization fostered by threats to the long-run integrity of the special-interest group also requires a high degree of compliance (both coercive and voluntary) by the members to promote its ends.

4. As a fundamental institution that enables the group to persist as an identifiable entity (or to perpetuate its position in society) over generations, kinship too is governed by rules emphasizing centripetal tendencies.

5. The mobilization of centripetal kinship groups to draw members inward would encourage strong collective efforts to maintain firm group boundaries and to sustain family stability.

6. Consequently, groups characterized by socioeconomic, religious, or other special interests that depend for their perpetuation upon centripetality in kinship would, over a series of generations, adopt family and marriage norms that foster this inward movement. Such norms would include endogamy, reluctance to resort to divorce, high priority given to the maternal role, and special meanings applied to fertility.

7. Since Standard American and particularly Parentela Orders kinship models appear to represent centripetal approaches to kinship organization, the norms specified above should be more pronounced among persons holding these orientations than they are among people with Civil Law, Genetic, or Canon Law orientations.

Complementing this set of statements on centripetal kinship norms is another set showing how communalism as an ideology is associated with centrifugal kinship norms:

1. When people regard any special-interest group as functionally equiva-

lent to other groups in the society, they have little stake in the perpetuation of any given social entity. (But where any particular group is considered indispensible for everyone's benefit, e.g., the Catholic community, the aim is generally to universalize that community, to identify it with the common good.)

2. Instead, people consider it to be important that special interests of different groups be subordinated to the common good and that the power of these special-interest groups be eliminated.

3. The power of special-interest groups is minimized if individuals are placed under cross-pressures as much as possible. With conflicting loyalties, people are less likely to be mobilized to give priority to a special interest.

4. Cross-pressures are maximized when boundaries between groups are vague and there are strong centrifugal tendencies in group organization.

5. As a fundamental institution in a society, kinship also would be governed by centrifugal rules that stress the creation of as many networks among families as possible.

6. The diffuseness of centrifugal kinship networks would minimize the perpetuation of special-interest groups, while at the same time, it would maximize the number of individual relatives with whom personal ties (and personal demands) can be sustained.

7. Consequently, families characterized by centrifugal kinship norms would emphasize personal ties in domestic relationships. In their attentiveness to personal qualities in domestic relations, these families would be inclined to be tolerant about departures from endogamy, decisions to divorce, the performance of the maternal role, and rates of fertility.

8. Since Genetic and especially Canon Law kinship models appear to represent centrifugal perspectives in kinship organization, the norms listed above should be prevalent among persons with these kinship orientations.

The succeeding sections of this chapter are devoted to testing the relationship between kinship orientations and norms associated with centripetal versus centrifugal tendencies.

KINSHIP ORIENTATION AND DIVORCE

Social scientists have noted that prevalence of divorce is related to the ways societies are organized. Using the Human Relations Area Files, Ackerman (1963) has shown that divorce rates are consistently low in those bilateral societies where there is community endogamy and first-cousin marriage and in those unilineal societies in which the levirate is present. In addition, Murdock (1970) reports that in societies permitting first-cousin marriage, relationships between cousins are seldom formal; similarly, in unilineal societies with levirate or with sororal marriage, brothers-in-law and sisters-in-law tend to be informal in interaction. This tendency toward informality (and often sexual license) implies a sense of closeness among these relatives. Noting that societies displaying a high degree of factionalism also tend to be characterized by community endogamy, first-cousin marriage, or the levirate, Farber (1975) found that societies with factional regimes also tend to have low divorce rates, while societies with communal regimes have high divorce rates. Finally, cross-cultural research on industrial societies indicates that divorce rates are inversely related to socioeconomic status (Goode, 1962). Given this array of findings on the relationship between social structure and divorce in societies with varying degrees of complexity, it seems reasonable to expect that kinship orientation—which also appears to be associated with locus in the social structure—is related to divorce.

Insofar as kinship orientation has an ideological basis, its impact should be felt throughout the respondents' families—not only in the parental generation but also among brothers and sisters. Table 6-1 presents data on the prevalence of divorce among the respondents' parents, by kinship orientation and by the religion in which the respondents were raised. The table indicates that for the different religious groups, prevalence of divorce is lowest among parents of Jewish respondents and next lowest among Protestants and Catholics, and divorce is most widespread among parents of persons raised in secular homes. When kinship orientation is taken into account for each religious group, the results are as follows:

1. While Jewish respondents with divorced parents are underrepresented in the Parentela Orders classification, they are fairly high in the remaining categories of kinship orientation, although still low in comparison with the other religious groups.

2. Protestants with different kinship orientations show little variation in prevalence of parental divorce: there is, however, a slight tendency for divorce among parents to be overrepresented in the Genetic and Canon Law category.

3. For Catholics, divorce occurs least often among fathers and mothers of persons in the Parentela Orders class and most frequently among those in the Civil Law, Genetic, and Canon Law categories.

Table 6-1 also presents information on prevalence of divorce among respondents' parents for different socioeconomic groups. In the table, persons are classified by their father's occupation prior to the adulthood of the respondents. Consistent with other investigations, the data show a clearcut relationship between socioeconomic status and divorce: fathers and mothers in the professional, managerial, and administrative class are least likely to divorce, while the blue-collar parents are the most inclined. But within socioeconomic strata, kinship orientations still differ in prevalence of marital disruption. For all three strata, divorce is widespread in the Genetic and

TABLE 6-1. Prevalence of Divorce among Respondents' Parents, by Kinship Orientation, Religion in Which Respondent Was Raised, and Father's Occupation

	Parentela orders	Standard american	Civil law	Genetic or canon law	Total
Religion in which respondent was raised					
No religious					
preference (%)	30.0			33.3	31.4
N	20			15	35
Jewish (%)	6.7[b]	13.6[a]		11.8	11.1
N	15	22		17	54
Protestant (%)	22.4	18.8	20.8	26.2[a]	21.2
N	67	197	72	84	420
Catholic (%)	15.8[b]	21.3	26.7[a]	25.0	21.9
N	38	89	30	44	201
Father's occupation while respondent was growing up					
Professional,					
managerial, or					
administrative					
(%)	11.5	12.4	16.7[a]	15.4[a]	13.4
N	52	113	42	39	246
Clerical, sales, or					
craft (%)	20.0[b]	23.1	23.7	28.3[a]	23.8
N	35	108	38	46	227
Blue collar (%)	29.7	27.5	24.3[b]	35.3[a]	29.2
N	37	91	37	51	216
Entire sample (%)	19.0	19.5	21.6	27.7[a]	21.4
N	126	333	116	141	716

[a] Ratio of cell percentage to total percentage is 1.2 or over.

[b] Ratio of cell percentage to total percentage is .8 or under.

Canon Law category, and except for the blue-collar group, it is least prevalent in the Parentela Orders category.

The overall pattern of prevalence of divorce among the respondents' parents is generally repeated in the next generation. Table 6-2 reports the percentage of respondents' siblings with previous marriages. (Some of these siblings have remarried; others have remained as divorced persons.) The percentage of previously married brothers and sisters is lowest in the Parentela Orders category (19.8 percent as compared with 19.0 percent for their parents), and it is highest for siblings of persons falling into the Genetic and Canon Law class (27.2 percent as compared with 27.7 percent for parents). The percentages for siblings of persons with Standard American and Civil Law orientations are intermediate. Thus, as anticipated, both parents and siblings of persons with a Parentela Orders orientation show the highest degree of marital stability, and families of individuals in the Genetic and

TABLE 6-2. Kinship Orientation and Percentage of Respondents' Siblings with Previous Marriages (Whether or not Currently Married)

Respondents' siblings	Parentela orders	Standard american	Civil law	Genetic or canon law
Percent with previous marriages	19.8	21.9	24.7	27.2
Total number of siblings[a]	308	675	247	298

[a] Includes siblings born before 1961 for siblings groups of six or fewer brothers and sisters. For each size of the sibling group up to the point, there are at least 20 families; the N decreases rapidly for larger sized sibling groups.

Canon Law classification have the greatest propensity toward marital breakup. These tendencies still persist even when the considerable effects of religion and socioeconomic status are taken into account.

KINSHIP ORIENTATION AND RELIGIOUS ENDOGAMY

Rules governing religious and ethnic endogamy can be regarded as extensions of those covering kinship endogamy. Of particular interest in European history are the Jewish *stetl* and German kinship arrangements, in that both systems applied the Parentela Orders procedure in determining collaterality. Both Jewish *stetl* and the old German kinship structure involved a highly integrated bilateral kindred—the Jewish *mishpokheh* and the German *maegth* or *magschaft*. (See Huebner, 1968, v. 4, p. 587.) Significantly, both Jewish and old German systems had rules of preferential marriage with close relatives. Early German law permitted marriages between any kindred outside the nuclear family, and evidently, "so-called endogamous marriages seem to have been the rule; that is, marriages between members of the same sib (Huebner, v. 4, p. 594 and 604)." In Jewish *stetl* kinship, cousin marriage was also widespread and strong bonds were maintained between co-parents-in-law, who were often times siblings. There is, hence, some basis for speculating that Parentela Orders kinship orientation is associated with endogamous rules of marriage.

Table 6-3 presents data regarding the extent to which the parents of persons with different kinship orientations married across boundaries of major religious groups—Judaism, Protestantism, Catholicism, or secularism. The table refers to the religions in which the parents had been raised: it does not take into account premarital or postmarital conversions. Even though the data may conceal some conversions, they still reveal considerable variation in religious intermarriage by kinship orientation.

Since the prevalence of intermarriages among Jewish parents is low (below ten percent), Table 6-3 describes only the extent of intermarriage for women reared as Protestants or Catholics. For respondents' mothers raised as Protestants, intermarriage is considerably less widespread among parents of persons in the Parentela Orders and Standard American categories than of those in the Civil Law, Genetic, or Canon Law classes. For those whose mothers had been reared as Catholics, however, only persons with a Parentela Orders orientation consistently come from homes in which both parents had been raised as Catholic. Similarly, for the entire sample, the Parentela Orders category stands out as exhibiting religious endogamy among parents of respondents.

The relationship between kinship orientation and religious homogeneity of families is particularly clear when the religion of the respondents' brothers and sisters is examined. Table 6-4 shows the percentages of respondents whose siblings are all in the same religion. The table excludes persons who are only children or who have just one sibling. The table does not take into account, however, shifts in religious identity that have occurred among siblings during their adulthood. Still, if religious ideology is a strong determinant of kinship orientation, then religious homogeneity among siblings does suggest the stubborn persistence of kinship orientation as a family attribute even after the married children have established their own homes. For this analysis, the diversity among Protestant denominations is seen as representing somewhat divergent kinship ideologies, and when siblings appear in two or more Protestant categories basically different in doctrine (i.e., Reformation Era, Pietistic, Neofundamentalist, or Mormon), they are classified as being hetergeneous in religion.

Table 6-4 indicates that religious homogeneity among siblings is highest among Jewish respondents, next among Catholics, then Protestants, and lowest among secularists. The findings on kinship orientation is as follows:

1. For persons with at least one sibling with no religious preference, hom-

TABLE 6-3. Percent of Respondents' Parents Who Intermarried Across Religious Groups, By Kinship Orientation[c]

Religion in which mother was raised	Parentela orders	Standard american	Civil law	Genetic or canon law	Total
Total sample (%)	14.8[b]	26.0	27.7	27.3	24.6
N	108	273	101	132	614
Mother raised as Protestant (%)	20.0[b]	24.1	31.2[a]	32.4[a]	26.4
N	55	158	64	71	348
Mother raised as Catholic (%)	9.7[b]	26.3[a]	25.9[a]	22.7	22.5
N	31	76	27	44	178

[a] Ratio of cell percentage to Total percentage is 1.2 or over.

[b] Ratio of cell percentage to Total percentage is .8 or under.

[c] Intermarriage here refers to marriage between persons raised in different major religious groups—Jewish, Protestant, Catholic, or secular (i.e., no religious preference).

TABLE 6-4. Kinship Orientation and Percentage of Respondents Whose Siblings Are all in the Same Religion

Religion of at least one sibling	Percentage of families in which respondents' siblings are all in same religion[c]				
	Parentela orders	Standard american	Civil law	Genetic or canon law	Total
No preference (%)	50.0[a]	51.5[a]	22.2[b]	21.1[b]	40.0
N	14	33	9	19	75
Jewish (%)	91.3		[d]	[d]	85.7
N	23				28
Protestant[e] (%)	52.9	57.2	58.8	45.5[b]	54.6
N	51	138	51	55	295
Catholic (%)	86.7[a]	70.7	71.4	68.2	72.9
N	30	75	28	44	177
All religious groups (%)	65.4	61.5	59.1	46.5[b]	58.9
N	104	252	88	113	557

[a] Ratio of cell percentage to total percentage is 1.2 or over.

[b] Ratio of cell percentage to total percentage is .8 or under.

[c] Excludes families in which respondent is only child or has only one sibling.

[d] Fewer than 5 cases. Included in computations for total percentages.

[e] Categories of Protestant denominations are Reformation Era, Pietistic, Neofundamentalist, and Mormon. When siblings appear in two or more Protestant categories (or as Jews, none, or Catholics), they are classified as being in different religions.

ogeneity among brothers and sisters is greater among Parentela Orders and Standard American respondents than among those in the Civil Law, Genetic, or Canon Law categories.

2. Among Jews, religious homogeneity among siblings is high regardless of kinship orientation. Yet, the percentage is slightly higher among persons in the combined Parentela Orders and Standard American category than among the few individuals in the remaining classifications.

3. Protestants reveal most sibling homogeneity with respect to religion in those kinship categories most often associated with Protestantism—the Standard American and Civil Law models. Like the other religious groups, though, Protestants show least homogeneity in the Genetic and Canon Law classification.

4. Unlike Protestants, Catholics in the Parentela Orders category are most homogeneous but, like Protestants, Catholics in the Genetic and Canon Law class indicate greatest diversity in siblings' religion.

When all religious groups are combined, the results are quite clear: Parentela Orders category is highest in percentage of homogeneous sibling groups, and the Genetic and Canon Law class the lowest. Therefore, the findings on the religious homogeneity among siblings, like those on parental endogamy, are consistent with the characterization of Parentela Orders kinship orientation as centripetal and Genetic and Canon Law perspectives as centrifugal.

KINSHIP ORIENTATION AND AGE AT MARRIAGE

The timing of events which mark transitions in life cycle appears to reflect modes of insitutional participation. Traditionally, marriage has represented one of the most significant transitions in a person's life, and the significance of age at marriage depends upon its relationship to other status changes that occur in the life course. Historical analysis suggests that age at marriage is related to social constraints on the decision to marry. "People have become relatively more free to marry according to preference [and timing] because structure conditions impose fewer obstacles to matrimony than was once the case (Modell, Furstenberg, and Strong, 1978, p. S129)." In recent decades, social conditions indeed, seem to "pose fewer impediments to arranging the life course ad lib (Modell, Furstenberg, and Strong, 1978, p. S147)." As a result, "The basis for 'decision' about marriage timing has changed . . . from involuntary to preferential, from a structurally constrained to an individually determined basis (Modell, Furstenberg, and Strong, 1978, p. S133)."

Given the norm of free marital choice, in the absence of social constraints, there is little reason to delay marriage once the right spouse has been found. Insofar as centripetal kinship systems generally place greater constraints upon life-course transitions than do centrifugal systems, one would anticipate that these constraints would operate in marriage as well. Previous analyses in this chapter have already indicated a lower prevalence of divorce and greater degree of religious homogamy among parents and siblings of persons in the Parentela Orders category. One would expect then the application of restraint also in entering marriage. On the other hand, given the emphasis in Canon Law orientations to create new ties to other kinship groups, Canon Law persons would be encouraged to marry early. Consequently, the Phoenix data should reveal that parents of persons in the Parentela Orders category are highest in age at marriage and parents of those in the Genetic and Canon Law class are the lowest.

Table 6-5 describes the relationship between kinship orientations and median age of mothers at the time they married the respondents' fathers. In the table, two control variables are introduced: religion in which the respondents were raised and their fathers' occupation at that time. Consistent with the findings of other studies, the data indicate that Jewish respondents' parents tend to marry late and Protestants early and that more persons in professional, managerial, and administrative positions generally delay marriage than do those in blue collar jobs.

TABLE 6-5. Kinship Orientation and Median Age at Marriage of Respondent's Mother, by Religion in Which Respondent Was Raised and Father's Occupation

	Parentela orders	Standard american	Civil law	Genetic or canon law	Total
Religion in which respondent was raised					
No religious preference (yrs.)	20.8			20.0	20.5
N		19		14	33
Jewish (yrs.)	22.0	23.7	25.5	21.3	23.3
N	14	22	8	9	53
Protestant (yrs.)	20.5	19.9	19.3	18.9	19.6
N	62	182	64	67	375
Catholic (yrs.)	22.6	20.5	20.3	20.1	20.8
N	35	78	26	35	174
Father's occupation at time when respondent was growing up					
Professional, managerial or administrative (yrs.)	22.2	21.3	21.0	20.6	21.4
N	49	111	40	36	236
Clerical, sales or craft (yrs.)	21.5	21.0	20.1	20.7	20.8
N	33	101	35	42	211
Blue collar (yrs.)	20.0	20.1	19.9	18.9	19.8
N	34	83	27	43	187
Entire sample (yrs.)	21.4	20.9	20.4	20.3	
N	117	305	103	125	

The general pattern of results in Table 6-5 is that, despite minor variations in different religious and socioeconomic groups, mothers in the Parentela Orders category have the highest median age at marriage, and those in the Genetic and Canon Law classification have the lowest median age. Among religious groups, this tendency is clearest for Protestants and Catholics; among socioeconomic groups, this tendency is sharpest for both the top (professional, managerial, and administrative) and the bottom (blue-collar) categories. The Jewish mothers, who marry late anyway, show little systematic variation kinship orientation on age at marriage. But, despite this deviation, as a whole, the data for mothers support the contention that persons with a Parentela Orders orientation will tend to be constrained to marry late, while persons with a Genetic or Canon Law orientation will be free (and perhaps encouraged) to marry early.

The data for fathers are somewhat more ambiguous than those for mothers. Table 6-6 presents the median age at marriage for the respondents' fathers. Like the previous table, this one also applies religion and father's occupation as control variables. As in the case of mothers, Jewish fathers are oldest at marriage and Protestant fathers the youngest, but whereas the professional, managerial, and administrative fathers have the highest median age, it is the middle-range white-collar workers (rather than blue-collar workers) who have the lowest median. This shift in pattern of of findings results from the large age discrepancy between husband and wife in the blue-collar class (i.e., a median difference of over 5 years).

A review of the general configuration of the data in Table 6-6 reveals that, whereas the median age for fathers of Parentela Orders respondents tends to be high (as expected), no definitive pattern emerges for the remaining kinship orientations. The complexity of the findings suggests that numerous constraints have impinged upon the marital decision of the fathers of the respondents to affect age at marriage. Since many of these men had been married in the years between 1935 and 1955, their life course seems to have been complicated by familial, occupational, and educational adaptations arising from World War II and the Korean conflict. (Unfortunately, data were not collected for age at marriage of respondents' siblings.)

TABLE 6-6. **Kinship Orientation and Median Age at Marriage of Respondent's Father, by Religion in which Respondent Was Raised and Father's Occupation**

	Parentela orders	Standard american	Civil law	Genetic or canon law	Total
Religion in which respondent was raised					
No religious					
preference (yrs.)	23.0		26.0		24.0
N	16		14		30
Jewish (yrs.)	25.0	27.7	27.0	26.5	27.0
N	14	21	8	9	52
Protestant (yrs.)	24.9	23.3	23.1	23.0	23.4
N	57	171	63	56	347
Catholic (yrs.)	25.8	24.5	23.0	24.7	24.7
N	31	74	24	30	159
Father's occupation at time when respondent was growing up					
Professional, managerial or					
administrative (yrs.)	25.9	24.8	23.8	23.9	24.9
N	49	108	39	36	232
Clerical, sales or craft (yrs.)	23.8	22.9	24.0	23.2	23.1
N	31	96	34	39	200
Blue collar (yrs.)	24.3	24.0	23.3	24.7	24.0
N	27	73	26	38	164
Entire sample (yrs.)	25.0	23.9	23.7	24.0	
N	107	286	100	115	

THE MATERNAL ROLE AND FERTILITY

The mobilization of family ties to promote the interests of the family suggests that the maternal role in centripetal kin groups differs considerably from that in centrifugal groups. Insofar as family members can be regarded as "assets," one would anticipate that with centripetal organization, the maternal role would be oriented toward maximizing the "worth" of each member. The investment in human capital among families and kin organized centripetally may lead to high fertility rates and certainly to special efforts by mothers to instil in their children values and skills that would facilitate "success" in later years. Since a strong commitment to the maternal role is time consuming, it seems likely that mothers in centripetal systems would be less apt to work outside the home than mothers in centrifugal systems. (See Hill, 1977). In terms of kinship models, one would expect that in families organized on the basis of the Parentela Orders model, mothers would be employed less frequently than would mothers in families organized on the basis of the Genetic or Canon Law model.

This section is divided into two parts. The first part pertains to employment of the respondents' mothers during the childrearing years; the second deals with levels of fertility.

Maternal Employment

Table 6-7 displays percentages of mothers who had been employed while the respondents were growing up. The working arrangements had been quite diverse: some of these mothers had worked full-time, others part-time; some had held a job continuously, others sporadically. Because it would be difficult to accommodate the large variation in patterns of work, the table refers merely to employment at any time prior to the respondent's adulthood. Perusal of Table 6-7 reveals that the major determinant in maternal employment is the number of children in the family; the larger the number of children, the less likely is the mother to work. Whereas over half of the mothers with only-children had been employed outside the home, only a fourth worked when there were four or more children.

However, when the number of children is taken into account, Table 6-7 indicates that fewer mothers of persons in the Parentela Orders category were employed while the respondent was growing up than were mothers in the other categories. By way of contrast, in families with four or more children, mothers of persons in the Standard American classification tended to be employed more often than did other mothers. In general, though, the data reveal only that mothers of respondents in the Parentela Orders category are less inclined than others to work while their children are growing up. At least

TABLE 6-7. Kinship Orientation, Mothers Who Had Been Employed While Respondents Were Growing Up, and Number of Respondent's Siblings

Number of respondent's siblings	Percent of mothers employed while respondents were growing up				
	Parentela orders	Standard american	Civil law	Genetic or canon law	Total
Respondent only child (%)	45.5[b]	51.5	63.7	63.7	57.6
N	11	33	11	11	66
One to three (%)	37.1	38.7	40.8	37.0	38.5
N	70	217	76	73	436
Four or more (%)	13.3[b]	30.0[a]	27.6	28.6	25.8
N	45	83	29	56	213
All families (%)	29.3[b]	37.8	39.5	36.4	36.5
N	126	333	116	140	715

[a] Ratio of cell percentage to total percentage is 1.2 or more.

[b] Ratio of cell percentage to total percentage is .8 or under.

in this respect, the findings support the speculation that commitment to the maternal role is associated with centripetal tendencies in kinship orientation.

Patterns of Fertility

Table 6-8 describes the fertility of the respondents' parents. This table takes into account the religion in which the respondent was raised, the occupation of the father at the time that the respondent was growing up, and the respondent's kinship orientation. In order to avoid fertility histories complicated by divorce and widowhood, the table includes only full siblings of the respondent.

Both religion and paternal occupation influence fertility rates. The rank ordering by religion shows Catholics with the highest mean (3.42 siblings of the respondent), Protestants next (3.09), secularists third (2.69), and Jews last (1.59). This ranking is consistent with the large number of fertility studies over the past generation (e.g., Freedman et al., 1959; Rainwater, 1960). Findings by father's occupation also follow a familiar pattern, with blue-collar parents highest (3.40), clerical, sales, and craft workers next (2.76), and professional, managerial, and administrative workers lowest (2.56). Thus, the findings indicate that the parents of the respondents are not atypical in their fertility history.

TABLE 6-8. Kinship Orientation and Mean Number of Full Siblings of the Respondent, by Religion in Which Respondent Was Raised and by Father's Occupation[a]

Religion in which respondent was raised or father's occupation	Mean number of full siblings				
	Parentela orders	Standard american	Civil law	Genetic or canon law	Total
Religion					
No religious preference	2.55[c]		2.87[c]		2.69
N	20		15		35
Jewish	2.20[b]	1.36	1.35[c]		1.59
N	15	22	17		54
Protestant	3.25	2.63	2.79	*4.43*	3.09
N	67	196	72	74	409
Catholic	3.26	3.19	3.50	*3.98*	3.42
N	38	90	30	44	202
Father's occupation					
Professional, managerial or administrative	2.73	2.35	2.79	2.74	2.56
N	52	116	42	38	248
Clerical, sales or craft	3.06	2.39	2.94	*3.26*	2.76
N	35	108	38	46	227
Blue collar	3.86	3.11	3.03	*3.92*	3.40
N	37	99	35	51	222
Entire sample	3.13	2.69	2.87	*3.97*	
N	122	326	114	138	

[a] Father's occupation at the time that respondent was "growing up." Excludes cases where father had died during respondent's childhood.

[b] The highest mean for each religious or socioeconomic group is in italics.

[c] Categories combined because N in either category is under 10.

Whether one scans the fertility data in Table 6-8 by religion or by socio-economic level, three regularities are apparent:

1. Parents of persons in the Standard American category generally have the fewest children regardless of religious or socioeconomic status.
2. Except for Catholics, within each religious or socioeconomic grouping, fathers and mothers of individuals in the Parental Orders category have a higher mean fertility than does that grouping as a whole.
3. Parents of people classified as Genetic or Canon Law generally have the largest number of children of any kinship orientation.

The tendencies in fertility clearly indicate that, at least in the parental generation, kinship orientation is associated with child-bearing. The overall pattern for the entire sample reveals the proclivity of the Standard American parents to limit the number of children; the Parentela Orders fathers and mothers to be above average in childbearing; and the parents of persons with a Genetic or Canon Law to be highest in child production.

When the fertility of the respondents' siblings are examined in Table 6-9, some differences by generation emerge. Whereas the parents of Genetic and Canon Law respondents are highly prolific, the fertility of their children (other than the respondent) shows a marked decline relative to the other kinship orientations. This drop is most dramatic among siblings of respondents raised as Catholics and among those whose parents are in the lower socioeconomic levels. This shift mirrors the findings of recent fertility stud-

TABLE 6-9. Kinship Orientation and Mean Number of Siblings' Children by Religion in Which Respondent Was Raised and by Father's Occupation[a]

Religion in which respondent was raised or father's occupation	Mean number of siblings' children				
	Parentela orders	Standard american	Civil law	Genetic or canon law	Total
Religion					
No religious preference	3.28[b]	2.53	1.54		2.20
N[c]	7[d]	51	37[e]		95
Jewish	2.13	.82	1.29		1.44
N[c]	29	28	21		78
Protestant	2.10	1.92	2.26	2.13	2.06
N[c]	232	464	208	237	1141
Catholic	2.19	1.89	1.60	1.67	1.84
N[c]	141	281	107	215	744
Total	2.15	1.91	2.01	1.87	
N	409	824	336	490	
Father's occupation					
Professional, managerial or administrative	2.04	1.74	2.04	2.08	1.93
N[c]	157	263	117	108	645
Clerical, sales, or craft	1.66	1.74	1.68	1.59	1.68
N[c]	104	223	111	148	586
Blue collar	2.44	2.16	2.31	1.92	2.17
N[c]	152	336	113	237	838
Total	2.09	1.92	1.99	1.86	
N	413	822	341	493	

[a] Father's occupation at the time that respondent was "growing up." Cases omitted where father had died during respondent's childhood.

[b] The highest mean for each religious or socioeconomic group is in italics.

[c] Includes both full and half siblings.

[d] Although mean is based on a very small N, the data are presented in order to show the contrast between Parentela Orders and Standard American fertility.

[e] Categories combined because N in either category is under 10.

ies, which portray a picture of shrinking differences in the production of children among the various religious and socioeconomic groupings (Westoff and Ryder, 1977).

Apart from the shift in fertility patterns among siblings of persons in the Genetic and Canon Law category, however, the relationship between kinship orientation and number of children is substantially the same as that for the respondents' parents. For the remaining kinship orientations, the brothers and sisters of persons in the Parentela Orders category have the largest families and the siblings of those with a Standard American orientation have the smallest. The findings suggest that families with these orientations are not as sensitive to changes in the social structure as those with Genetic or Canon Law orientation.

Particularly, the results indicate a changing pattern of adherence to Catholic family ideology. As in previous years, Westoff and Ryder (1977, p. 338) report that, "The number [of children] wanted among Catholics . . . [still] varies directly and strongly with simple measures of religious commitment." That being the case, recent events—perhaps pertaining to the changing role of women in modern society—appear to have affected the Catholic family more than they have the families of Jews or Protestants. Moreover, the findings imply that this change has occurred most profoundly among those Catholic families with a Genetic or Canon Law orientation—precisely the orientation associated traditionally with the Church—leaving the other orientations relatively unaffected.

SUMMARY: KINSHIP IDEOLOGY AND FAMILY OF ORIENTATION

This chapter has dealt with the relationship between kinship orientation and attributes of the respondents' parental family. The analysis has utilized the concepts of centripetal and centrifugal kinship organization. Theoretically, centripetal kinship emerges (or is sustained) in a situation in which a special interest group is vying with other groups for economic, political, or religious "goods". Centrifugal kinship, however, is fostered when special interests are subordinated to the broader concerns which extend beyond the particular group. As a general rule, centrifugal systems are organized in ways that individuals are placed under as many cross-pressures as possible and kin group boundaries are vague. These modes of organization yield distinct norms regarding marriage, divorce, and the maternal role.

The theoretical discussion also proposed that the models of kinship orientation under investigation can be placed upon a continuum in the extent to which they represent centripetal versus centrifugal properties. Moreover, the kinship models represent ideological stances that are transmitted from parents to children.

To support the above propositions, I have presented data to show that the norms imputed to the models are held by the parents as well as by the siblings of respondents with given kinship orientations. These data reveal differences according to kinship model in such characteristics as prevalence of divorce in the family; religious endogamy between parents; religious homogeneity among siblings; age at which the parents married. the maternal role; and fertility. (Obviously, the data would have been more definitive had each parent and sibling been interviewed personally. But using the respondent as family informant on objective matters—such as divorce, age at marriage, and fertility—maternal employment does lend plausibility to the assumption that the data are fairly reliable.)

This chapter focused upon the family of orientation as the source of the respondent's kinship ideology. The following chapter shifts the attention to the respondent as the transmitter of the ideology to the next generation.

Family of Procreation

The previous chapter on parents and siblings of respondents outlined characteristics of family relationships associated with the appropriation of particular kinship orientations by individuals. These characteristics included such diverse phenomena as age at marriage, religious homogeneity in the family, the maternal role, and fertility. The interpretation offered was that the configurations of these attributes express family ideologies associated with the kinship orientations under investigation.

Here I shall continue the analysis of the content of family norms and values connected with kinship orientations—this time in the respondents' own families of procreation. I shall discuss topics that are similar to those handled in the previous chapter, except that greater emphasis is given to marital ties between the respondents and their spouses. Moreover, whereas in the previous chapter I utilized a typology of centripetal and centrifugal kinship organization to interpret the data, I now translate that typology into competing models of family organization in contemporary society.

MODELS OF FAMILY ORGANIZATION

The dichotomy of centripetal and centrifugal kinship organization appears to be reflected in the distinction between "natural" and "legal" models of family organization. The "natural" family model rests upon a clear discrimination between natural and human creations. Consistent with this model, historically family law in Western Europe has distinguished between "artificial" and "natural" nuclear-family relationships. According to the "natural" model, the nuclear family derives its authorization or charter for existence from a source outside the state—in religion, in the mystique of blood relationships, in the maintenance of estates, or in other sources of traditional values (Schneider, 1968). Artificial family ties, in this context, are merely a creation of secular legislatures and derive their legitimation from the state.

The natural family model provided the basis for American family law from its very beginning. In colonial New England, "positive law, that is, the law made by man, was believed to have to comport with a higher, divine law for its validity. This idea of higher law, although later secularized, was to become an enduring legacy of the colonial period (Haskins, 1960, p. 140)." Some aspects of Mosaic law were thought of as natural and immutable—other aspects as modifiable and positive. The assumptions that underlay Puritan social theory in "the conception of the social convenant and the emphasis upon a God-given fundamental law were the genesis of ideals which flowered in the eighteenth century and shaped political and legal thinking in the early days of the Republic (Haskins, 1960, p. 229)." Because the natural or ascriptive family derives its authorization for existence outside the state, the household may be regarded as extraterritorial government coming under state jurisdiction only insofar as it impedes or interferes with the normal life of the community. This assumption lay behind John Locke's statement in his "Second Treatise of Civil Government" that:

> A child is born a subject of no country or government. He is under his father's tuition and authority until he comes to age of discretion, and then he is a freeman, at liberty what government he will put himself under, what politic he will unite himself to . . . The power that a father hath naturally over his children is the same wherever they be born, and the ties of natural obligations are not bounded by the positive limits of kingdoms and commonwealths.

An alternative cultural model emerging to replace the "natural" family is the conception of the family as a mere legal entity. In this model, since family relationships exist only as a category comparable to business enterprises, the difference between natural and artificial family ties disappears. The state is then the only chartering agency for the legitimation of family relationships (Farber, 1973).

In contrast to the Puritan conception that Election to Grace produces a natural hierarchy among men, the Enlightment doctrines (that *all* men are created without differential status ascribed by birth, and all are endowed with the same civil rights) assume a lack of "natural" institutional structure. A natural structure would imply that there be differential treatment between some men and others and that those who support the natural structures should be rewarded, while those who do not should be punished. Presuppositions of the lack of natural structure imply that any structure is created by man-made rules, which are then codified in law. Hence, in this conception of law, one need not posit "natural" ends or purposes of institutions in providing for the perpetual continuity of social institutions. Inasmuch as institutions are seen as continuing to exist for reasons other than those that brought them into being, particular "natural" ends become irrelevant.

Whereas traditional conceptions of the family have presupposed a fixed set of functions derived from "nature," law in contemporary society is faced with the problem of providing continuity in social structures without presupposing fixed ends for these structures. To solve this problem, family law has had to assume that the perpetuation of social structures (such as the family) is desirable only insofar as people have reason to continue them. Any given structure might have to accommodate a variety of values and goals. Consequently, governments have had to modify laws in ways that admit a multiplicity of ends and that assume an equivalence of different value systems. The idea that all domestic groups have equal rights and standing in the society thereby opposes the notion that congeries of families should be encouraged to perpetuate homogeneous clusters (or factions) organized on the basis of social class, religion, ethnicity, or some other ascriptive criterion denoting a set of "naturally" derived values.

The distinction between "natural" and "legal" family models implies also a difference between corporate and individual privacy. The concept of privacy itself rests upon the degree of autonomy from the general community. To the extent that conduct is not subject to public surveillance and accountability, it remains private. In corporate privacy, it is the "natural" family whose autonomy is to be protected; in personal privacy, it is individual autonomy that is paramount.

The coexistence of both "natural" and "legal" family models is indicated by the justifications that have been supplied in landmark decisions of the U.S. Supreme Court. For example, the Court decision in *Griswold v. Connecticut* (381 U.S. 479) relies heavily upon corporate privacy in marriage. This decision proposes that:

We deal with a right of privacy older than the Bill of Rights—older than our political parties, older than our school system. Marriage is a coming together for better or for worse, hopefully enduring, and intimate to the degree of being sacred. It is an association that promotes a way of life, not causes; a harmony in living, not political faiths; a bilateral loyalty, not commercial or social projects. Yet it is an association for as noble a purpose as any involved in our prior decisions.

Concurring with the Court decision in *Griswold*, Justice Goldberg cites "the traditional relation of the family" as being "a relation as old and as fundamental as our entire civilization" and suggests that:

The entire fabric of the Constitution and the purposes that clearly underlie its specific guarantees demonstrate that the rights to marital privacy and to marry and raise a family are of similar order and magnitude as the fundamental rights specifically protected.

Holding that the Ninth Amendment to the U.S. Constitution implies a recognition of additional basic and fundamental rights omitted from the Bill of Rights, Justice Goldberg concludes that:

To hold that a right so basic and fundamental and so deep-rooted in our society as the right of privacy in marriage may be infringed because that right is not guaranteed in so many words by the first eight amendments to the Constitution is to ignore the Ninth Amendment and to give it no effect whatsoever.

Yet the interpretation of marriage as a fundamental relationship acts as counterpoint to the interpretation put forth in other cases that "outside of areas of plainly harmful conduct, every American is left to shape his own life as he thinks best, do what he pleases, go where he pleases (Cited in *Roe v. Wade*, 35 L Ed 2d 147)." Indeed, in *Eisenstadt v. Baird* (105 U.S. 438), the Court contends that:

> It is true that in Griswold the right of privacy in question inhered in the marital relationship. Yet the marital couple is not an independent entity with a mind and heart of its own, but an association of two individuals each with a separate intellectual and emotional makeup. If the right of privacy means anything, it is the right of the *individual*, married or single, to be free from unwarranted government intrusion into matters so fundamentally affecting a person as the decision whether to bear or begat a child.

In *Planned Parenthood of Missouri v. Danforth*, the Court explicitly *rejects* the following argument of corporate privacy, namely, that:

> Recognizing that the consent of both parties is generally necessary . . . to begin a family, the legislature has determined that a change in the family structure set in motion by mutual consent should be terminated only by mutual consent (Brief for Appellee Danforth 38).

That rejection would also discount the views that the decision to complete the birth process involves obligations by both husband and wife and that, in case of disagreement, the wife already has veto power over her husband's desire for abortion.

Instead, the *Planned Parenthood of Missouri* decision takes the position that the husband's rights with regard to abortion are not considered to be fundamental to the structure of the family, but rather, that they are delegated by the State:

> We are not unaware of the deep and proper concern and interest that a devoted and protective husband has in his wife's pregnancy and in the growth and development of the fetus she is carrying. Neither has this Court failed to appreciate the importance of the marital relationship in our society . . . . Moreover, we recognized that the decision whether to undergo or to forgo an abortion may have profound effects on the future of any marriage, effects that are both physical and mental, and possibly deleterious. Notwithstanding these factors, we cannot hold that the State has the constitutional authority to give the spouse unilaterally the ability to prohibit the wife from terminating her pregnancy, when the State itself lacks the right . . . Even if the State had the ability to

delegate to the husband a power it itself could not exercise, it is not at all likely that such action would further, as the District Court majority phrased it, the 'interest of the state in protecting the mutuality of decisions vital to the marriage relationship'.

The distinction between corporate and individual privacy suggests the existence of a relationship between modes of kinship orientation and norms relevant to family privacy. The emphasis on line of descent in the Standard American and (particularly) the Parentela Orders models implies that holders of these models tend to bracket ascendants and/or descendants (in addition to parents and children) within their conceptions of especially close kin. Since grandparents and grandchildren are not normally included within the household, this bracketing seems to denote a corporate conception of kinship and family ties and, consequently, a conception of family organization in terms of corporate privacy and autonomy. At the other extreme, the Genetic and Canon Law models do not reveal any particular structure on the basis of generational distinctions or any particular bracketing of kin; as a result, the Ego-centeredness of these models appears to reflect a stress upon individual privacy and autonomy in family relationships. (The Civil Law model seems to be intermediate between the two extremes).

Insofar as corporate privacy is associated with centripetal kinship norms and individual privacy with centrifugal norms, the findings in the chapter on Family of Orientation should be replicated in the respondents own families of procreation. The data that are presented in the succeeding sections of this chapter are expected to show further support of the relationship between family ideology and kinship orientation with regard to such significant matters as (a) religious homogeneity within the family; (b) disillusionment with the spouse in the marital relationship; (c) proclivities toward early marriage and divorce; (d) norms governing family roles; and (e) ideas on fertility.

KINSHIP ORIENTATION AND RELIGIOUS HOMOGENEITY

One of the marks of a coherent corporate structure is the unity of underlying principles by which the collectivity operates. Basic values in the family are generally grounded in religious ideals and interests. To the extent that kinship orientations represent a range in corporate characteristics, one would expect them to vary also according to religiosity and religious homogeneity in marriage.

Religiosity

Among Protestants and Catholics, one of the chief indicators of religiosity is the frequency of church attendance (Glock and Stark, 1965). Table 7-1 shows the number of times per month that Protestants and Catholics report attending church services. For both Catholics and Protestants, more persons in the Parentela Orders category than in the remaining kinship orientations are weekly church goers. Among Protestants, those in the Genetic and Canon Law classifications are least likely to attend frequently, while among Catholics, the lowest attendance appears among those persons with Standard American and Civil Law orientations. Hence, insofar as church attendance reflects religiosity, both Catholics and Protestants in the Parentela Orders category reveal a greater religious interest than do persons with other kinship perspectives, while among Protestants, the data clearly show least interest among those in the Genetic and Canon Law grouping.

Religious Intermarriage and Homogenization

Given current courtship practices, whereby religion ordinarily plays a minimal role in selection of serious-dating partners, chances of religious intermarriage are considerable. Under these circumstances, the religious unity between man and woman—as an expression of corporate existence—may operate less frequently in marital selection than might be achieved later in the marriage itself. Table 7-2 displays the percentages of intermarriages and mixed marriages by the kinship orientation of the respondents. In this study, intermarriage refers to those couples in which husband and wife have been raised in different religions (whether or not there has been a conversion prior to the marriage itself.) Whereas *intermarriages* ordinarily are defined as marriages in which bride and groom differ in religion at the time of the wedding, *mixed marriages*, however, are those marriages in which the husband and wife continue to maintain their separate religious identities afterwards.

TABLE 7-1. Kinship Orientation and Frequency of Attending Church Services by Protestants and Catholics

Frequency of attending church services	Parentela orders	Standard american	Civil law	Genetic or canon law
Protestants				
At least once a week (%)	37.1	30.4	31.5	28.2
1 to 3 times per month (%)	17.7	16.3	21.4	12.7
Less than once a month (%)	45.2	53.3	47.1	59.2
N	62	184	70	71
Catholics				
At least once a week (%)	45.9	32.5	33.3	35.1
1 to 3 times per month (%)	24.3	21.7	18.5	28.6
Less than once a month (%)	29.7	45.8	48.1	38.1
N	37	83	27	42

In Table 7-2 Jewish respondents show the least amount of intermarriage and mixed marriage, and Catholics the most. As for kinship orientation, persons with a Parentela Orders generally are least apt to intermarry regardless of the couple's religion. Among Protestants, both Parentela Orders and Standard American perspectives are lower in percentage of intermarriage than are Civil Law, Genetics, or Canon Law; but among Jews and Catholics, only Parentela Orders and Civil Law categories are relatively low in percentage of intermarriage. The findings on mixed marriages are generally similar to those on intermarriage (except that Catholics in the Standard American and Civil Law categories tend more often to stay in mixed marriages than do those in the Parentela Orders, Genetic, or Canon Law classification).

The similarity in findings between intermarriages and mixed marriages informs us only that the greater the original heterogeneity in religion, the more often it will persist. But perhaps the distinctive mark of a corporate entity is special proclivity toward homogenization of values that had been different initially. Table 7-3 shows the extent to which religious groups differ in homogenization. This table presents percentages of intermarriages that remain as mixed marriages among the different religious groups and kinship categories. Even given the smallest number of intermarriages among the

TABLE 7-2. Percentages of Intermarriages and Mixed Marriages, by Religion and Kinship Orientation

Religion of one of the spouses	Parentela orders	Standard american	Civil law	Genetic or canon law	Total
Religion in which raised			Intermarriages		
Protestant (%)	49.4	47.3	50.6	55.1	49.6
N	81	256	85	98	520
Jewish (%)	33.3	50.0	22.2	42.9	40.3
N	18	26	9	14	67
Catholic (%)	60.4	70.1	60.9	66.2	66.2
N	53	137	46	65	301
All cases[a] (%)	52.1	62.0	59.7	60.4	
N	117	321	109	134	
Religion now			Mixed marriages		
Protestant (%)	25.8	27.1	42.3	40.0	32.1
N	66	203	78	80	427
Jewish (%)	12.5	29.2	22.2	27.3	23.2
N	16	24	9	11	60
Catholic (%)	38.6	50.5	44.7	38.5	44.9
N	44	111	38	52	245
All cases[a] (%)	30.9	31.9	42.2	41.4	
N	140	332	116	140	

[a] For "all cases" only, intermarriages and mixed marriages include marriages between major Protestant classifications: Reformation era denminations, Pietistic Protestants, Neofundamentalist sects, and Latter Day Saints.

TABLE 7-3. Percentage of Marriages (in Which Persons Had Been Raised in Different Religions) Which Remain as Mixed Marriages

Religion of one of the spouses	Parentela orders	Standard american	Civil law	Genetic or canon law	Total
Protestant	52.2	57.3	83.6	72.6	64.7
Jewish	37.5	58.4	100.0	63.6	57.8
Catholic	63.9	72.0	73.4	58.2	67.8
All cases[a]	59.3	51.5	70.7	68.5	—

[a] For "all cases" only, intermarriages and mixed marriages include marriages between major Protestant classifications: Reformation era denominations, Pietistic Protestants, Neofundamentalist sects, and Latter Day Saints.

religious groups, Jewish respondents are most likely to homogenize the religions of husband and wife; that is, among Jews the percentage of mixed marriages remaining (58 percent) is lower than it is for Protestants (65 percent) or Catholics (68 percent).

Overall, fewer persons in the Parentela Orders and Standard American classifications remain in mixed marriages than do those in the Civil Law, Genetic, or Canon Law categories. Among religious groups, this tendency toward religious homogenization holds in particular for Jews and Protestants; for Catholics, homogenization is greater in the Parentela Orders, Genetic, and Canon Law classes than it is for persons with a Standard American or Civil Law perspective. Thus, except for Catholics, the data on religious homogenization of intermarriages indicates that marriages of Parentela Orders and Standard American persons show greater evidence of corporateness than do marriages of persons with Civil Law, Genetic, and Canon Law viewpoints. The data for Catholics, however, suggest that for them, the Standard American and Civil Law orientations represent a falling away from the norms associated with the Church and perhaps a Protestantization of views on the family.

Kinship Orientation and Religious Homogeneity: Summary

Collectively, the data pertaining to kinship orientation and religious homogeneity confirm the expectation that Parentela Orders (in particular) and Standard American kinship (to a lesser extent) are related to greater religious interest and homogeneity than are the Civil Law, Genetic, and Canon Law approaches to kinship. Persons with a Parentela Orders orientation are the most constant churchgoers and they (along with those in the Standard American category) generally homogenize the religion of the couple in intermarriages. Insofar as the coalescence of a common value system is a mark of corporate structure, the findings on homogenization of religion supports the view that Standard American and particularly Parentela Orders models express corporate conceptions of family organization.

IDEALIZATION, DISILLUSIONMENT, AND MARITAL INSTABILITY

Before midcentury, when Freudian psychology was popular in sociological analysis, the roots of marital disruption were sought in the irrationalities of marital selection. At that time, much research was devoted to the prediction of marital adjustment (e.g., Burgess and Cottrell, 1939; Burgess and Wallin, 1953; Horst, 1941; Locke, 1951; and Terman, 1938). Of particular interest was the phenomenon of idealization whereby an individual projects unreal virtues upon a beloved. According to Willard Waller's (1951, p. 120) description of idealization, "In romantic love one builds up an almost completely unreal picture of a person which he calls by the same name as a real person, and vainly imagines to be like that person, but in fact the only authentic thing in the picture is the emotion which one feels toward it." According to this theory, when the couple settles down to a routine of living together after marriage, realism is bared, disillusionment ensues, and the marriage flounders.

But the view that idealization during courtship is at fault in producing marital maladjustments has not survived the test of evidence. Studies of courtship and marital prediction have shown that most relationships eventuating in marriage are not intense, romanticized affairs; instead the findings reveal that courtships ordinarily consist of companionate relationships that become progressively more intimate with the passage of time (Burgess and Wallin, 1953). On the whole, marital-prediction research shows that couples have a realistic view about their partners' faults and virtues.

But despite the realism that dominates during courtship, over the years couples do exhibit signs of disenchantment with their spouses. The Burgess longitudinal study has indicated that after fifteen or so years of marriage, "Regardless of initial level of [marital] adjustment, the majority of husbands and wives suffered decline in level of adjustment. Clearly, this is not simply a change built into the mate selection process; nor does it seem that husbands and wives are simply regressing to a theoretical mean level of adjustment (Dizzard, 1968, p. 13)." It seems that, rather than a dissipation of idealization, there is instead a progressively increasing disappointment in the spouse. This shift in perception of the spouse evokes questions about the processes by which disillusionment occurs and marriages may eventually disintegrate.

Irreligiosity of the Spouse

When marriage is regarded as a mechanism for unifying basic values and attaining collective ends, then it achieves a corporate identity that embodies the individual personalities of husband and wife; however, without a consensus on values, marriage tends to signify only a relationship between two individuals in a household arena. For example, earlier I indicated how kinship orientations vary in the extent to which homogenization of initially different religions occurs (with Parentela Orders being highest in homogenization, and Genetic and Canon Law the lowest). Instead, if people regard their marriages as relationships between individuals, then with disillusionment and increased maladjustment, they would project upon their spouses those attributes that conflict with their own. As a result, they would likely view their spouses as differing in values and aims. As a means of self protection, these individuals, faced with disillusionment in marriage, would tend to see their spouses as holding more profane ideas than they themselves do. This profanity can be expressed in respondents' perceptions of their spouses as generally maintaining an irreligious posture relative to their own.

Putatively, the kinship models under investigation represent a continuum of corporateness. Parentela Orders and, to a lesser extent, Standard American models, insofar as they give much weight to line of descent, imply a corporate, enduring existence of the family (or "house"). While the Civil Law model is in an intermediate position, the Genetic and Canon Law models are Ego-based. Given this continuum, one would expect that persons with a Genetic or Canon Law orientation would be more likely to be vulnerable to disillusionment in marriage and to project profane ideas upon the spouse than would those with a Parentela Orders or Standard American perspective.

The relationship between general disillusionment and kinship orientation is indicated in Table 7-4. The data in this table refer to Srole anomia scale, which deals with general disillusionment—loss of faith in the future, discouragement of having children, and lack of trust in others and in the political process. (A high score on the anomia scale implies extensive disillusionment.) According to the table, persons with a Genetic or Canon Law orientation tend more often than others to ascribe to themselves and to their spouses a high level of disillusionment, while most of those with a Parentela Orders perspective view themselves and their spouses as low in disillusionment. Respondents with a Standard American or Civil Law conception of kinship are intermediate, but those individuals with a Civil Law viewpoint tend somewhat more often to assign both themselves and their spouses a low anomia score. The findings in Table 7-4 hence clearly indicate a variation by kinship orientation in extent of general disillusionment.

A connection between kinship orientation and view of the spouse as irreligious is suggested in Table 7-5. This table presents ratios of ratings for self and spouse on the extent to which various religious beliefs are held. A ratio

TABLE 7-4. Kinship Orientation and Percentage of Married Persons with Low Anomia Score for Self and Spouse

Score on srole anomia scale	Parentela orders	Standard american	Civil law	Genetic or canon law
Both self and spouse assigned low score (%)[a]	53.7	39.9	47.8	35.6
Respondent has low anomia score (%)[a]	58.6	47.3	58.3	38.8
Spouse has low anomia score (%)[a]	56.6	44.2	49.0	40.8
N	106	256	96	98

[a] A low anomia score is 0 or 1, and it denotes a low degree of disillusionment with the society; a high anomia score is 2, 3, 4, or 5, and it denotes much disillusionment.

greater than *one* indicates that the respondents tend to regard themselves as more religious (or to hold a more fervent religious position) than their spouses; a ratio less than *one* indicates that the individuals see their spouses as more fervent.

Three statements about religious belief are presented. The most general statement merely asks, "How important would you say that religion is to you (your spouse)?" The second statement refers to the role of God in everyday life, and the third, which is most specific in content, pertains to the belief that "the institution of marriage and family was established by God"—and

TABLE 7-5. Kinship Orientation and Ratio of Ratings for Self and Spouse on Extent to Which Religious Beliefs Are Held[a]

Religious beliefs	Parentela orders	Standard american	Civil law	Genetic or canon law
How important would you say that religion is to you (your spouse)? Would you say it is *very important, fairly important, fairly unimportant,* or *not important at all?*	1.40	2.40	2.25	2.87
Extent of agreement with statement, "I am convinced that God plays a strong part in what happens in our daily lives."[b]	.93	1.50	1.64	2.20
Extent of agreement with statement, "The institution of marriage and family was established by God."[b]	.53	.60	.75	1.67

[a] A ratio greater than *one* indicates that respondents tend to view themselves as more religious than their spouse; a ratio less than *one* indicates that the individuals see their spouse as more religious.

[b] The response categories are: *strongly agree, agree, not sure, disagree,* and *strongly disagree.*

therefore, by implication, more fundamental than secular law. For all three statements, respondents in the Parentela Orders category have the lowest ratios, thereby revealing the least tendency toward attributing profane views to the spouse, whereas the persons in the Genetic and Canon Law category uniformly have the largest ratios, and consequently appear most likely to impute such views to the spouse. Ratios for the Standard American and Civil Law respondents lie in the middle of the range. Hence, the data support the contention that Parentela Orders, as representing a corporate conception of kinship, permits least latitude in seeing the spouse as irreligious, and that Genetic and Canon Law views, as representing individualistic conceptions of kinship, are most conducive to disparaging the spouse's religious ideas.

Like the findings on general disillusionment, the evidence regarding the spouse as irreligious lends credence to the position that kinship orientations are associated with modes of family organization reflecting the centripetal-centrifugal kinship continuum.

Kinship Orientation and Marital Status

One would expect that, where corporate conceptions of kinship predominate, kinship ideologies would militate against marital instability. Specifically, one would expect to find less divorce and a later age for marriage among persons with Parentela Orders and Standard American perspectives than among persons with other kinship orientations. Indeed, the data in the chapter on respondents' parents and siblings show such tendencies.

For the respondents themselves, information on marital status appears in Table 7-6. Among men, chances are greater for divorced than for married persons (either in first or subsequent marriages) to fall into the Standard American grouping, and the probability is especially high for the divorced to be in the Genetic and Canon Law categories. Among women, however, there is little relationship between kinship orientation and marital status. The data on marital status (by sex of respondents) are thus equivocal in that they indicate a relationship between kinship orientation and divorce among men (albeit a complex one) but not among women.

However, when data on marital stability are examined by religion of respondents (in Table 7-7), a somewhat different picture emerges. Comparisons between those in the Genetic and Canon Law category (where women predominate) and the entire sample reveal that, except for Catholics, persons with Genetic and Canon Law orientations tend less often to be in their first marriage than the average for the total sample. For Catholics, the Genetic and Canon Law category (presumably reflecting Catholic doctrine) shows about the same percentage of first-marriages as the total sample does. Hence, when religion is taken into account, the data indicate that Ego-based kinship orientations do generally hold fewer first-marriages than the average.

Table 7-7 also displays the percentage of first marriages for both self and

TABLE 7-6. Respondent's Marital Status and Kinship Orientation

Kinship orientation	Now married First marriage	Now married Remarriage	Divorced, not now married
Men[a]			
Parentela orders (%)	22.6	22.4	7.7
Standard american (%)	46.6	44.9	56.4
Civil law (%)	18.3	14.3	0.0
Genetic and canon law (%)	12.5	18.4	35.9
N	208	49	39
Women[b]			
Parentela orders (%)	15.2	18.4	13.6
Standard american (%)	48.9	35.5	45.7
Civil law (%)	15.9	21.1	16.0
Genetic and canon law (%)	20.1	25.0	24.7
N	264	76	81

[a] For men, Chi square = 19.245; d.f. = 6; p = .01.

[b] For women, Chi square not significant. For total distribution (men and women combined), Chi square = 14.597; d.f. = 6; p = .02.

spouse in the Genetic and Canon Law category. Whereas about 67 percent of the married persons in the entire sample report that both are currently in their first marriage, only 57 percent of the persons in the Genetic and Canon Law category reveal that neither husband nor wife has been married before.

TABLE 7-7. Kinship Orientation and Percentage of Respondents Now in Their First Marriage for Persons in the Genetics and Canon Law Classification as Compared with the Entire Sample, by Religion and Marital Status of Spouse

Religion and spouse's marital status	Genetic and canon law classification	Total sample
Religion		
No religious preference (%)	46.7	54.7
N	15	75
Jewish (%)	55.6	74.1
N	9	54
Protestant (%)	50.7	64.9
N	71	387
Catholic (%)	69.0	69.3
N	42	189
Marital status of spouse		
Both respondent and		
spouse in first marriage (%)	57.0	67.4
Number of married couples	107	596

These data therefore bolster the findings on religion that the Genetic and Canon Law kinship orientations (except as an expression of Catholic ideology) are associated with marital instability—past or present.

Marital instability is particularly prevalent among persons married in the teenage years, especially among those women marrying under the age of eighteen (U.S. Health Resources Administration, 1974). Table 7-8 reports the percentages of women married before the age of eighteen for the various kinship orientations of the respondents. The table includes not only the women respondents themselves but also the wives of the male respondents. Because wives may not always hold the same kinship orientations as their husbands, greater weight should be given in interpreting the data to the distributions for the women respondents themselves than to those for wives of respondents.

In Table 7-8, except for persons now divorced, the data for women respondents indicate a fairly uniform progression among the kinship orientations with regard to the percentage married before reaching the age of eighteen. Married women (now either in their first or subsequent marriage) in the Parentela Orders class are least likely to marry before the age of eighteen,

TABLE 7-8. Kinship Orientation of Respondent and Percentage of Women Married Before Reaching the Age of Eighteen

Marital characteristics	Parentela orders	Standard american	Civil law	Genetic or canon law	Total
All persons					
Wives of men respondents	16.3	14.8	11.6	23.8	16.3
N	61	135	43	46	285
Women respondents	10.8	11.9	19.8	20.9	14.9
N	65	193	71	91	420
Persons now in first marriage					
Wives of men respondents	11.1	13.5	11.1	16.0	12.9
N	45	96	36	25	202
Women respondents	5.0	9.3	14.3	15.3	10.7
N	40	129	42	52	263
Persons now remarried[a]					
Wives of men respondents	00.0	14.3	—	23.1	16.2
N	3	21	—	13	37
Women respondents	00.0	8.1	7.7	20.0	9.8
N	11	37	13	20	81
Persons now divorced					
Wives of men respondents	38.5	22.3	14.3	40.0	30.4
N	13	18	7	8	46
Women respondents	35.6	29.6	43.8	36.8	35.6
N	14	27	16	19	76

[a] Age at previous marriage.

while those with a Genetic or Canon Law perspective are most apt to do so. Of those women now in their first marriage, fewer of those in the Standard American category marry before eighteen than do those in the Civil Law category, but this difference disappears among the remarried. Curiously, however, among divorced women, those with a Standard American orientation least often enter marriage prior to eighteen, while those in the Civil Law group most often do so. Still, the overall findings do indicate a relationship between emphasis on line of descent in kinship orientation and age at marriage.

The findings in Table 7-8 for wives of respondents do not, however, permit as clear an interpretation as those for the women respondents themselves. The data for wives of respondents suggest only that men in the Genetic and Canon Law classifications are more prone to marry teenage women than are men in the other kinship categories.

In summary, the data on age at marriage, like those pertaining to marital status, support the position that emphasis on line of descent in kinship orientation expresses a corporate conception of family and inhibits the disillusionment with the spouse. These findings are consistent with those pertaining to the respondents' parents and siblings, which reveal a similar connection between kinship orientation and such characteristics as marital status and age at marriage. The weight of evidence thus seems to imply a qualitative difference in family structure among the various kinship orientations. The following section on family roles and statuses elaborates further on this difference.

KINSHIP ORIENTATION AND FAMILY ROLES

The existence of a distinction between "natural" and "legal" cultural models of family organization assumes a corresponding distinction in definitions of appropriate family roles. Insofar as the "natural" family presupposes a conception of corporate privacy, one would expect that family roles suitable for this model would emphasize the need for conduct that would delimit family boundaries in order to defend the family domain against external encroachment. Consequently, families operating with "natural" model assumptions would be inclined:

1. Not to permit the immediate situations in everyday life to dictate conduct governing family relationships, but instead to be guided by general principles aimed at protecting the privacy of the family as a corporate unit.

2. Not to allow extrafamily obligations to subvert household demands, but to give priority to home and family on case of conflict.

3. Not to emphasize the personal aspects of social relationships over those qualities pertaining to legitimate status, but instead to demarcate family boundaries as distinct in quality from interpersonal relations.

In contrast to those families organized on the basis of the "natural" model, families working with a "legal" model would hold opposite views. To a greater extent, the members of these families would tend:

1. To adapt their conduct to accommodate specific situations and thereby reveal greater role flexibility.

2. To weigh each case of conflict between home and extrafamily obligations on the basis of personal desires and wishes.

3. To emphasize interpersonal ties rather than familial status in organizing conduct related to marriage, the home, and fertility.

This section deals with the relationship between conceptions of roles, which are associated theoretically with the "natural" versus "legal" family models, and types of kinship orientation, which are putatively expressions of varying degrees of corporateness of kinship structure. This analysis rests on the assumption that family is an inherent substructure of the kinship unit. The connections between family roles and kinship orientation are examined in two segments: (a) age, sex, and household composition as revealing the extent to which family roles are situationally determined and (b) the salience of marital roles as indicating social demarcations of family boundaries.

Age, Sex, and Household Composition

A focus on age, sex, and household composition provides information relevant for investigating the influence of ideology versus situational factors in kinship orientation. Age and sex constitute distinctions for conduct in almost every society. But although all societies make use of age and sex in ascribing roles, the specific content of these roles varies from group to group. The first question to be addressed, however, is whether age and sex influence kinship orientation at all.

Table 7-9 displays the kinship orientations of respondents according to their age and sex. For men, Parentela Orders and Genetic and Canon Law responses vary by age, while Standard American and Civil Law categories are not affected. Although 27 percent of the men born from 1932 to 1939 fall into the Parentela Orders category, only 17 percent of the men born in the period 1950 to 1959 do so. Conversely, whereas just 9 percent of the men in the earlier cohort (1932–1939) are classified as Genetic or Canon Law, fully 23 percent of the later cohort (1950–1959) are. However, as noted above, age seems to have little bearing on the Standard American and Civil Law distributions among men.

According to Table 7-9, age influences kinship orientations of women differently from those of men. For women, Civil Law, Genetic, and Canon Law orientations appear to be unaffected by age. The major influences of age are on the Parentela Orders and Standard American perspectives. As for men, the probability of falling into the Parentela Orders category is greater for

TABLE 7-9. Kinship Orientation and Respondents' Year of Birth, by Sex of Respondent

Kinship orientation	Year of birth					
	Men respondents[a]			Women respondents[b]		
	1932–1939	1940–1949	1950–1959	1932–1939	1940–1949	1950–1961
Parentela orders (%)	27.0	18.2	17.2	21.5	16.5	5.8
Standard american (%)	47.2	49.0	45.3	38.5	46.2	54.8
Civil law (%)	16.9	14.7	14.1	18.5	15.4	17.3
Genetic or canon law (%)	9.0	18.2	23.4	21.5	22.0	22.1
N	89	143	64	135	182	104

[a] For men, Chi square not significant.

[b] For women, Chi square = 13.573; d.f. = 6; $p = .05$.

older than younger women—22 percent in the 1932–1939 age cohort as compared with 6 percent in the 1950–1961 cohort. But the chances of having a Standard American orientation decrease with age—55 percent for younger women (born 1950–1961) in contrast to 39 percent for older women (born 1932–1939).

In brief, the influence of age on kinship orientations shows these tendencies: (a) there is a greater probability among both men and women to hold a Parentela Orders orientation at older (than younger) age levels; (b) whereas younger men tend to fall more often into the Genetic and Canon Law category, younger women more frequently have a Standard American orientation.

The presence of age and sex differences in kinship orientation evokes a further question as to whether these variations can be attributed to stage in the family life course or to the differences in the historical contexts in which the individuals grew up. Research on family life cycles is concerned with the effects of transitions in role and status on the lives of the family members. As Reiss (1960) has found, interaction with relatives varies at different stages of the family development. If kinship orientation is situationally determined, then one would expect that persons shift in orientation as their children grow and eventually leave home. However, it is also possible that age and sex differences derive not so much from life course transitions, but from the diverse historical experiences of different birth cohorts. The economic depression of the 1930s may have influenced the kinship ideologies of the older respondents; World War II and the Korean conflict may have affected kinship ideas of the middle-range respondents; and movements toward equal rights may have swayed the younger respondents. Or, since kinship ideologies appear to be transmitted in families, the particular historical experiences of the respondents' parents and grandparents may have been influential in shaping the respondents' own ideas about kinship. While it may not be possible to delve into the precise impact of historical periods on kinship orientation, it may be possible to determine whether age differences can be attributed to birth cohorts or, conversely, to family life cycle events.

At first glance, the findings on the concordance of age and sex on kinship orientation suggest that as people get older, their institutional involvements stabilize and their interest in line of descent increases. But there are puzzling elements in the findings. Especially baffling is that, among young people (generally those below thirty), men and women appear to differ in their perceptions of the role of kinship in social endurance. Whereas younger men tend to regard kinship structure from an Ego-centric perspective (i.e., Genetic and Canon Law viewpoint), younger women more often see kinship as a means for social placement. Possibly, the women born after 1950 have been influenced significantly by the recent feminist movements, affirmative action programs, and career concerns. One would then expect that young women would display considerable interest in upward social mobility and would, with declining birth rates, give greater attention to ascending generations in their structuring of kinship ties. Perhaps only later do familial influences operate.

Insofar as age differences in kinship orientation among women may represent cohort shifts in occupational orientation and the role of women in society instead of life cycle transitions, a further analysis by educational level may shed light on this issue. Table 7-10 shows kinship orientation and educational level by sex of respondent. For men, educational level affects kinship orientation in ways similar to age. Those men with a high education level (i.e., graduate work or professional school) tend to fall into the Parentela Orders category, while men at low educational levels (i.e., less than a high school graduate) are overrepresented in the Genetic and Canon Law grouping. Since the findings for men do not discriminate between age and education as influences in kinship orientation, these findings are equivocal as far as the life cycle versus cohort issue is concerned.

Among women, however, age and education seem to differ in their effects on kinship orientation. Unlike the age data, educational level of women is not related to holding a Parentela Orders orientation. Instead, while those women at low educational levels (i.e., less than a high school graduate) are overrepresented in the Genetic and Canon Law class, women at high levels (i.e., graduate or professional school), as well as being young, are more often in the Standard American category. Hence, there appear to be two separate influences affecting the relationship between age and kinship orientation among women — one of them related to Parentela Orders, derived from maturation, and the other related to Standard American kinship, derived from the historical events affecting the birth cohort.

TABLE 7-10. Kinship Orientation and Educational Level Achieved, by Sex of Respondent

Kinship orientation	Educational level				
	Graduate work	Some college	High school graduate	Less than high school graduate	Total
Men respondents[a]					
Parentela orders (%)	29.0	20.8	19.2	15.2	20.6
Standard american (%)	45.2	49.4	46.2	45.5	47.6
Civil law (%)	16.1	13.0	19.2	15.2	15.2
Genetic or canon law (%)	9.7	16.9	15.4	24.2	16.6
N	31	154	78	33	296
Women respondents[b]					
Parentela orders (%)	17.6	14.8	13.2	21.1	15.4
Standard american (%)	58.8	49.0	49.1	25.4	45.8
Civil law (%)	5.9	16.8	18.6	18.3	16.9
Genetic or canon law (%)	17.6	19.5	19.2	35.2	21.9
N	34	149	167	71	421

[a] Chi square not significant.

[b] Chi square = 20.478; d.f. = 9; $p = .015$.

The interpretation that the data on age and sex may reflect both cohort and maturation influences on kinship orientation suggests still another analysis based on household composition. Data relevant to the family life cycle are presented in Table 7-11 which describes characteristics of the respondents' children and households. This table includes reports on whether the children had been born to the respondent, ages of children, residence of children in the household, and marital status of adult children. The findings in Table 7-11 are:

1. Recruitment of children. The question as to whether children in the respondents' families have been born to the respondent points to the distinction between the "natural" family and those domestic relationships formed through adoption, marriage, or foster placement. The data indicate that persons with a Genetic or Canon Law orientation more often than others have children in their families who had not been born to them. This finding is of course consistent with that on marital status, which has indicated that relatively fewer couples in the Genetic–Canon Law category than others in the sample are in their first marriages. (See Table 7-7.)

2. Ages of children. The data on ages of children are classified in Table 7-11, generally according to level of schooling—5 or under corresponding to preschool, 6–12 to elementary school, 13–17 to high school, and 18 or over to college or independent residence. The overall data indicate that children of parents in the Parentela Orders, Genetic, and Canon Law categories are slightly older than children with Standard American or Civil Law parents. The differences among kinship orientations, however, are generally less than five percent (and always less than ten percent) for any age group. Variations in kinship orientation by age of respondent far exceed those according to age of children. (See Table 7-9.) Hence, few findings regarding respondents' ages appear to derive from differences in family life cycle stage among kinship orientations.

3. Residence of children. As in the case of children's ages, the data on residence do not provide explanatory power for difference among kinship orientations. There is a slight tendency for respondents in the Genetic and Canon Law category to be overrepresented in the "empty nest" stage (i.e., where all children have left home) and to be underrepresented in households in which all children are still in the home. But these findings do not seem sufficient to provide a reasonable explanation for variations in respondents' age among kinship orientations.

4. Marital status of adult children. The percentages of respondents with at least one married child do show a considerable difference by kinship orientation. More respondents with a Genetic or Canon Law orientation have at least one child who has married than do respondents with other orientations. Certainly, some of this tendency can be explained by the relative ages of children whose parents are in the Genetic and Canon Law grouping. Still, by way of contrast, although children of parents with a Parentela Orders perspective are also generally older than are those of Standard American or Civil Law parents, they appear to leave home late and to marry late. These data are consistent with the findings that the parents of respondents in the Parentela Orders category, as well as the respondents themselves, tend to marry at a late age, while those in the Genetic and Canon Law classification more often marry at an early age. (See Tables 6-5, 6-6, and 7-8.) Hence, although marriage of adult children is the only family life cycle variable that is clearly associated with variation in kinship orientation, it appears to be influenced by kinship orientation rather than the reverse.

The overall findings on age, sex, and household composition suggest that whereas age and sex differences in kinship orientation do occur, these differences seem to derive more from maturation and cohort experiences—for example, economic depression, women's movement, or war—rather than from transitions in the family life cycle. This set of results appears to provide further support for the contentions that kinship orientation is more a product of ideology than personal adaptation to family situations.

TABLE 7-11. Kinship Orientation and Characteristics of Children and Household

Characteristics of children and household	Parentela orders	Standard american	Civil law	Genetic and canon law
Recruitment of children				
Percent of respondents whose children are all "natural", (i.e., none is adopted, step, or foster)	69.6	62.9	67.6	55.2
Ages of children				
18 or over (born before 1960) (%)	28.7	25.2	26.5	31.9
13–17 (born 1961–1965) (%)	25.6	22.4	22.2	24.0
6–12 (born 1966–1972) (%)	29.0	31.6	29.1	30.1
5 or under (born 1973–1978) (%)	16.6	20.7	22.2	14.0
Total (%)	99.9	99.9	100.0	100.0
Number	355	745	302	329
Residence of children				
Percent of households in which all children have left home	8.0	10.2	9.5	13.8
Percent of households in which all children are still in home	68.8	68.8	74.3	63.8
N	112	285	105	116
Marital status of adult children				
Percent of respondents with at least one married child	44.2	51.2	45.5	62.2
Number of respondents with at least one child born 1960 or earlier	43	84	33	37

The Salience of Marital Roles

In contemporary society, the emergence of popular movements pertaining to equal rights and equal treatment of all individuals (regardless of ascribed characteristics or of personal beliefs) have had significant effects on the family. While critics of family life for centuries have urged changes in marital relationships (e.g., John Milton and Frederick Engels), apparently only recently has the state of technology, literacy, and standard of living been sufficient to permit the enactment of such changes. The women's movements in particular have encouraged freedom of choice regarding domestic versus occupation role and, in some instances, legal-marriage versus living-together. Insofar as kinship orientations seem to reflect ideological stances, one would expect that labor force commitment as well as willingness to live together prior to marriage would be related to conceptions of kinship. This section deals with respondent's views on the issues of work versus domestic commitment by women and of the propriety of cohabitation. These issues bear on the maintenance of family boundaries in social space and time.

Table 7-12 shows the percentages of women in the labor force (or in college), classified by kinship orientation and year of birth. The data for women respondents show clearly that among younger women (i.e., born 1940 or later), those in the Parentela Orders category are underrepresented in the labor force, while Standard American women are overrepresented. Among wives of men respondents, the percentage of younger women in the Parentela Orders category is also low; however, there is little difference in labor force participation among women in the other kinship categories. (The data for older women, i.e., born in the 1930s, are less significant than those for younger women in that most of the former women do not have young children in the home.)

Table 7-12 indicates further that most women in the study are employed. To determine relative commitment to household versus occupational demands (at least in the abstract), the respondents were asked the extent to which they agreed (or disagreed) with the statement, "In a conflict between demands of home and job, a woman's first loyalty should be to her home." Since the number of children living in the household may affect the degree to which people give priority to the home, respondents with no or one child in the home are compared separately from those with two or more children. The findings appear in Table 7-13.

In Table 7-13, the data for women reveal that in small families, those in the Parentela Orders category are most prone to favor familial demands over job demands, whereas women in the Genetic and Canon Law group are least apt to do so (80 versus 59 percent). For larger families, the trend is in the opposite direction: Parentela Orders women are least willing to describe their

TABLE 7-12. Kinship Orientation and Percentage of Women Either in Labor Force or in College, by Year of Birth

Year of birth	Parentela orders	Standard american	Civil law	Genetic or canon law
Women respondents				
Born 1940 or later (%)	58.3	75.2	66.7	66.7
N	36	141	48	63
Born in 1930's	79.3	63.5	76.0	75.9
N	29	52	25	29
Wives of men respondents				
Born 1940 or later	50.0	57.7	57.0	58.1
N	38	97	30	31
Born in 1930's	61.1	68.2	50.0	
N	18	22	16	

TABLE 7-13. Kinship Orientation and Percentage of Respondents Who Agree with Statement: "In a conflict between the demands of home and job, a woman's first loyalty should be to her home," by Sex of Respondent and Number of Children Living Home

	Women respondents		Men respondents	
	None or one child in home	Two or more children in home	None or one child in home	Two or more children in home
Parentela orders (%)	80.0	78.3	84.2	91.9
N	15	46	19	37
Standard american (%)	76.3	86.0	72.7	94.0
N	76	107	55	67
Civil law (%)	71.4	88.6	78.6	81.5
N	21	44	14	27
Genetic or canon law (%)	59.4	92.7	77.3	93.8
N	32	55	22	16

first loyalty as being to the home, and the Genetic and Canon Law women are most willing (78 percent versus 93 percent). Note however that for women in the Parentela Orders category, size of family appears to make little difference in the precise percentage agreeing with the statement (80 versus 78 percent); I interpret this similarity in percentages to mean that, for Parentela Orders women, degree of loyalty to home versus job is a matter of principle and not circumstance. At the other extreme, with a great discrepancy in percentage by family size among Genetic and Canon Law women (59 versus 93 percent), presumably situational factors play a more significant role in determining one's first loyalty.

The data for men in Table 7-13 are less conclusive than those for women. Aside from the slightly larger percentage of Parentela Orders men in small families agreeing with the statement, there is little similarity between findings for men and for women. For most categories, the men show a greater proclivity to agree with the statement than do women—regardless of kinship orientation.

The salience of marital role over occupational role among Parentela Orders women is parelleled by views of these women on restricting female-male cohabitation to married couples. The percentages of respondents who agree with the statement that, "It is a good idea for a man and a woman to live together for a while before they marry," are presented in Table 7-14. For men, there is little distinction among kinship orientations with regard to agreement with this statement. Among women, however, there is a wide variation by kinship orientation. Whereas only 15 percent of the women in the Parentela Orders category approve of premarital cohabitation, fully 46 percent of those in the Genetic and Canon Law classes are in agreement with

144

TABLE 7-14. Kinship Orientation and Percentage of Respondents Who Agree with the Statement: "It is a good idea for a man and woman to live together for a while before they marry."

Kinship orientation	Men respondents who agree	Women respondents who agree
Parentela orders (%)	44.3	15.3
N	61	65
Standard american (%)	51.0	34.7
N	141	193
Civil law (%)	44.5	25.3
N	45	71
Genetic or canon law (%)	51.0	45.6
N	49	92

the statement. Hence, the data on premarital cohabitation reinforce the interpretation that orientations regarding kinship ties express conceptions of family life along a dimension of corporateness—with Parentela Orders symbolizing the greatest salience of status in a corporate group and Canon Law and Genetic models the least.

Kinship Conceptions and Family Roles: Summary

This section has focused on the connections between conceptions of kinship and family roles in two ways: first, by examining whether the family life cycle played an important part in determining kinship orientation and, second, by comparing the salience of marital and domestic roles with other commitments. The findings with regard to family life cycle influences indicate the following:

1. Age of respondents is associated with kinship orientation. Whereas younger men in the sample are overrepresented in the Genetic and Canon Law classification, older men tend to fall more often into the Parentela Orders category. But while older women are also clustered more than expected in the Parentela Orders class, younger women more frequently are classified as Standard American.

2. Among men, age and education converge in their influence on kinship orientation, but for women, their effects are divergent. Instead, among women, high educational level (i.e., graduate or professional school) is associated with the Standard American model. This finding reflects the increasing educational levels among younger women.

3. In contrast to the marked differences among kinship orientations found for age and educational level, analysis by ages of children—intended to

indicate family life cycle influences on orientations—fails to yield comparable distinctions. Hence, family life cycle variations by themselves seem insignificant in determining kinship orientation.

4. The only noteworthy findings with regard to household composition pertain to the large number of Genetic and Canon Law families with step and adopted children and the relatively small percentage of families in the Parentela Orders category with adult married-children. These data, however, appear to reflect influences of kinship orientation rather than household attributes as causative factors.

The contrast between findings by age (coupled with education) and those by family life cycle suggests that the historical factors affecting entire birth cohorts are at least as influential as life-course transitions within the family in determining shifts in kinship orientation.

The conclusion that age differences are partly a function of the historical context in which a birth cohort grew up implies that kinship orientation will itself give meaning to life cycle transitions and family roles. Findings pertaining to family roles include:

1. Among younger women (i.e., born in 1940 or later), those respondents in the Parentela Orders category are underrepresented in the labor force, while Standard American women are overrepresented.

2. Among women in small families, respondents in the Parentela Orders category most often favor giving priority to familial commitments over job demands, whereas women in the Genetic and Canon Law grouping least often do so. In large families, the trend is in the opposite direction. But for women in the Parentela Orders category, size of family appears to make little difference in choosing home over job, while for Genetic and Canon Law women, family size itself has a considerable impact. Presumably, among Parentela Orders women weighing loyalties between home and job is a matter of principle, and among Canon Law and Genetic model women situational factors play an important part in determining priorities.

3. As opposed to women in the Parentela Orders class, women in the Genetic and Canon Law category endorse the notion that, "It is a good idea for a man and a woman to live together for a while before they marry." These findings suggest the strong significance of the status of marriage for women with a Parentela Orders perspective in contrast to the views of women classified as Genetic or Canon Law.

4. The data for men on the relationship between kinship orientation and family role are generally inconclusive.

Hence, the findings on family role, like those pertaining to age and sex differences, support the view that the kinship orientations represent different degrees of corporateness in family and kinship ties. While generally kinship orientations tend to be transmitted in families, cohort and educational effects are more important than family life cycle influences in modifying kinship conceptions; meanings of work and marriage are then structured in ways consistent with kinship orientations in protecting family boundaries.

KINSHIP ORIENTATION AND FERTILITY

In contemporary society, every married couple faces the decision of the eventual size of its family. Insofar as kinship orientations represent ideologies governing family relationships, these orientations would also have implications for fertility decisions. Moreover, since kinship orientations seem to persist in family lines over generations, one would anticipate that fertility rates would vary not only among respondents themselves but also among their parents, siblings, and children in ways consistent with the respondents' kinship orientations.

Two models of collaterality under investigation differ in the extent to which they distinguish between closeness of ascending versus descending generations. The Parentela Orders model assigns a greater proximity to Ego's descendants then to his ascendants, while the Standard American model stresses the closeness of ancestors. On the basis of differential weighting of ascendants and descendants, one would expect that persons with a Parentela Orders orientation would have a larger-than-average number of children, whereas those with a Standard American perspective would have relatively small families. The remaining models—Civil Law, Genetic, and Canon Law—give equal weight to proximity of ascendants and descendants; as a result, these models do not provide any clues per se of implications for fertility rates. Instead, they appear to accommodate a greater flexibility in fertility rates, and birth prevalence would depend to a greater extent (than would be the case for Parentela Orders and Standard American) upon the specific social contexts.

This section is divided into two parts: the first part deals with the fertility of close relatives of the respondents and the second pertains to the respondents' projections with regard to their own fertility.

Fertility of Close Relatives

The ability of kinship orientation to circumscribe fertility among close relatives is described below in two tables, the first referring to fertility over generations and the second to the multiplier effect of kinship orientation.

Table 7-15 presents data on the fertility of the respondents' parents, siblings, and children (as well as the respondents' own child-bearing experiences and projections). There are several regularities in the data. Across generations, with minor exceptions:

1. Close relatives of persons with Parentela Orders or with Genetic or Canon Law orientations tend to have high fertility levels.

2. Close relatives of persons with a Standard American orientation tend to have low fertility levels.
3. Close relatives of persons with a Civil Law orientation are intermediate in fertility.

The exceptions to these general tendencies occur where birth histories are perhaps most incomplete—among the Genetic and Canon Law respondents and among the married children of Parentela Orders respondents.

Hence, the findings on the fertility of respondents' parents, siblings, and children appear to support the proposition that pattern of collaterality expressed by kinship models is related to fertility level. Moreover, data on age at marriage (Tables 6-5 and 7-8) indicate that kinship orientation operates independently of marital age in affecting fertility.

Possible effects of differential fertility upon the distribution of kinship orientations in a population are suggested in Table 7-16. This table displays the mean number of the respondents' nieces and nephews for the different kinship orientations and takes into account the respondents' religion and father's occupation. The data on religion show clearly the long term consequences of low fertility among Jewish respondents (2.3 nieces and nephews)

TABLE 7-15. Kinship Orientation and Mean Number of Children Born to Respondents and to Respondents' Parents, Siblings, and Children

Parentage	Parentela orders	Standard american	Civil law	Genetic or canon law
Mean number of respondents' full siblings	3.15	2.56	2.91	3.27
N	126	334	116	141
Mean number of children born to respondents	2.82	2.23	2.60	2.33
N	126	334	116	141
Mean number of children anticipated eventually by respondents	2.86	2.49	2.75	2.63
N[a]	106	261	97	96
Mean number of children born to respondents' siblings	3.02	2.71	2.70	2.87
Number of siblings with children	302	591	254	322
Mean number of grandchildren per married child	2.00	1.35	2.13	3.04
Number of married children	19	43	15	23

[a] The respondents not included in these calculations gave nonquantifiable answers, such as "Whatever happens," "It's up to God," "As many as possible," "We haven't decided yet," and so on. Divorced respondents also excluded.

as contrasted with the traditionally high Catholic birth rate (7.2 nieces and nephews). Similarly, the data indicate the high contribution that blue collar families have made to the population of Phoenix. As for kinship orientation, with only minor departures (among Catholics, Jews, and blue collar workers), the results are similar to respondents' own fertility rates; the mean number of nieces and nephews is highest in the Parentela Orders, Genetic, and Canon Law categories and lowest in the Standard American class.

Insofar as the Standard American orientation is most prevalent among the nonminority, educated middle class, the findings on numbers of nieces and nephews of respondents (taken in conjunction with the respondents' own fertility) seem to have significant implications for social stratification. The low prevalence of grandchildren of the Standard American respondents' parents presumably operates to diminish the number of middle-class candidates for desirable occupational positions and leaves at least some slots open for upwardly mobile individuals. More than that, the low productivity of children also minimizes the possibility of having surplus children who cannot maintain a given socioeconomic status. It thereby enhances the probability of the family's retention of a high socioeconomic status, while simultaneously permitting upward social mobility of other families.

TABLE 7-16. Kinship Orientation and Mean Number of Nieces and Nephews of Respondents by Respondents' Religion and Occupation of Fathers[a]

Religion and fathers' occupation	Parentela orders	Standard american	Civil law	Genetic or canon law	Total
Religion					
No preference	7.60			2.08	6.33
N	20			13	33
Jewish	4.43	1.21	2.38	1.14	2.33
N	14	19	8	7	48
Protestants	7.73	5.09	6.91	7.35	6.28
N	63	175	68	69	375
Catholics	8.35	6.26	5.90	8.78	7.15
N	37	85	29	41	192
Fathers' occupation[a]					
Professional, managerial, or administrative	6.29	4.37	6.13	6.62	5.43
N	51	105	39	34	229
Clerical, sales, or craft	5.58	4.05	5.34	5.36	4.78
N	31	96	35	44	206
Blue collar	10.31	7.83	7.68	9.46	8.60
N	36	93	34	48	211
Total with adult siblings	7.33	5.36	6.36	7.26	6.26
N	118	294	108	126	646

[a] Fathers' occupation at time respondents were growing up.

Projected Fertility of Respondents

Inasmuch as the sample in this investigation is limited to persons between ages of 18 and 45 virtually all respondents are capable of bearing more children than they already have. Although most respondents may have already completed their families, some of them may anticipate having additional children. Consequently, in the interview, the respondents were asked the number of children they anticipated having eventually. (This question was omitted from interviews with divorced persons.) While the number projected by the respondents may not in all instances correspond to the actual number they ultimately produce, the projected number may provide a more realistic estimate of fertility than the number of children they now have.

Table 7-17 describes the levels of fertility eventually anticipated by respondents with different kinship orientations and diverse social characteristics. For the various sections of the table, the results are as follows:

1. Men and Women. Except in the Standard American category, women generally anticipate having a larger number of children than men do. Both men and women in the Parentela Orders category tend to anticipate a large number of children and those in the Standard American class a small number, with individuals in the Civil Law grouping between them. Among kinship orientations, however, men and women in the Genetic and Canon Law category differ considerably in expected fertility. In that category, men provide the lowest mean number of children anticipated (as compared with the means in the other categories); but the mean for women in that category is as high as that for Civil Law respondents. This difference in anticipated fertility between men and women in the Genetic and Canon Law grouping persists in the other sections of the table despite independent influences of other social characteristics.

2. Religion. Within each kinship orientation, for both men and women, there is a general tendency for Jewish respondent to anticipate fewest children and Catholics most, with Protestants between them. Overall, except for Protestant men in the Parentela Orders category, differences within religion follow the patterns of fertility according to kinship orientation. Hence, although religious identity itself does affect fertility, this influence seems less profound than that of kinship orientation.

3. Education. Like religion, education exhibits a moderate influence on fertility as compared with kinship orientation. The most significant impact of education is that those persons with at least a high school education anticipate having fewer children than individuals who have not graduated from high school. As for kinship orientations, the Parentela Orders men and women who had had some college (but not graduate study) expect to have

TABLE 7-17. Kinship Orientation and Anticipated Eventual Fertility, by Various Social Characteristics

Social characteristics	Mean number of children expected eventually			
	Parentela orders	Standard american	Civil law	Genetic or canon law
ALL MARRIED RESPONDENTS				
Men	2.72	2.51	2.60	2.18
N	55	114	40	34
Women	3.02	2.48	2.86	2.87
N	51	147	57	62
RELIGION				
Men				
Jewish	3.00	2.00	2.20	—
N	6	9	5	—
Protestant	2.44	2.51	2.52	2.28
N	25	58	25	18
Catholic	3.06	2.71	2.60	2.33
N	16	31	5	12
Women				
Jewish	2.28	1.82	2.38	
N	7	11	8	
Protestant	2.96	1.97	2.82	2.97
N	27	92	34	31
Catholic	3.86	2.56	2.93	3.23
N	14	32	15	22
EDUCATION				
Men				
Graduate study	2.83	2.36	1.43	
N	6	11	7	
Attended college	2.33	2.44	3.06	2.05
N	30	62	18	19
High school	3.00	2.58	2.46	2.43
N	15	31	13	7
Less than high school graduate	4.25	2.90	2.50	
N	4	10	10	

(continued)

fewer children than other persons with that orientation. Otherwise, the data (with minor exceptions) fall into the overall fertility pattern by kinship orientation found for men and women generally.

4. Woman's employment status. The data on the employment status of women respondents and wives of men respondents reinforce the often replicated findings that homemakers have (and anticipate) more children than mothers who are employed outside the home. Yet, even with maternal employment taken into account, the force of kinship orientation on anticipated

TABLE 7-17 *(continued)*

Social characteristics	Mean number of children expected eventually			
	Parentela orders	Standard american	Civil law	Genetic or canon law
Women				
Graduate study	2.60	1.79	2.20	
N	5	14	5	
Attended college	2.22	2.46	2.65	2.37
N	18	61	20	19
High school graduate	3.38	2.38	2.88	2.41
N	16	58	24	22
Less than high school graduate	3.92	3.21	3.36	4.06
N	12	14	11	18
WOMAN'S EMPLOYMENT STATUS				
Men respondents' wives				
Now employed	2.35	2.38	2.09	1.53
N	28	56	22	15
Homemaker	3.12	2.74	3.38	2.73
N	26	47	16	15
Women respondents				
Now employed	2.52	2.33	2.38	2.63
N	27	84	32	32
Homemaker	3.67	2.73	3.42	2.88
N	21	52	19	26
MARITAL STATUS				
Men				
Now in first marriage	2.51	2.47	2.61	2.12
N	45	92	33	26
Now remarried	3.60	2.68	2.57	2.38
N	10	22	7	8
Women				
Now in first marriage	3.03	2.44	2.90	2.75
N	37	122	41	48
Now remarried	3.00	2.64	2.75	3.29
N	14	25	16	14

fertility is a significant one. The only departure from the general pattern is that homemakers in the Civil Law category expect to have an especially high number (and conversely working mothers a low number) of children.

5. Remarriage status. Table 7-17 also includes a tabulation comparing persons in their first marriage with those in subsequent marriages. Apart from the Civil Law respondents, remarried persons (both men and women) anticipate having a greater number of children eventually than do those in their first marriages. Inasmuch as fertility pertains to children from both marriages, presumably some remarried persons consider having two sets of children—one set in each marriage. Since this number represents anticipated (rather than actual) fertility, age does not appear to be an important factor in this estimate. However, even when remarriage status is held constant statistically, kinship orientation still affects anticipated fertility. The patterns of fertility expectations by kinship orientation of remarried persons are similar to those found for the entire sample.

6. Contact with mother. Another possibly confounding variable related to kinship is the frequency of contact with one's own mother. Perhaps, insofar as one's mother often remains as a significant figure in influencing family decisions (either directly or as a reference person), it seems plausible that frequent contact with one's parents would reinforce fertility in the adult children. (This statement assumes that parents are usually pronatal in outlook.) Data pertaining to the relationship between anticipated fertility and contact with mothers appear in Table 7-18. For the purpose of this analysis, frequent contact is interpreted as "at least once a month." As the table clearly shows, for each kinship orientation (outside of women in the Genetic and Canon Law grouping), those men and women who see their mothers at least once a month expect to have more children than those persons who see their mothers less often. Yet, although maternal contact does affect anticipated fertility, kinship orientation retains its mark upon childbearing.

TABLE 7-18. Kinship Orientation and Anticipated Eventual Fertility, by Frequency with Which Respondent Sees Own Mother

Frequency with which mother is seen	Number of children expected eventually			
	Parentela orders	Standard american	Civil law	Genetic or canon law
Men				
Mother seen at least once a month	3.14	2.59	2.58	2.21
N	21	45	19	14
Mother seen less than once a month	2.37	2.29	2.28	2.13
N	27	48	18	15
Women				
Mother seen at least once a month	3.07	2.51	3.07	2.62
N	15	69	29	29
Mother seen less than once a month	2.58	2.41	2.50	2.72
N	26	61	22	18

In brief, the percentages reported in table 7-17 and 7-18 verify the important role of kinship orientation in fertility rates even when other characteristics which ordinarily affect childbearing are controlled. These other characteristics—sex, religion, education, maternal employment, remarriage status, and maternal contact—while they each exert an independent constraint, are for the most part subordinate to the impact of kinship orientation upon anticipated fertility.

Kinship Orientation and Fertility: Summary

The data on fertility generally reflect the weighting of ascendants and descendants in the collaterality models over generations of families. Parentela Orders, which emphasizes closeness of descendants, tends to yield fairly large families; the Standard American model, which stresses ascendance, produces small families; and the remaining models, which are ego-centered, tend to be flexible in fertility—sometimes (for Genetic and Canon Law models) resulting in large families in the parental generation and small families among the respondents' siblings.

The continued influence of kinship orientation on fertility over a series of generations has a multiplier effect on the proportions holding each orientation within a population. The differential fertility among the kinship orientations is magnified with each new generation (as the data on nieces and nephews indicate). (In *none* of the social categories in Table 7-17 is the expected fertility highest in the Standard American classification.) The consistently low fertility rates of persons with a Standard American orientation carry various implications for social stratification. The small number of children in these families permits maximum concentration in expenditure of resources upon these children and thereby serves to sustain a desirable socioeconomic position for the family members (or to enhance chances of upward social mobility) in the succeeding generation. In addition, the continual lack of a large surplus of children minimizes the probability of marrying someone of lower socioeconomic status. In a growing economy, the small number of children produced by persons with a Standard American orientation would necessitate recruiting new families into the middle class as managerial, administrative, and professional positions multiply. In a contracting economy, families with a Standard American orientation would not be burdened by an excess of children whose marital choices and careers would be problematic in hard times. Overall, the relatively low fertility rates which characterize the Standard American families yield long-run effects over generations in ways which sustain the socioeconomic positions of these families.

The pervasive influence of kinship orientations on childbearing is suggested not only by the stability of family size for respondents' parents, siblings, and children (as well as for themselves) but also by the data on number of children anticipated by the respondents. The impact of variables normally associated with fertility rates—sex, religion, education, maternal employment, remarriage, and maternal contact—is ordinarily less than the influence of kinship orientation in determining the number of children anticipated by the respondents.

SUMMARY: KINSHIP ORIENTATION AND FAMILY ORGANIZATION

The typology of centripetal versus centrifugal kinship organization generates a corresponding typology of "natural" versus "legal" family models. Traditionally conceptions of the family have presupposed a fixed set of functions derived from "nature". Law in contemporary society, however, is faced with the problem of dealing with continuity in social structures without presupposing fixed ends or corporate "reality" for these structures. Consequently, family law assumes that social structures exist for whatever reasons individuals have. As a result, laws have to accommodate a variety of ends and to consider different value systems as being of equal worth. The idea that all domestic groups have equal rights and standing in the society thereby opposes the notion that congeries of families should be encouraged to sustain homogeneous clusters on the basis of "naturally" derived criteria.

The distinction between "natural" and "legal" family models implies also a difference between corporate and individual privacy. The concept of privacy itself rests upon the degree of autonomy from the general community. To the extent that conduct is not subject to public surveillance and accountability, it remains private. In corporate privacy, it is the "natural" family whose autonomy is to be protected; in personal privacy, it is individual autonomy that is paramount.

The dichotomy of corporate versus individual privacy denotes a relationship between norms pertaining to family privacy and modes of kinship orientation. The emphasis on line of descent in the Standard American and particularly in the Parentela Orders model suggests that people who conform to these models tend also to conceive of family organization mainly in terms of corporate privacy; the Ego-centeredness of the Genetic and Canon Law models, however, appear to reflect a stress upon individual privacy in family relationships. The data presented here examine the extent to which kinship orientations express varying degrees of corporateness in the respondents' families of procreation.

Prevalent sociological conceptions of the family generally focus on the here-and-now and the domain of the family is frequently delimited to the household. Attention is then usually directed to attributes of the household family: (a) social pathologies, such as personal abuse, alcoholism, delinquency, mental illness, or not "getting along," (b) explorations of alternative life styles, (c) socialization and social placement, (d) effects of socioeconomic or ethnic variables upon interpersonal ties, and so on. Although these concerns with the household family are often interesting and of practical importance, they fail to take into account the fact that relevant family ties may extend beyond the household in time and space. Indeed, the very crucial elements for understanding interaction within the household may inhere in characteristics of kinship that have little to do with residence.

When the household family is regarded as the basic unit of analysis, then the temporal span is limited to life course transitions of the husband and wife. The span normally covers the period from the establishment of a new household by a married couple to the time that the household is dissolved by their death. But if the field of family relationships is defined by the organization of kinship statuses, the household family is merely one segment of an entity that can stretch over several generations. For example, individuals who stress line of descent as a source of identity may incorporate ancestors from the dim past—long dead—into the operational family boundaries. Similarly, yet-unborn descendants—though necessarily anonymous—may be pulled inside the family boundaries as "kinship gives life meaning by providing people with a mechanism by which both their substance and their personal values . . . survive them (Craig, 1979, p. 95)."

The symbolic extension of the family in time yields a coherent set of goals and norms that organizes the conduct of the family members into a corporate body and constrains their conduct. The material in this and the previous chapter has suggested that the kinship models represent family ideologies (implying varying degrees of corporateness) that exert their influence over generations in significant ways. Latent consequences of separatist (or pluralist) models (e.g., Parentela Orders) differ considerably from those of communal models (e.g., Canon Law). The corporateness implied by the separatist models influences the homogenization of basic values in the family, stabilization of the marriage, inhibition of disillusionment, establishment of the priority of family status over other (perhaps more personal) commitments, and the maintenance of fertility norms over a series of generations.

These findings support the view that the kinship models represent pervasive ideologies that influence the conduct of the constituent household families among closely related kin. Much of what is happening in the household of one person probably has its ideological roots in the parental household; very likely this conduct is being repeated in the households of siblings; and it stands a good chance of affecting the succeeding generation.

Relatives and Strangers

There is considerable evidence that increasingly in modern urban settings we are becoming strangers to our relatives—even to our spouses, parents, and children. This alienation often occurs not so much as a result of ideological revisions, but because the high degree of mobility in modern societies does not permit many of us to have an intimate relationship with relatives, and our diversity of personal interests draws us away from domestic life itself. There is, thus, some tendency for social scientists to consider family and kinship roles as continually diminishing in significance in modern life (Bahr, 1976, p. 61).

Accompanying this view regarding the languishing of kinship, there has been a prolonged controversy over whether the family is becoming "structurally isolated"—a tightly bounded, relatively autonomous sub-system in society (Morgan, 1975). This controversy has stimulated considerable investigation into the ties between the nuclear family and relatives. These investigations have shown that, generally, families rely on relatives in time of crisis (Lopata, 1973; Adams, 1968; Bahr, 1976); women form the major communication agents with kin (Adams, 1968; Bahr, 1976); parents transfer wealth to married children over the life course (Sussman and Burchinal, 1962); people use siblings as reference markers for evaluating their own degree of success (Adams, 1968); and so on. The major point, however, is that, despite the persistence of these uses of kin, the weight of evidence shows a movement toward more and more structural isolation. This trend has indicated to Schneider (1968) that American kinship is not based on a uniform set of social roles, but that it is coming to be defined as a system of statuses based on biogenetic ties and emptied of specific rights and obligations upon which most people agree.

Although the trend toward structural isolation of the nuclear family has changed modes of interaction with relatives, the institution of kinship endures as a social category in modern culture. But, having acknowledged its endurance, we are obliged to ask: Given the broad range of life circumstances, how does the fact that people are related to one another genealogically impinge upon their lives? Once having assigned "kinship" an existential status, people must deal with it and integrate it into their outlook in the world. I shall now consider topics relevant to ways in which people handle kinship as a social category.

KINSHIP AND SOCIAL EXCHANGE

If kinship statuses are divorced from specific role prescriptions in modern society, then one can anticipate a broad range of orientations with regard to appropriate interactions with relatives. Depending upon circumstances, at one extreme, people can regard their kinship ties as uniquely important and, at the other extreme, they can ignore these ties. This variation suggests that kinship ties can be regarded as a commodity in social exchange—valued highly in some situations and easily expendable in others.

Peter Blau (1964) proposes that, "There are a number of similarities between social exchange and economic exchange . . .The principle of the eventually diminishing marginal utility applies to social as well as economic commodities (314–315)." One would anticipate that where the persistence of the family expresses a special interest, marginal utility in the maintenance of ties would be quite different from the situation in which the family must compete with other institutions for supplying these satisfactions to the individual. "Competition occurs not only among like social units that have the same objective but also among unlike units with different objectives (Blau, 1964, p. 331)."

Past research on the family and kinship offers a wide range of assumptions regarding the uniquesness of kinship as a commodity of social exchange. These conceptions of kinship can be placed on a continuum to produce a series ranging from the uniqueness of kinship ties to the irrelevance of such ties. Each point on the continuum seems to be expressed by a metaphor of giving and taking. Meyer Fortes depicts kinship norms in terms of generosity; Lewis Coser portrays institutions as greedy; Michael Anderson describes kinship in terms of risk, uncertainty, and profit; while Erving Goffman discusses social relationships as fraudulent manipulation. These conceptions are described below as they relate to the Parentela Orders, Standard American, Civil Law, Genetic, and Canon Law models.

Kinship and Generosity

Using a political analogy, Meyer Fortes (1969, pp. 97–99) concerns himself with kinship as a unique domain of social order:

> I suggest that the social and cultural elements and processes that make up a given social system fall into determinate sectors of organization. Each sector—which I call a domain—comprises a range of social relations, customs, norms, statuses, and other analytically discriminable elements linked up in

nexuses and unified by the stamp of distinctive functional features that are common to all . . .A domain is not merely a classificatory construct. It is a matrix of social organization in the sense that its members derive their specificity from it . . .A status can be defined as a position held by a person in a given domain, specified by the social relations distinctive of that domain, and deployed in activities and attitudes conforming to the norms and customs and material apparatus that are distinctive of that domain.

Kinship as a domain is governed, according to Fortes, by a norm of generosity, a rule of amity. By amity, Fortes does not mean "love" but instead a "consensus in accepting the value of mutual support in maintaining 'a code of good conduct' for the realization of each person's 'legitimate interests,' . . .even by acts of violence regarded as legitimate (Fortes, 1969, p. 110)." He suggests further that this prescriptive altruism is a universal characteristic of kinship (Fortes, 1969, p. 234).

At least in his emphasis on prescriptive altruism, Fortes takes a position consistent with that of Lévi-Strauss. According to Lévi-Strauss (1969), corporate structure is stabilized when there are obligations that cannot be paid off—the indebtedness is always greater than the amount returned. The Fortes position implies that the debt of being a kinsman is always greater than any activity that the individual can perform for his relative. This norm of generosity, thus, represents an ideal condition that sustains a corporate structure of kinship.

The conception of kinship as a domain governed by a norm of generosity implies that social space is partitioned into a complex of categories (i.e., corporate units), each of which is governed by a unique set of reciprocity norms. This connection between social category and reciprocity norms suggests that people who apply norms of generosity to kin have a categorical rather than a gradational perspective of relatives. Accordingly, one would anticipate that people conforming to the *Parentela Orders* model of genealogical structure would tend to apply the norm of generosity to broad classes of relatives. Inasmuch as the *Standard American* model, like Parentela Orders, derives its structure from categories based on line of descent, it too implies the norm of generosity in organizing kinship ties.

Kinship and Conflict

One view of kinship as a political domain produces the Fortes conception of ties between relatives as resting upon the norm of amity (or of generosity). Another perspective, however, denotes a conflict either within the kinship group or between kinship obligations and those pertaining to competing institutional commitments.

A problem in the maintenance of kinship ties emerges when conflicting demands are placed on individuals by kinship ties as opposed to obligations derived in another institutional setting (e.g., employment). Under such conditions, people may regard their kinship ties (as well as other commitments) as excessive. Coser applies the anthropomorphic metaphor of "greediness" to those organizations and groups that "make total claims on their members and which attempt to encompass within their circle the whole personality (Coser, 1974, p. 4)." Extending the metaphor further, Coser suggests that the demands of "greedy" institutions upon the person are "omnivorous" and insatiable. No matter how much time and effort the individual devotes, the institution calls for more.

Suppose that familial and civil institutions are "greedy" in their demands, both of them offering in return unique kinds of satisfaction to the individual. William Goode (1960, pp. 494–495) proposes that "role demands made by one institutional order conflict with those made by another. . . . The individual cannot fully satsify all demands, and [he] must move through a continuous sequence of role decisions and bargains, by which he attempts to adjust these demands . . . The social structure determines how much freedom in manipulation he possesses."

Coser further suggests that incompatibility in the individual's allocation of time is not itself the significant factor in the conflict between "greedy" institutions. Rather, it is a matter of personal investment: sacrifice and devotion. "Since it is very difficult to repudiate objects in which one has invested so much, the more one invests in an object, the greater the hold that object has on the person (Coser, 1974, p. 91)." If the person then invests heavily in "time, energy, and affect" in both family and employment, the potential conflict between the "norm of generosity" in family matters and the norm of achievement is heightened.

The study of kinship patterns of Jewish families in New York by Leichter and Mitchell (1956) showed that conflict generally arose when relatives considered the demands or expectations of other relatives as excessive. The general complaint was that the relative either was taking advantage of the person, was ignoring the closeness of the relationship, or had been untrustworthy. For some relatives, this breakdown in consensus on reciprocities resulted in a complete rupture of ties; for others this breakdown was followed by a long period of "not talking to each other." Despite the conflict, there is an underlying consensus that people ought to maintain a series of reciprocities with relatives; the disagreement arose over the extent to which kinship ties were too "greedy."

The conception of kinship ties as "greedy" somehow echoes the concerns of the Roman civilization at the time of the formulation of the Twelve Tables. The rise of the Plebians when the Roman Republic was founded gave voice to the contention that the Patrician class too often directed its efforts to the promotion of the special interest of its own families. Henceforth, the devotion to family was to be matched by devotion to civil society. Implicit in this change was the need to strike a series of bargains to accommodate conflicts in demands by family as opposed to civil society. At this time, prohibition of intermarriages between Plebian and Patrician families was lifted, and the *Civil Law model* somewhat weakened the emphasis upon ancestral line of descent implied by the Parentela Orders model, but it retained (through succession *per stirpes*) a focus on family continuity.

Kinship as Market

If kinship ties are regarded as exchanges in market place, interaction between relatives is based on a "market price," an equilibrium of supply and demand. Relatives are assumed to be free-acting agents—no longer strongly constrained by corporate injunctions to perform certain acts. Without such injunctions, "the establishment of exchange relations involves making investments that constitute commitments to the other party. Since social exchange requires trusting others to reciprocate, the initial problem is to prove oneself trustworthy (Blau, 1964, p. 98)." The degree of trustworthiness to reciprocate through services of equal value then defines one's standing in an exchange relationship. Whereas two people may trust each other to reciprocate in transactions that involve immediate exchange or services of little value, they may hesitate when the reciprocation may never occur or when the value of the initial service is very high. In such instances, kinship status counts for little in the maintenance of relations with particular persons. Specific relatives must, like anyone else, then "earn" their standing by gaining personal trust.

In an analysis of reliance upon kin in 19th century England, Michael Anderson conceived of kinship as a source of "goods" like those in any other institution. For Anderson, kinship is a source of goods in competition with other sources for similar goods: material help, personal or intimate ties, certainty of delivery of services, emergency assistance, and so on. There is then nothing unique about kinship that establishes it as a social category that on its own merits deserves to endure. For Anderson, "The highest probability that a kinship relationship of a functional kind will come into being between kinsman A and kinsman B will be when A has resources inadequate to solve one or more problems alone *and* when B also has or expects to have problems which A is or will be able to help him solve because he (A) has a surplus of the required resources, *and* when neither of them have open to them alternative suppliers of resources which they are in need who will demand a lower expenditure of resources by them in reciprocation (Anderson, 1971, p. 171)."

The conception of kinship ties as a commodity that competes on the open market with alternative relationships—friendships, social agencies, neighbors—for meeting personal satisfactions erases the idea of kinship as perpetual order. Instead, the endurance of any social structures rests upon its continuing to supply a balance of personal gratifications. Social distance is a function of personal intimacy rather than similarities between classes. The *Canon Law model* of genealogical distances seems particularly appropriate as an expression of personal intimacy in that it yields gradiations of relatives by the number of collateral or lineal links between them and EGO's nuclear family.

Kinship and Fraudulent Manipulation

Drawing upon the metaphor of the theater, Erving Goffman (1956) has analyzed the ways by which the people try to manage the impressions they make on others. He writes that, "When an individual appears before others he will have many motives for trying to control the impression they receive of the situation . . . .The issues dealt with by stage-craft and stage-management are sometimes trivial but they are quite general; they seem to occur everywhere in social life, providing a clear-cut dimension for formal sociological analysis (Goffman, 1956, p. 8)." As in the various ideologies regarding acting, impression management can be sincere (perhaps the performance is intended to shield or benefit the other person) or it can be cynical or fraudulent—primarily to manipulate the other person to respond in ways which will benefit the impression manager. From Goffman's perspective, however, both actors are involved in one way or another in impression management. Indeed, Goffman's major thesis is that people are judged by others according to their conformity to some set of moral standards. "But, *qua* performers, individuals are concerned not with the moral issue of realizing these standards, but with the amoral issue of engineering a convincing impression that these standards are being realized . . . .As performers we are merchants of morality (Goffman, 1956, p. 162)." In kinship as drama, relatives are the audience, "strangers" who are witnesses to a performance.

If in the establishment of reciprocities, we are dealing with exchanges of moral acts, we intend to receive genuine moral acts in exchange for our pretenses. We seek love and good will for our payment of empty niceties. Carried to its extreme, impression management eventuates in a norm of fraud—a trade of morality for immorality, a trade of the genuine for the fake. In kinship, impression management often results in the obligation to present a friendly front, as long as the price is not exhorbitant, and to apply much tact in interaction. The metaphor of fraudulent manipulations symbolizes estrangement from kin.

Range of Models and Reciprocity

In summary, each model of kinship-mapping seems to imply a specific mode of reciprocity. The Parentela Orders model appears to express the norm of generosity. It emerged in societies that depended for their persistence upon the endurance of "houses" or belief systems passed down through the generations from parents to children. The Standard American model, with attention more to the past than the future, seems to provide a bridge between the Parentela Orders and Civil Law models. The Civil Law model appears to be related to institutional greediness. It emerged in a society in which civil institutions were in conflict with an elite of powerful families. The Genetic model, by virtue of its modification of the Civil Law computational formula, $[(i-1)+j]$ instead of $[i+j]$, stands between the Civil and Canon Law models. The Canon Law model seems to give form to the marketplace conception of kinship reciprocity. The Canon Law model developed at a time in late medieval Europe when the Church and the state were both centralized institutions, forcing the family into a subordinate position in competition with them for the satisfaction of needs. Each mode of reciprocity thus seems to reflect a different set of norms and values appropriate to a specific kinship model.

The remainder of this chapter deals with the topics of residential location, interest in kinship ties, and the discrepancy between actual and desired contact with kin as all of these are related to kinship orientations and metaphors of social exchange.

LOCATION OF RESIDENCE

In the study of kinship organization, anthropologists give considerable attention to the location of the residence of married couples. Following Murdock (1949), the position usually taken is that the relative contribution of men and women in the division of labor determines the location of the marital residence. In those societies where the man's contribution is greater, the couple will live near his people (i.e., virilocality); where the woman's contribution is greater, the rule is for couples to live near the wife's people (i.e., uxorilocality); and where male and female contributions are equal, residence is either neolocal or utrolocal (i.e, near either spouses's people). In the preindustrial cultures used in these analyses, however, economic production is not isolated from residence and its environs, as it generally is in contemporary society.

In modern industrial society, marital residence has (if anything) tended toward uxorilocality (Adams, 1970). Closeness of residence to the wife's relatives permits not only the persistence of intimate ties but also the development of coalitions and mutual welfare networks within maternal kindreds. In fact, a primary determinant of interaction with relatives is proximity of residence (Klatzky, n.d.; Adams, 1968).

There are two separate components that describe spatial aspects of marital residence. The first component concerns the extent to which persons live near relatives at all; it pertains to the degree to which movement away from one's consanguine family occurs. The amount of such movement depends upon a variety of factors—economic opportunities, climate, cultural amenities, accessibility to educational or health facilities, and so on. The second component deals with the distinction between husband's and wife's relatives— uxorilocality, virilocality, or utrolocality. Although circumstances pertaining to degree of movement may dictate neolocality (i.e., isolation from both sides), there may still be a preference on the part of husband and wife to live near one set of relatives.

General Residential Proximity

Table 8-1 presents data on the percentages of close relatives residing in Arizona. In this table, close relatives refer to members of the respondents' (and their spouses') families of orientation. Arizona (rather than Maricopa County) was chosen as describing nearby residence because the major populations centers in the state are within a two-hour drive from Phoenix; the population in the remaining areas is sparse.

In Table 8–1, the percentage for women clearly show a wide range in residential patterns by kinship orientation. Women in the Parentela Orders category have the fewest parents and siblings in Arizona, and those with a Genetic or Canon Law perspective have the most. For example, whereas only 36 percent of the mothers of Parentela Orders women reside in Arizona, 75 percent of the mothers of those with a Genetic or Canon Law orientation do so. As for in-laws, while the women with a Parentela Orders conception again have the smallest percentages of their husbands' families in Arizona, women in the Standard American category have the largest. For instance, for mothers-in-law, the percentage is 37 for Parentela Orders women and 54 for those women in the Standard American category. Thus, the data indicate that Parentela Orders women are most likely to live apart from their own and their husbands' families of orientation, while Genetic and Canon Law women are most apt to live near their own families and Standard American women near their husbands' families.

For men, the data in Table 8–1 reveal a somewhat different picture. Distinctions among kinship orientations are somewhat blurred. Except for fathers and sisters second nearest in age to the respondents, relatives of Parentela Orders men (unlike women) are similar to men with other orientations in percentages living in Arizona. The only noteworthy finding is the tendency for men with a Genetic or Canon Law orientation to have a comparatively high percentage of close relatives in Arizona.

Table 8–1 indicates that while both men and women in the Genetic and Canon Law categories tend to have a high percentage of close consanguineal relatives in Arizona, it is just the women in the Parentela Orders classification whose families are particularly prone to be out-of-staters.

TABLE 8-1. Percentages of Close Relatives Residing in Arizona, by Sex of Respondent

Relatives	Parentela orders	Standard american	Civil law	Genetic or canon law
Ego's family of orientation (Women)				
Father	31.7	51.5	50.0	59.6
Mother	35.8	54.4	55.0	75.0
Brother closest in age to ego	26.0	32.0	48.0	54.5
Sister closest in age to ego	35.3	45.5	42.0	55.1
Brother second closest in age to ego	30.3	35.0	34.3	48.8
Sister second closest in age to ego	26.7	44.6	50.0	61.4
In-Laws				
Father-in-law	38.2	58.6	50.5	56.0
Mother-in-law	37.0	54.1	58.5	48.5
Wife's brother best known to ego	24.4	44.8	49.1	38.9
Wife's sister best known to ego	23.4	46.0	45.6	25.8
Ego's family of orientation (Men)				
Father	29.7	50.5	55.3	52.8
Mother	47.2	51.3	54.5	52.5
Brother closest in age to ego	38.3	32.7	35.7	48.5
Sister closest in age to ego	42.6	38.5	45.5	42.5
Brother second closest in age to ego	37.5	34.4	31.2	47.8
Sister second closest in age to ego	21.7	42.9	42.1	41.7
In-Laws				
Father-in-law	59.6	61.2	47.1	48.6
Mother-in-law	56.9	54.9	52.5	57.5
Husband's brother best known to ego	51.2	45.4	46.9	54.3
Husband's sister best known to ego	54.3	48.4	53.1	51.6

Virilocal and Uxorilocal Tendencies

In modern America with its high degree of residential mobility, people have many reasons for moving to new localities—or remaining in the same one. But apart from extent of mobility, there is the question whether being near "family" differentially influences moving and staying decisions of men as compared with women.

Table 8–2 presents the ratios of relatives residing in Arizona for men and women holding each particular kinship orientation. The percentages used are taken from Table 8–1. For example, for mothers of persons with a Parentela Orders orientation, the ratio is 47.2 percent over 35.8 percent or 1.32. A review of the data in Table 8–2 reveals that for the respondents' own families of orientation, the findings are: Parentela Orders is marked by virilocal tendencies (mean ratio = 1.17); Genetic and Canon Law models by uxorilocal tendencies (mean ratio = 0.79); while the Standard American and Civil Law groupings are utrolocal (mean ratio = 0.95 for each).

As for residence of in-laws, an apparent anomaly occurs. To be sure, the findings are consistent in indicating uxorilocality for persons with a Genetic or Canon Law perspective (mean ratio = 1.33) and utrolocality for Standard American and Civil Law respondents (mean ratio = 1.0). Yet, paradoxically, they also show an uxorilocal tendency among Parentela Orders respondents (ratio = 1.88); that is, with disproportionately more men living near in-laws. The anomaly, however, is more apparent than real. Since the men and women in the Parentela Orders category are not married to each other, this finding could readily occur if the men with a Parentela Orders orientation are utrolocal (i.e., living near either set of relatives) in comparison with the neolocal proclivities of Parentela Orders women, which would isolate the women from both parents and in-laws.

In general, the overview of virilocal as opposed to uxorilocal tendencies suggests that Genetic and Canon Law perspectives are uxorilocal; Standard

TABLE 8-2. For Each Kinship Orientation, the Ratio of Percentage of Close Relatives Living in Arizona for Men to that for Women (Percent of *Men's* Relatives in Arizona / Percent of *Women's* Relatives in Arizona)

Relatives	Parentela orders	Standard american	Civil law	Genetic or canon law
Ego's family of orientation				
Father	.94	.98	1.11	.70
Mother	1.32	.94	.99	.70
Brother closest in age to ego	1.47	1.02	.74	.89
Sister closest in age to ego	1.21	.85	1.08	.77
Brother second closest in age to ego	1.24	.98	.91	.98
Sister second closest in age to ego	.81	.96	.84	.68
Mean ratio	1.17	.96	.95	.79
Ego's in-laws				
Father-in-law	1.56	1.04	.93	.71
Mother-in-law	1.54	1.01	.90	1.19
Spouse's brother best known to ego	2.10	1.01	.96	1.40
Spouse's sister best known to ego	2.32	1.05	1.16	2.00
Mean ratio	1.88	1.03	.99	1.33

American and Civil Law conceptions are utrolocal; but that, although Parentela Orders men tend toward utrolocality, Parentela Orders women are highly neolocal. These different patterns in turn define those groups of relatives with whom reciprocities are established.

Insofar as women tend to provide the major links in interaction with kin, the data on residence suggest considerable differences in day-to-day contact by kinship orientation. Families with a Genetic or Canon Law orientation can be expected to have the highest levels of interaction with relatives, while those with a Parentela Orders perspective will likely have the least. However, as the following section indicates, variations in frequency of visiting relatives should not be confused with diverse degrees of interest in kin.

INTEREST IN KINSHIP TIES

Familism has generally been treated in sociological research as opposite of degree of isolation of the nuclear family from larger kinship attachments. This treatment has placed much emphasis on residential propinquity as a factor in the maintenance of strong kinship ties and in the persistence of a strong personal influence of relatives.

But if one makes a distinction between the family as a collectivity and the family as an aggregate of related persons, then familism changes in meaning. Insofar as the kindred is endowed with corporate qualities, it has a "reality" beyond its individual members. Corporate entities provide guidelines for conduct *in principle*. This attribute permits corporate units to perform functions of a symbolic nature over and above the mundane services of any individuals. These symbolic functions often pertain to the promotion of religious, ethnic, moral, or material values. It is this symbolic function that is absent from current conceptualizations of familism by sociologists.

The introduction of symbolic functions, however, implies that there are not only differences among people in degree of familism but in types of familism as well. First, a particular society may foster many mundane personal services while inhibiting symbolic functions (or vice versa). But, the performance of symbolic functions may not require the same degree of actual interaction as personal services. Instead, ritual occasions, ceremonies, and norms indicating the desirability of contact may serve to sustain the sense of corporateness required for the persistence of the symbolism of the "family," the "tribe," the "clan," or the numerous other names applied to the kindred.

This section deals with four aspects of interest in kinship ties. The first aspect pertains to general norms regarding kinship obligations and a sense of trust associated with Fortes' concept of axiom of amity. The second aspect involves interest in information about one's "roots." The third aspect of interest in kinship concerns the extent to which contact is maintained over long distances when relatives are seen infrequently. The fourth aspect is a negative one: lack of interest in kinship and unwillingness to respond to questions on kinship priorities.

Trust and Obligation

Despite the many connotations of the terms *friend* and *relative,* both kinds of relationships generally involve bonds of trust and a commitment to undertake obligations on behalf of another person. In many instances, friends are regarded as sufficiently close to warrant the use of kin terms such as Auntie or Uncle (Laumann, 1966). At other times, especially among upwardly mobile individuals, kin and friends are carefully segregated (Litwak, 1960a; Babchuk, 1965). But in any case, to be a *true* friend denotes the epitomy of loyalty and conformity to the axiom of amity (Fortes, 1969).

In the Phoenix study interview, two items pertained to the axiom of amity. For the first item, respondents were asked the extent of their agreement with the statement, ''A person's relatives usually turn out to be his or her truest friends.'' Table 8–3 describes the pattern for ''strongly agree'' responses. This pattern bears a relationship to kinship orientation. Whereas 17 percent of the Parentela Orders respondents reported that they strongly agree with the statement, only 6 percent of those in the Genetic and Canon Law category did so; persons with Standard American and Civil Law perspectives were intermediate, with slightly over ten percent of them expressing strong agreement. The table also indicates that the respondents generally regard their spouse's views as similar to their own.

TABLE 8-3. Kinship Orientation and Percent Agreeing Strongly with Statements about Relatives

Statements	Parentela orders	Standard american	Civil law	Genetic or canon law
A person's relatives usually turn out to be his or her truest friends[a]				
Respondent's view (%)	16.7	10.5	12.1	5.7
N	126	334	116	141
View attributed to spouse (%)	15.2	10.1	10.0	5.0
N	112	268	100	101
A person has a greater duty to help a relative than to help a nonrelative[a]				
Respondent's view (%)	16.8	14.1	11.2	4.3
N	125	333	116	141
View attributed to spouse (%)	18.3	16.1	15.0	10.8
N	109	273	100	102

[a] Response categories are strongly agree, agree, not sure, disagree, and strongly disagree.

The second item bearing upon the axiom of amity is extent of agreement with the statement, "A person has a greater duty to help a relative than to help a nonrelative." This item deals more directly than the previous one with obligations to promote the general welfare of kin. Table 8–3 shows that pattern of responses for the assistance item is similar to that for the friendship question. Again, Parentela Orders respondents display the greatest amount of strong agreement (17 percent), and persons with Genetic or Canon Law orientations the least agreement (4 percent), while those individuals with Standard American or Civil Law positions are in the middle. And again, the pattern for views attributed to spouses follows the persons' own positions (but with a slight tendency here for regarding the spouse as more agreeable than one's self in giving priority to relatives over nonrelatives).

The findings for the questions on true friendship and on the duty to help relatives both reveal a variation among kinship orientations in fervency with which the axiom of amity is held. Persons with a Parentela Orders view have the most commitment to the axiom of amity, and those with a Genetic or Canon Law perspective have the least commitment. These findings are consistent with the position that the Parentela Orders model implies the greatest degree of corporateness of kinship ties, while Genetic and Canon Law models express individualistic ideas. Without an assumption of corporateness, it would be difficult to hold general norms having to do with the assignment of trust and obligation to an entire social category—relatives as opposed to nonrelatives.

Information about "Roots"

In contemporary society, kinship biography can become an important mechanism for sustaining one's personal identity. Insofar as the line of descent (in Parentela Orders and Standard American models) provides a basis for identifying family boundaries, kinship takes on a corporate character that extends far beyond the individual. One's corporate existence both stretches back to ancestors in history and projects forward to future generations. The symbolic estate that one inherits from the past consists, in large part, of biographical information of antecedents and collaterals who are socially (and presumably genetically) incorporated into one's idea of self. This collection of biographies yields for the individual a fixed point in a set of coordinates for charting one's "world" and a sense of belonging to a particular domain. But just as property estates vary in value, so do symbolic estates. In individualistic kinship models (e.g., Genetic or Canon Law), personal ties with relatives overshadow symbolic connections. When individuals have no stake in seeking identification through knowledge of biographies, there is little reason to collect or to communicate biographical knowledge. Such communication may rattle skeletons best forgotten, uncover symbols of failure and degradation, or disinter relics from an irrelevant past. Still in corporate kinship models, it is through these symbolic family estates that kinship groups persist with their unique identities and facilitate social differentiation—religiously, socioeconomically, and ethnically. (See Farber, 1971.)

Interest in information about one's "roots" is perhaps best indicated by knowledge about grandparents. Most of the individuals in the Phoenix study no longer have grandparents; many of them never knew their grandparents well even when children. For a majority of respondents, information about grandparents would have to have been passed along through the parents. This is particularly true for paternal grandparents, who are generally older than maternal grandparents. One piece of information which many respondents would not have been able to obtain directly is the birthplace of their grandparents (and certainly their spouse's grandparents). Presumably, the greater the interest of the family in biographical information of ancestors, the greater is the probability that birthplace information about grandparents would be passed along.

Table 8–4 presents data on the percentages of respondents who know the general locations of the birthplaces of their own and their spouses' grandparents. In each instance—for own or spouses' or for maternal versus paternal grandparents—the results are similar: The percentage is highest for Parentela Orders respondents and lowest for those with a Genetic or Canon Law orientation. While differences among orientations are not large, they are consistent. The findings thus suggest that greatest interest in one's symbolic family estate is associated with the Parentela Orders model, and least interest is associated with the Genetic and Canon Law models.

TABLE 8-4. Percentages of Respondents Who Know General Locations of Birthplaces of Own and Spouse's Grandparents

Classification of grandparents	Parentela orders	Standard american	Civil law	Genetic or canon law
Own grandparents				
Both maternal grandparents	92.1	90.6	90.4	87.9
Both paternal grandparents	94.4	85.6	84.3	83.7
Spouse's grandparents				
Both maternal grandparents	82.5	75.2	81.7	68.8
Both paternal grandparents	82.5	74.8	79.1	64.5
N	126	333	115	141

For own grandparents, the respondents were asked to locate birthplace in the following sections of the United States (or to specify country of birth): Northeast, South, West, Arizona, Alaska or Hawaii, or don't know where born. For spouse's grandparents, the respondents were asked, "Do you know in what country any of your (husband's/wife's) grandparents were born?" If the answer was affirmative, the next questions were, "Which grandparents? What country?".

Contact over Long Distances

Adages are generally partial truths. On the one hand, "Absence makes the heart grow fonder," and on the other hand, "Out of sight out of mind." Presumably, the more intense is the quality of corporateness in conceptions of kinship, the greater are the chances that contact with family will be maintained despite long distances and infrequent visiting. The corporate identity itself would provide a basis for continued contact by mail or telephone.

The purest measure of kinship-interaction norms (by eliminating barriers such as money, distance, and competing relationships) is the extent of mail and telephone contact between relatives living in different states. In this study, a basic proposition is that kinship groupings organized on the basis of special (or factional) concerns favor higher levels of kinship interaction as a general principle than do those groupings organized on the basis of general (or communal) concerns. Factional grouping encourages the maintenance of corporate-like structures. Three indices of special-concern organization are applied—kinship orientation, religion, and socioeconomic position. The theoretical discussions and findings in the previous chapters of this monograph point to Parentela Orders, Judaism, and professional-managerial-and-administrative positions as appropriate indicators of special-concern (or pluralistic) social organization, while Genetic and Canon Law models, Catholicism, and blue-collar occupations imply universalistic (or communal) conceptions.

Table 8–5 describes the percentages of respondents who have frequent contact by telephone or mail with parents and in-laws when these relatives are seen less than once a month. Generally, these relatives live out of state. The data on kinship orientation, while falling into the anticipated pattern, offer only weak confirmation of the proposition; the percentage differences between Parentela Orders and Genetic-and-Canon-Law respondents are quite small for the parents and, for in-laws, only the Genetic and Canon Law category differs appreciably from the other orientations (albeit in the expected direction). For religion and socioeconomic position, however, the results are quite striking. Jewish respondents have the most frequent contact with parents and in-laws and Catholics the least, and the differences for in-laws exceed those for parents. For example, whereas there is a spread of only 16 percentage points (94 versus 78) between Jews and Catholics for mothers, the gap increases to 30 points (65 versus 35) for mothers-in-law. For socioeconomic position, the findings also definitely confirm the proposition. Respondents in households where the husband is in a professional, managerial, or administrative occupation are much more likely to have frequent contact with parents and in-laws than are those in blue-collar families; for fathers there is a 27 percent difference between them (72 versus 45). Thus, particularly for religious and socioeconomic indicators the data support the proposition that kinship groupings organized on the basis of a special concern tend to promote kinship interaction as a general norm more than do groupings organized on the basis of communal, universalistic concerns.

The weakness of the findings on kinship orientation suggests that a second test of the proposition be applied. Salience of kinship orientation for maintaining long-distance ties would be even more clearly evidenced when face-to-face interaction rarely takes place—less than once a year. Table 8–6 shows data regarding the extent to which Ego reports frequent contact by mail or telephone with parents and siblings despite the fact that face-to-face interaction occurs less than annually. For all of Ego's family seen less than once a year, persons in the Parentela Orders category have most contact by mail or telephone (and Standard American respondents somewhat less), while generally those classified as Genetic or Canon Law are least likely to maintain long-distance contact. For persons with a Genetic or Canon Law perspective, the rule often seems to be, "Out of sight, out of mind," even when the

TABLE 8-5. Percentages of Respondents Having Frequent Contact by Telephone or Mail with Parents and In-Laws in Cases Where these Persons Are Seen Less than Once a Month, by Kinship Orientation and Social Characteristics

Kinship orientation and social characteristics	Father	Mother	Father-in-Law	Mother-in-Law
Respondent's kinship orientation				
Parentela orders (%)	67.3	82.3	46.5	55.6
N	55	62	43	54
Standard american (%)	66.1	81.3	41.5	50.3
N	124	139	123	145
Civil law (%)	64.9	82.2	52.5	52.3
N	37	45	40	44
Genetic or canon law (%)	62.0	74.4	28.0	30.2
N	50	43	50	53
Respondent's religion				
Jewish (%)	80.8	93.5	60.0	65.4
N	26	31	20	26
Protestant (%)	67.3	81.3	46.1	53.6
N	153	171	152	192
Catholic (%)	58.6	77.9	32.3	34.7
N	70	68	62	72
Occupation of male co-head in respondent's household				
Professional, managerial, or administrative (%)	72.3	82.4	55.6	62.0
N	119	136	99	129
Clerical, sales, or craft (%)	65.1	80.6	46.3	57.3
N	86	108	82	96
Blue collar (%)	44.7	76.9	40.4	38.9
N	47	39	57	54

relative is a parent or a sibling, and reciprocity seems to represent for them a personal rather than a corporate phenomenon in kinship.

The Refuseniks

One percent of the respondents failed to provide valid answers to the questions about priorities among relatives in cases of intestacy. Although these persons were not unusual in some ways, a majority have come from broken families, none has gone to college, generally they hold blue-collar jobs, and they never attend church services. As far as kinship is concerned, they have smaller kindreds than do other respondents in the sample. Of the 24 relatives about whom information is sought in the interview, the refuseniks have an average of 10.6 relatives in their kindred as compared with 13.4 for the total sample. Most significant, however, is the fact that, with one exception, the refuseniks do not care to see even those relatives they have. Whereas in the total sample, respondents want to see a majority of their relatives (58 percent) at least"once a month," the seven remaining refuseniks want to see only 20 percent of their relatives that often. In answering questions about desired frequency of contact with relatives, the refuseniks react strongly:

TABLE 8-6. Percentage of Respondents Having Frequent Contact by Telephone or Mail with Parents and Siblings in Cases Where these Relatives Are Seen Less than Once a Year[a]

Relatives	Parentela orders	Standard american	Civil law	Genetic or canon law
Father (%)	66.7	24.1	30.8	28.6
N	9	29	13	14
Mother (%)	75.0	60.9	45.5	44.4
N	16	23	11	9
Brother closest in age to ego (%)	28.1	27.6	4.8	15.0
N	32	58	21	20
Sister closest in age to ego (%)	43.3	31.0	23.5	27.3
N	30	42	17	22
Brother second closest in age to ego (%)	27.8	30.4	7.7	14.3
N	18	23	13	28
Sister second closest in age to ego (%)	44.4	26.9	0.0	0.0
N	18	26	10	13

[a] For relatives seen less than once per month, the respondents were asked, "Do you have frequent contact by mail or phone, occasional contact by mail or phone, or no cntact at all by mail or phone?" The definition of "frequent" is thus subjective.

"No, I don't want to see any of them." (Int. 299)

[After responding "Never" for all relatives in the question on frequency of contact], "That's it if you really want to know. I can get along with them or without them." (Int. 220)

"[My brother] lives up the block, but I only see him about once a year." (Int. 107)

In sorting cards to indicate frequency with which she wanted to see relatives, at first the respondent laughed and placed the cards for all relatives in the "Never" category. Then, referring to her brother, she said, "No, let's see, I guess I could stand him once a month." The interviewer noted, however, that the respondent betrayed much antagonism toward her brother when she answered questions about him. (Int. 541)

Apparently, any interaction between refuseniks and their relatives involves exploitation, pretense, and the norm of avarice.

Summary: Kinship Interest

This section has explored various aspects of interest in kinship ties. Focusing on symbolic elements in kinship, I have found that persons holding a Parentela Orders perspective reveal the greatest interest in kinship ties and persons with Genetic or Canon Law views show least interest. Those taking Standard American or Civil Law positions are intermediate in their concerns. These relationships between kinship orientation and interests hold for such topics as: (a) the axiom of amity (i.e., trust and obligation), (b) information about one's ancestral roots, and (c) maintenance of contact with kin over long distances (with little face-to-face interaction). The data also indicate that, when there is little concern with kinship, respondents refuse even to consider establishing any series of priorities among relatives.

ACTUAL AND DESIRED CONTACT

Research on kinship ties ordinarily rests upon the implied assumption that if people really want to see their relatives often, they will arrange their lives to do so: they do not move away from parental homesteads; they organize their calendars to fit social occasions around family visits; and they maintain a maximum of personal interdependence with their relatives. This assumption of a social market treats contact with relatives as a "good" in competition with other goods: economic achievement, friends, cultural events, and so on. But the competitive assumption does not take into account the diverse qualities of family interest in different groups. One can have a profound sense of obligation to relatives without giving them the highest priority in time expenditure. Moveover, one may dislike certain kin. Rather, interest in family and kin appears to be expressed by an absolute scale. Regardless of competing interests and goods, to what extent does one want to have considerable interaction with relatives? For the individual who has few competing interests or obstacles, this interest in family ties can be readily accommodated, and much time can be spent with relatives. For the individual with numerous competing interests and obstacles, this interest in family must generally be held in abeyance; other interests may be more pressing.

The interpretation of kinship ties as a form of social exchange requires a model of an interactional marketplace comparable to the conception of ideal conditions for perfect competition in economics. The model of a free market assumes (among other things) that all buyers are equally accessible to all sellers (and vice versa) and that none of the buyers or sellers is sufficiently large and powerful enough to dominate the general market conditions. Yet in the analysis of kinship ties in contemporary urban populations, most observers base their interpretations upon frequency of contact, and they ignore selection factors in and consequences of differences in the proximity of residence and the size of the kin universe. (See Adams, 1970.) Klatzky (n.d., p. 2), however, notes that, "The studies which have explicitly included distance as a variable . . . show that kin contact is a monotonically decreasing function of distance—that is, the frequency of contact declines steadily as distance increases." Moreover, "In terms of daily living, kin seem more salient to working-class people (Adams, 1970, p. 586)," who do have larger families and therefore a greater chance to find relatives with whom to interact. If our interest is to investigate *norms* operating in social exchange, then the degree of residential proximity and the size and composition of a person's kinship universe limit the use of actual contact with relatives as a means for ascertaining which norms are operative. In the interview, the respondents were asked not only how often they saw their relatives but also to describe the frequency with which they would like to see each relative "if money or distance didn't matter."

The distinction between actual and desired interaction with kin permits examination of various kinds of discrepancies. Under ideal conditions, some people would like to see their relatives more often than they do, while others would prefer to see kin less often. Both alternatives with regard to desired contact with relatives are explored below.

Wanting More Face-to-Face Interaction

Generally, each individual has a reservoir of relatives in excess of those with whom it is necessary to interact on a regular basis. How then does an individual decide that he would like to increase the amount of face-to-face interaction with a relative? The norm of exchange with which the individual operates seems to provide a clue to the nature of this decision.

If the individual operates with a *norm of marketplace exchange* in inter-action with a relative, then any increase in interaction is motivated only when the individual perceives that relative as capable of meeting specific personal needs. Metaphorically, the purchase of that relative's interaction occurs when there can be an immediate, concrete exchange of services. If needs can be met more adequately elsewhere, then the individual does not have to choose an additional relative from the kin reservoir. Since distance and other inconveniences impede the practicality of immediate exchange, the individual limits interaction to those kin at hand. As a result, the amount of interaction with relatives tend to correspond to the amount that the individual desires; in general, desired contact would not exceed actual contact.

However, if the individuals operate in their kinship universe with a *norm of generosity* (or axiom of amity), then the relationship between the amount of desired as compared with actual contact should be different. According to this norm, specifics of given and take need not be identified; rather, the emphasis is on optimizing one's position to "give" in any relationship with kin. (See Joffe, 1949.) Distance and inconvenience are not supposed to dis-tract one from entertaining the possibility of reciprocal relations. The norm of generosity thus implies that an individual ought to want more interaction with relatives than actual circumstances dictate. Ideally, this excess of desired over actual interaction should occur regardless of personal qualities or im-mediate availability of the relative.

In the Phoenix study, in order to ascertain the extent to which kinship orientations incorporate norms of social exchange with kin, I sought to de-termine whether levels of desired interaction (e.g., weekly, monthly, and so on) would exceed the actual levels reported. The findings for parents and siblings and for relatives outside the nuclear family are described below.

Table 8–7 displays information about actual and desired interaction with one's family of orientation. The findings on actual interaction indicate a general progression in frequency of contact, with Parentela Orders persons seeing their parents and siblings least often, and those with a Genetic or Canon Law perspective seeing them most often. For example, only 23 percent of men in the Parentela Orders category see their mothers weekly, whereas 42 percent in the Genetic and Canon Law grouping see their mothers that often, and about 31 percent in the Standard American and Civil Law clas-sifications see their mothers at least once a week. While there are minor deviations from this pattern, overall the relationship appears to hold.

The percentages on actual contact in Table 8–7 might lead one to conclude that respondents in the Parentela Orders category are the least familistic, and those with Genetic or Canon Law orientations are most familistic. However, these variations in contact cannot be attributed to a differential lack of desire

176

TABLE 8-7. Parents and Siblings Seen Weekly and, for Those Seen Less Frequently, Percentages of Parents and Siblings Whom Respondents Would Like to See More Often

Parents and siblings	Parentela orders	Standard american	Civil law	Genetic or canon law
MEN RESPONDENTS				
Fathers				
Seen weekly (%)	18.4	29.5	31.6	33.3
Desire to see more often (%)	65.8	62.9	57.9	61.1
Total (%)	84.2	92.4	89.5	94.4
N	38	105	38	36
Mothers				
Seen weekly (%)	22.6	30.5	31.0	41.5
Desire to see more often (%)	64.2	59.3	57.1	56.1
Total (%)	86.8	89.8	88.1	97.6
N	53	118	42	41
Brothers closest in age to ego				
Seen weekly (%)	16.7	14.9	28.6	26.5
Desire to see more often (%)	70.8	77.2	67.9	58.8
Total (%)	87.5	92.1	96.5	85.3
N	48	101	28	34
Sisters closest in age to ego				
Seen weekly (%)	14.9	17.7	26.5	20.0
Desire to see more often (%)	66.0	66.7	52.9	70.0
Total (%)	80.9	84.4	79.4	90.0
N	47	96	34	40
Brothers second closest in age to ego				
Seen weekly (%)	25.0	15.6	15.8	30.4
Desire to see more often (%)	66.7	71.9	73.7	56.5
Total (%)	91.7	87.5	89.5	86.9
N	24	64	19	23
Sisters second closest in age to ego				
Seen weekly (%)	4.2	18.4	26.3	20.0
Desire to see more often (%)	87.5	75.5	68.4	72.0
Total (%)	91.7	93.9	94.7	92.0
N	24	49	19	25

(continued)

to see fathers, mothers, sisters, and brothers. A reverse pattern is noted for *desire* to see parents and siblings more often. Among persons who see their nuclear-family relatives less than weekly, those in the Parentela Orders category express the greatest desire to see them more often, and people in the Genetic-and-Canon Law class voice the least desire. In fact, when the percentage of persons who want to see their parents and siblings is added to

TABLE 8-7 *(continued)*

Parents and siblings	Parentela orders	Standard american	Civil law	Genetic or canon law
WOMEN RESPONDENTS				
Fathers				
Seen weekly (%)	14.6	34.1	35.6	30.5
Desire to see more often (%)	75.6	53.3	55.6	57.6
Total (%)	90.2	87.4	91.2	88.1
N	41	135	45	59
Mothers				
Seen weekly (%)	32.1	42.2	45.9	50.0
Desire to see more often (%)	62.3	49.1	47.5	40.3
Total (%)	94.4	91.3	93.4	90.3
N	53	173	61	72
Brothers closest in age to ego				
Seen weekly (%)	4.0	13.6	17.6	22.7
Desire to see more often (%)	82.0	73.6	78.4	63.6
Total (%)	86.0	87.2	96.0	86.3
N	50	125	51	66
Sisters closest to age to ego				
Seen weekly (%)	19.6	18.9	26.0	27.1
Desire to see more often (%)	64.7	72.7	66.0	62.9
Total (%)	84.3	91.6	92.0	90.0
N	51	132	50	70
Brothers second closest in age to ego				
Seen weekly (%)	3.0	11.7	14.3	9.3
Desire to see more often (%)	87.9	76.7	74.3	74.4
Total (%)	90.9	88.4	88.6	83.7
N	33	60	35	43
Sisters second closest in age to ego				
Seen weekly (%)	16.7	28.8	33.3	31.8
Desire to see more often (%)	76.6	66.7	60.0	54.5
Total (%)	93.3	95.5	93.3	86.3
N	30	66	30	44

those who actually see them frequently (i.e., at least weekly), differences among kinship orientations virtually disappear. Regardless of orientation, about 90 percent of the respondents either see or want to see their parents and siblings frequently. Hence, variations among kinship models in actual interaction with parents and siblings seem to be a function of diversity of competing interests and opportunities rather than a result of differing degrees of absolute interest in maintaining nuclear family ties.

178

The complexity of influences impinging on contact with family of orientation is suggested further in Table 8–8 on percentages of locally residing parents and siblings seen at least weekly by respondents. Overall, more respondents tend to see mothers and sisters weekly than they do fathers or brothers. In particular, ties to fathers of Parentela-Orders respondents seem especially weak, while the bonds to mothers in blue-collar families appear notably strong.

TABLE 8-8. Percentages of Close Relatives Living in Maricopa County Whom the Respondent Sees at Least Weekly, by Kinship Orientation, Occupation of the Male Co-Head of the Household, and Religion

Kinship orientation, male co-head's occupation, and religion	Father	Mother	Closest in age to ego		Second closest in age to ego	
			Brother	Sister	Brother	Sister
Kinship orientation						
Parentela orders (%)	52.5	70.3	38.5	50.0	43.8	54.5
N	23	37	26	32	16	11
Standard american (%)	70.8	76.6	42.4	46.1	41.0	59.5
N	106	137	66	89	39	42
Civil law (%)	72.2	73.5	53.3	64.5	50.0	59.1
N	36	49	30	31	16	22
Genetic or canon law (%)	63.6	77.8	53.7	53.5	34.6	56.7
N	44	63	41	43	26	30
Occupation of male co-head						
Professional, managerial, or administrative (%)	64.0	64.3	42.9	46.7	39.1	36.0
N	75	98	49	60	23	25
Clerical, sales, or craft (%)	62.9	68.2	37.5	49.2	40.6	65.7
N	70	85	56	59	32	35
Blue collar (%)	62.3	83.1	48.1	51.7	36.6	54.8
N	53	77	54	60	41	42
Religion						
Jewish (%)	84.6	93.3	75.0	77.8	a	a
N	13	15	8	9	2	4
Protestant (%)	65.0	73.6	40.7	42.3	36.0	43.4
N	117	163	86	104	50	53
Catholic (%)	65.2	77.4	44.9	64.0	46.9	67.3
N	69	93	69	75	49	652
No religious preference (%)	46.4	55.6	58.8	39.1	27.3	42.9
N	28	36	17	23	11	7

a Number too small to compute percentage.

In general, though, the data in Table 8–8 on kinship orientation and socioeconomic status reveal little about interaction with family of orientation. The percentages on religion, however, indicate an ideological impact. Among religious groups, Jewish respondents exhibit the greatest amount of contact with parents and brothers and sisters, and those persons with no religious preference show the least contact. With roughly 90 percent of the Jewish respondents having weekly interaction with locally residing parents, the findings appear to express the centrality of lineal ties in Judaism. By way of contrast, only about half of the respondents without a religious preference have frequent contact with their parents in Maricopa County. Among these secularists in particular, kinship ties seem to depend upon chance factors (50–50 probability) for frequent occurrence. These findings together point up the complexity of influences upon interaction with parents.

For relatives outside the respondents' families of orientation, the data (reported in Table 8–9) regarding desire to increase interaction are more eloquent. First actual contact with these relatives will be described and afterward desired contact.

Because most people in the Phoenix area have immigrated from other sections of the United States since 1950, only a small minority of uncles, aunts, and cousins reside locally, and only a tiny proportion of these is seen monthly. But since persons with Genetic and Canon Law orientations are the most likely to be Arizona natives, they tend to see uncles and aunts more often than do persons with other orientations. As Table 8–9 indicates, differences in interaction among kinship orientations are slight, however, seldom more than 10 percent. As in other investigations, women see maternal relatives more often than paternal relatives, but unlike most other studies, this tendency is not found for men (Adams, 1968, 1970; Schneider and Cottrell, 1975, is an exception.) Since the percentages seeing relatives are small, no special significance can be attached to this finding. Thus, as a whole, little significance can be determined from the data on actual interaction with aunts, uncles, and cousins.

Despite the paucity of interpretable findings on actual interaction with relatives outside the nuclear family, the information on desired interaction is productive, at least for women respondents. Table 8–9 shows that, for women, the desire to increase interaction with relatives is more a function of kinship orientation than (unlike parents and siblings) degree of actual contact. Except for the mother's brother, the tendency for wanting to increase face-to-face interaction is strongest in the Parentela Orders group and least among women classified as Genetic or Canon Law. For example, whereas six percent of Parentela Orders women actually see their best-known paternal aunt (Father's Sister) monthly, about 74 percent want to see her more often; in contrast, and while eight percent of Genetic or Canon Law women see

TABLE 8-9. Percentages of Persons Desiring More Contact with Uncles and Aunts than Actually Occurs, by Kinship Orientation

Uncles and aunts	Parentela orders	Standard american	Civil law	Genetic or canon law
WOMEN RESPONDENTS				
Father's brother best known to ego				
Desire more contact (%)	77.5	71.8	66.0	57.4
Actual contact at least once				
monthly (%)	0.0	4.8	12.7	11.6
N	40	124	47	54
Father's sister best known to ego				
Desire more contact (%)	73.5	70.4	76.7	52.4
Actual contact at least once				
monthly (%)	5.9	5.1	4.6	7.9
N	34	135	43	63
Mother's brother best known to ego				
Desire more contact (%)	69.8	72.3	88.9	61.4
Actual contact at least once				
monthly (%)	7.0	7.0	11.1	17.6
N	43	130	45	57
Mother's sister best known to ego				
Desire more contact (%)	81.4	77.4	71.1	68.1
Actual contact at least once				
monthly (%)	11.6	14.5	6.6	13.0
N	43	124	45	69

(continued)

Note: Data for cousins are comparable to those for aunts and uncles. There was a tendency among respondents to place a cousin in the same category of desired contact as that cousin's parent.

their best-known paternal aunt that frequently, only 52 percent want to increase their interaction with her. Clearly, the two percent difference in actual contact between the two kinship categories cannot account for the 22 percent difference in desired contact. (The data for other relatives yield similar interpretations.) Given the assumptions made regarding desired frequency of interaction and norms of reciprocity, the data indicate that the Parentela Orders models represent the highest proclivity toward prescriptive altruism and the Genetic and Canon Law orientations the least.

For men, the data on desired interaction with kin outside the nuclear family do not reveal consistent trends. Instead, they are ambiguous and seem to reflect the incursion of a variety of competing elements into desire for kinship ties. Kinship norms may not be as compelling for men as they are for women. (Perhaps men use more nonkinship criteria than do women in interacting with

TABLE 8-9 *(continued)*

Uncles and aunts	Parentela orders	Standard american	Civil law	Genetic or canon law
MEN RESPONDENTS				
Father's brother best known to ego				
Desire more contact (%)	66.7	65.2	74.2	67.6
Actual contact at least once				
monthly (%)	7.8	4.2	3.2	8.8
N	39	95	31	34
Father's sister best known to ego				
Desire more contact (%)	58.5	81.5	66.7	61.0
Actual contact at least once				
monthly (%)	0.0	2.8	6.1	9.8
N	41	108	33	41
Mother's brother best known to ego				
Desire more contact (%)	72.5	75.7	65.6	52.8
Actual contact at least once				
monthly (%)	2.5	12.6	12.6	19.4
N	40	111	32	36
Mother's sister best known to ego				
Desire more contact (%)	72.9	73.3	66.7	75.0
Actual contact at least once				
monthly (%)	4.2	16.2	0,0	3.1
N	48	105	27	32

kin. For men, such interaction may indeed involve choices made on the basis of relatives-as-persons.)

In summary, the findings on desire for increased interaction with kin reveal that:

1. Despite the greater amount of actual interaction of Genetic and Canon Law persons with parents and siblings, differences among kinship orientations are dependent upon competing interests and differential opportunities rather than variations in absolute interest in the maintenance of nuclear family ties.

2. For persons with parents living in Maricopa County, Jews have most contact with fathers and mothers, while persons with no religious preference have the least contact. Kinship orientation and socioeconomic status show little overall influence on actual interaction with parents.

3. For women in particular, desire for increased contact with kin outside the nuclear family is associated with kinship orientation; those with a Parentela Orders perspective show the greatest desire for increased interaction, and women in the Genetic and Canon Law grouping show the least.

Wanting Less Face-to-Face Interaction

Negative aspects of social exchange are ordinarily discussed in terms of imbalanced reciprocities, inequality, exploitation, and power differentials (Ekeh, 1974). Indeed, studies of modern kinship have generally ignored potentially exploitive features in the maintenance of kinship ties. (Leichter and Mitchell, 1956, is an exception.)

Forced exchange is generally considered to be, at a minimum, "unfair." The idea of exchange ordinarily implies an ability to dispose of one's goods at will. Under conditions of forced exchange, though, an individual participates only to decelerate depletion of his stock of resources. Often, but not necessarily, an individual may submit to exploitation by one party with an eye to recouping those losses through increasing the indebtedness of a third party. For instance, a man may endure contact with his authoritarian father to reap the benefits of interaction with his mother, or he may submit to visiting his domineering mother-in-law to mollify his spouse. But this forced exchange places a premium upon the added value of the rewards expected from the third party (i.e., in these examples, from the mother or spouse). (See Ekeh, 1974.) If the increment of reward for these sacrifices is not forthcoming, the relationship between the individual and the third party may suffer disproportionately.

This description of forced interaction, however, assumes that all social goods are personal (e.g., the services of the spouse or mother). But in some kinship groups, the costs of personal ties can be compensated for by corporate rewards, such as the perpetuation of the religious identity or of socioeconomic position. Corporate conditions, then, operate to inhibit the breakdown of systems of reciprocity. This inhibition could occur in two ways. First, since the compensations for corporate interaction have nothing to do directly with the offending individual, the offences (or costs) of such interaction are minimized in their consequences; rather, it is the offending individual's role in the corporate structure that counts and not his obnoxious characteristics. Second, there is little additional obligation placed upon a third party to compensate for the forced relationship with an offending party. Consequently, the probability of disillusionment with the third party for failing to supply an increment of satisfactions would be reduced. The earlier chapters have indicated that Genetic and Canon Law individuals have a tendency toward disillusionment with the spouse; at least a part of this tendency may reside in the inability of the spouses to compenste (under individualistic conditions) for the depletion of one's social and psychological resources in unwanted kinship interaction. Instead, a corporate conception of family and kinship (as in Parentela Orders) may shield the spouse from such demands.

Authority and power seem to provide conditions for exploitation in social interaction. Generally, in kinship, such inequality occurs in relationship between generations. The authority of parents over children and the subservience of the children would characterize a corporate kinship structure. In societies with a disintegrating patrilineal tradition. such as ours, one would expect this residual corporate authority to reside in the father and his relatives. In corporate kinship, the father and paternal relatives might be seen as overstepping the normal bounds of influence—as meddling in one's affairs. However, in kinship systems without organized corporate aspects, the crucial bond tying families into networks is the husband-wife relationship (Parsons, 1949; Schneider, 1968). In those systems, intrusion into the affairs of the couple would then be seen often by the couple as in-law interference.

Table 8–10 shows comparisons among relatives whom the respondents want to see less often than they actually see them. In the section of the table on generational distinctions, parents are compared with the siblings with whom the respondents have the most intimate relationships (Adams, 1968). Since ties with parents and siblings are usually close, percentages are small; but the trends in the data are fairly clear. For both Parentela Orders and Standard American orientations, more respondents would like to reduce their interaction with parents than with siblings—regardless of sex of respondent of or parent. Sex differences occur, however, in the other orientations. Findings

TABLE 8-10. Comparisons of Relatives Whom the Respondents Want to See Less Often than They Actually See Them, by Generation and Maternal Versus Paternal Tie

Relatives	Parentela orders		Standard american		Civil law		Genetic or canon law	
	Men	Women	Men	Women	Men	Women	Men	Women
By generation								
Father (%)	15.8	4.9	6.7	8.1	2.6	4.4	0.0	8.5
Brother closest in age to ego (%)	6.2	4.0	5.0	5.6	7.1	3.9	11.8	6.1
Greater percentage	Fa	Fa	Fa	Fa	Br	Fa	Br	Fa
Mother (%)	5.7	5.9	6.8	15.2	9.5	7.2	2.4	13.8
Sister closest in age to ego (%)	4.3	3.9	6.2	2.3	8.8	0.0	5.0	1.4
Greater percentage[b]	Mo	Mo	Mo	Mo	Mo	Mo	Si	Mo
Maternal versus paternal tie								
Father's brother (%)[a]	10.3	7.5	14.7	12.9	6.5	17.0	5.9	20.4
Mother's brother (%)[a]	2.5	4.7	9.0	5.7	6.3	0.0	11.1	10.5
Greater percentage	FaBr	FaBr	FaBr	FaBr	Equal	FaBr	MoBr	FaBr
Father's sister (%)[a]	9.8	11.8	13.0	11.1	9.1	9.3	14.6	19.0
Mother's sister (%)[a]	8.3	0.0	8.6	7.3	3.7	13.3	12.5	10.1
Greater percentage[c]	FaSi	FaSi	FaSi	FaSi	FaSi	MoSi	FaSi	FaSi

[a] Best known to respondent.

[b] Parental Percentage greater: 13; sibling percentage greater: 3.

[c] Father's side greater percentage: 13; mother's side greater percentage: 2; equal percentage: 1.

for women in the Civil Law, Genetic, or Canon Law categories are similar to those for Standard American and Parentela Orders classes. But men in these other categories are more likely to want to decrease interaction with siblings than with parents. These findings are clearly in line with expectations regarding the impact of residual authority of parents in families with a large component of corporateness in organization.

The contrastive desire to diminish interaction with paternal versus maternal kin is indicated in the second section of Table 8–10. As for parents, the findings in this section also suggest the residual effect of patrilineality on Parentela Orders and Standard American kinship. For both of these orientations, there is a greater tendency to wish for diminished interaction with paternal uncles and aunts than with maternal relatives. Departures from this pattern of responses are found again particularly among men in the Civil Law, Genetic, and Canon Law categories. Hence, for aunts and uncles, as for parents, the data support the interpretation that (particularly where corporateness provides a basis for kinship organization) the desire to cut down on interaction is associated with persistence of efforts at sustaining authority surviving from a patrilineal tradition.

Table 8–11 presents data on the desire to decrease interaction with in-laws, revealing that, regardless of kinship orientation, roughly 20 percent of the respondents would like to diminish the amount of face-to-face contact they now have with their fathers-in-law. On the other hand, mothers-in-law of Genentic or Canon Law men and women are distinctly unpopular. Thirty-two percent of the men and 27 percent of the women with these orientations would like to see their mothers-in-law less often; in contrast, only 14 percent of the men and 20 percent of the women in the Parentela Orders category prefer to interact with their mothers-in-law less frequently. Clearly, contact with mothers-in-law by persons with a Genetic or Canon Law perspective is

TABLE 8-11. The Desire to Decrease Interaction with In-Laws

In-law	Parentela orders	Standard american	Civil law	Genetic or canon law
Men				
Father-in-law (%)	21.3	22.5	14.7	20.5
N	47	111	34	35
Mother-in-law (%)	13.8	20.5	19.3	31.7
N	58	122	40	41
Women				
Father-in-law (%)	20.6	18.9	14.3	22.0
N	34	122	42	50
Mother-in-law (%)	19.6	18.1	17.0	26.9
N	48	126	46	67

a socially costly proposition. Presumably, Genetic and Canon Law kinship ideology cannot readily accommodate ties with the mother-in-law.

The findings on wanting less face-to-face interaction with kin reinforce the premise that one ought not equate amount of contact with relatives as a sign of voluntaristic familism. Whereas some individuals do not see their relatives often enough, others find frequent contact (particularly with parents, in-laws, or paternal kin) distasteful. However, unpleasantness in kinship ties seems to depend in part upon the kind of authority and power patterns associated with kinship orientation. Persons with a Parentela Orders or Standard American orientation are more likely to encounter overinteraction with parents and paternal kin, and those in the Genetic or Canon Law category more often have mother-in-law problems.

Summary: Actual and Desired Contact

The comparative isolation of the nuclear family from relatives in modern industrial society has led to the conclusion among many observers that kinship is becoming a relic, distance and the competition of other interests impeding visitation and assistance. From this perspective, functionally kinship loses its value as an institution. This view, however, ignores the symbolic value of kinship and the normative power of kinship ties. But if a distinction is made between actual and desired contact with relatives, the focus shifts instead to prescriptive aspects of relationships with kin.

This section has reported various connections between kinship orientations and interaction with relatives:

1. Although there are large variations among kinship orientations in the frequency with which people see their parents and siblings, these differences derive primarily from differential opportunities and competing interests. When desire to see parents, brothers, and sisters is taken into account, about 90 percent of the respondents either see or want to see their nuclear families frequently.

2. Because of their migrant status, few respondents see relatives outside their families of orientation frequently. Yet, although most women would like to increase their interaction with kin considerably, those with a Genetic or Canon Law orientation are fairly reluctant to do so. Men apparently apply nonkinship criteria to a greater extent than women do in evaluating the amount of contact they would like with relatives.

3. Kinship orientation influences the extent to which people would like to decrease contact with particular relatives. Presumably because of authority or unwanted intrusion, individuals in the Parentela Orders or Standard American categories may want to decrease interaction with their parents or paternal kin, while those with Genetic or Canon Law orientations may regard contact with their mothers-in-law as forced.

SUMMARY: TIES WITH KIN

In this chapter I have explored some relationships between kinship orientation and interaction with relatives. Specifically, I have shown how these orientations bear upon such topics as marital residence, interest in kinship matters, and the disparity between desired and actual contact with kin.

The findings here suggest that the kind of kinship orientation held is related to norms of social exchange. Suppose that we interpret the norm of generosity as a long-term exchange in which repayment for assistance may be long in coming and the norm of market exchange as a short-term exchange in which immediate reciprocation is expected. Then, in particular, Parentela Orders orientation is associated with stable kindreds, which can withstand much physical separation or petty annoyances. According to analyses reported earlier, persons who are characterized by high educational and income levels, Jewish upbringing, older ages, married, and with many progeny are overrepresented in the Parentela Orders category. One would then expect a norm of generosity to operate to a greater extent where people exhibit these attributes.

Moreover, if Genetic or Canon Law orientations are indicative of short-term reciprocities, the stability of the kindred in groups with those orientations is highly dependent upon maintaining residential propinquity. The dependence of working-class kinship ties upon propinquity is suggested by the fact that, in this sample, poor persons and/or those who are not high school graduates are overrepresented in the Genetic and Canon Law categories. In addition, the young, the unmarried, and those with few children are poorly motivated to operate with a norm of generosity. Thus, models of kinship orientation—Parentela Orders, Standard American, Civil Law, Genetic, or Canon Law—while referring to patterns of priorites among kin seem also to express different norms for social exchange and consequently different bases of kinship organization in diverse population segments. (Cf. Sahlins, 1965.)

Perspectives on Kinship: Concluding Remarks

9

In previous chapters, I have reported the findings on the distribution of kinship models in an urban population. This chapter will be consigned to the integration of the materials in the rest of the book and to an exploration of their implications for various theoretical and practical concerns. The first part of the chapter provides a summary of research and its theoretical underpinnings. The second part relates the findings to previous sociological and anthropological writings about kinship and social structure. The final section is a brief epilogue on the interpretation of ''kinship'' and its implications for social policy.

SUMMARY STATEMENT

This section draws together various theoretical and empirical materials that have been described in a more extensive manner throughout the book. Its topics range from a general portrayal of kinship ties to an integration of survey results. There are two subsections: the basic kinship grid as a starting point for analysis of models of collaterality and the relationship between the kinship models under investigation and social structures in which they appear to thrive.

THE KINSHIP GRID

The term kinship connotes a degree of relatedness through a biological (or quasi-biological) connection. One mode of representing this relatedness is to construct a grid of loci of kin ties deriving from birth and marriage. Because the genealogical locations of kin in any society can be defined from the perspective on one member, Ego, the elements in the matrix are identified by their relationship to Ego. Table 9-1 indicates a basic grid of kinship loci from Ego's perspective. This grid, which seems to represent a scheme prevalent in Western civilization, refers only to consanguines; a comparable grid can be constructed to show the loci of affines. Metaphorically, a basic kinship grid can be regarded as a physical map of kin loci generated from connections through birth. Upon this map, one can superimpose other information de-

188

scribing boundaries of clusters or priorities among kin—just as political boundaries and other social characteristics are superimposed upon maps showing only the physical features of a territory. Hence, a basic kinship grid can be considered as representing the physical basis for the creation of social arrangements based upon birth and marriage.

The construction of the kinship grid in Table 9-1 rests upon the assumptions that:

1. Relatedness of any kinship locus to Ego can be described in terms of (a) chains of generational links of parentage (i.e., links from children to parents) and (b) chains of descent linkages (i.e., links from parents to children).

2. In Table 9-1, relatedness to Ego in terms of parentage (j) is indicated by the number of generations up from Ego to an ancestor (or, for collateral kin, from Ego to the closest common ancestor): for example, for Ego's grandparent, $j=2$.

3. In Table 9-1, relatedness to Ego in terms of descent (i) is indicated by the number of generations downward from Ego (or Ego's ancestor) to a descendant. For example, for Ego's grandchild, $i=2$.

4. The characteristics of the social structure determine the topological features of the grid: how parentage and descent are differentially weighted in organizing kinship relations; how groups of kinship loci are partitioned; which kinship loci are ignored in terminology and conduct; and which ones are merged in larger classes, and so on. In modern society, the complexities of social stratification, occupational differentiation, religious and ethnic diversity, frequent contact with foreigners, and variations in domestic life styles all interact to sustain a broad spectrum of modes of kinship organization. These diverse organizational modes each rest upon ideologies regarding the relationship between family and society.

George Peter Murdock (1949, p.103) has identified collaterality as a basic dimension in the ordering of relationships among kin in virtually all societies. The term, collaterality, refers to aspects of kinship ties associated with genealogical distances among relatives. In the United States, in particular, collaterality seems to be a significant dimension in determining how relatives should be treated. (See Klatzky, n.d; Litwak, 1960a, 1960b; Rosenberg and Anspach, 1973; Adams, 1968; Schneider and Cottrell, 1975.) But if modes of kinship organization vary in different segments of American society, then it seems plausible that people vary also in the ways they interpret genealogical distances. The Phoenix study has explored the ways by which diverse models of collaterality express different modes of kinship organization. The models include Parentela Orders, Standard American, Civil Law, Genetic, and Canon Law.

The collaterality models, which provide the various values for the cells in Table 9-1, represent unique combinations of i and j. For *collateral* relatives

Table 9-1. Grid of Kinship Loci Defined by Parentage and Descent As Viewed from Ego's Perspective, with Loci Designated by American Terms for Relatives and Collaterality as Determined by Canon Law, Genetic, Civil Law, Standard American, and Parentela Orders Measures[a]

Number of descending generations from ego and ego's ancestors (descent generation) (i)	Number of ascending generations from ego and ego's descendants (parentage generation) (j)				
	0	1	2	3	4
0	Ego	Parents Canon: 1 SAM: 1 Genetic: 1 POM: 4 Civil: 1	Grandparents Canon: 2 SAM: 2 Genetic: 2 POM: 8 Civil: 2	Great grandparents Canon: 3 SAM: 3 Genetic: 3 POM: 12 Civil: 3	Great great grandparents Canon: 4 SAM: 4 Genetic: 4 POM: 16 Civil: 4
1	Children Canon: 1 SAM: 5 Genetic: 1 POM: 1 Civil: 1	Siblings Canon: 1 SAM: 6 Genetic: 1 POM: 5 Civil: 2	Aunts and uncles Canon: 2 SAM: 7 Genetic: 2 POM: 9 Civil: 3	Great aunts, Great uncles Canon: 3 SAM: 8 Genetic: 3 POM: 13 Civil: 4	Grandparents' aunts and uncles Canon: 4 SAM: 9 Genetic: 4 POM: 17 Civil: 5
2	Grandchildren Canon: 2 SAM: 10 Genetic: 2 POM: 2 Civil: 2	Nieces and nephews Canon: 2 SAM: 11 Genetic: 2 POM: 6 Civil: 3	First cousins Canon: 2 SAM: 12 Genetic: 3 POM: 10 Civil: 4	Parents' first cousins Canon: 3 SAM: 13 Genetic: 4 POM: 14 Civil: 5	Grandparents' first cousins Canon: 4 SAM: 14 Genetic: 5 POM: 18 Civil: 6
3	Great grandchildren Canon: 3 SAM: 15 Genetic: 3 POM: 3 Civil: 3	Grandnieces and grandnephews Canon: 3 SAM: 16 Genetic: 3 POM: 7 Civil: 4	First cousins' children Canon: 3 SAM: 17 Genetic: 4 POM: 11 Civil: 5	Second cousins Canon: 3 SAM: 18 Genetic: 5 POM: 15 Civil: 6	Parents' second cousins Canon: 4 SAM: 19 Genetic: 6 POM: 19 Civil: 7

[a] In Table, SAM refers to Standard American model; POM refers to Parentela Orders model.

in particular, each of the models combines the values for parentage generations (j) and descent generations (i) in a different way. For example, considering siblings ($i=1$; $j=1$) and grandchildren ($i=2$; $j=0$), we find that
Parentela Orders assigns a closer relationship to grandchildren (2 versus 5),
Civil Law regards them as equidistant (both siblings and grandchildren, 2),
while Standard American, Genetic, and Canon Law models place siblings
closer to Ego (respectively, 5 versus 10, 1 versus 2, and 1 versus 2). (The
computational formulae for all five measures of collaterality are summarized
in the Descriptive-Formulae column of Table 9-2.)

A componential analysis of the kinship models (reported in Chapter 4)
discloses that these models lie on a continuum in the extent to which they
stress degree of collateral removal from Ego's line of descent in allocating
priorities among kin. The analysis involves, among other procedures, a trans-
position of the basic kinship grid. In the transposed grid, the vertical and
horizontal axes are called G (generational distance) and R (collateral removal). Specifically, G is the number of generations above or below Ego in
which any given relative is located, and R is the lateral distance between
relatives in Ego's line of descent (including direct ancestors and descendants)
and Ego's other kin in that same generation as those relatives.

As Table 9-2 reveals, all models display the basic two dimensions, G and
R. But, in addition, apart from Canon Law, each model reveals at least one
other component. Moreover, the components of the models increasingly
stress R collateral removal (or, conversely, the centrality of Ego's line of
descent) as one moves from Canon Law to the Standard American and Parentela Orders conceptions:

1. The Canon Law model, in giving equal weight to G and to R, partitions
kin by placing them along gradients extending outward from Ego and the
nuclear family. It thereby essentially ignores line of descent in describing
degree of relationship.

2. The Civil Law model, in assigning a double weight to R as compared
with G, modifies the Canon Law pattern by emphasizing the *lineal* ties of
Ego to family of orientation (through parents) and to family of procreation
(through children). All other relatives are then distributed on the basis of
their distance from this abbreviated lineal core, which consists of Ego, his
parents, and his children. (The Genetic model is transitional between the
Canon Law and Civil Law models and it embodies characteristics of both.)

3. The Standard American model has three distinct components. The first
component is the basic Canon Law degree (G+R); the second component is
the R increment of the Civil Law degree; and the third is a unique factor that
is defined in Table 9-2 as $n(DG+R)$. The unique component apportions an
equal weight to all of those kin who are in a given descent generation (i)
from Ego and his ancestral line. For example, in Table 9-1, all kin in the

Table 9-2. Descriptive and Componential Formulations of Kinship Models

Kinship models	Descriptive formula	Componential formulation					
		Basic grid dimensions					Componential emphasis
		Generational difference	Collateral removal	Civil law contribution	Unique component		
Canon law	i or j, whichever is larger	[G	+	R]			Undifferentiated radiation
Genetic	$(i - 1) + j$	[G	+	R	+	$(R - f)$]	Intermediate between canon law and civil law
Civil law	$i + j$	[G	+	R	+	R]	Lineal core
Standard american	$(n + 1)i + j$	[G	+	R	+	R	$+ \; n(DG + R)$]	Lineality emphasis in ascending generations
Parentela orders	$i + (m + 1)j$	[G	+	R	+	R	$+ \; m(AG + R)$]	Classes of parentelae—lines of descent

Definitions of symbols: j = number of generational links between Ego and a descendant or between Ego's ancestor and that ancestor's descendant (e.g., Child - 1; Grandchild - 2); i = number of generational links between Ego and an ancestor (e.g., Parent = 1; Grandparent = 2); i = number of generational links between Ego and a descendant or between Ego's ancestor and that ancestor's descendant (e.g., Child - 1; Grandchild - 2); i = number of generational links between Ego and an ancestor (e.g., Parent = 1; Grandparent = 2); Sibling = 1; Niece = 2; G = $j - i$ (plus or minus sign of G ignored); R = j or i, whichever is smaller; n = largest j in a set of relatives for whom priorities are being computed; m = the largest i in a set of relatives for whom priorities are being computed; D = Descendancy coefficient; when j is greater than i, D = 0; when j is smaller, then D = 1 (when $i = j$, G = 0, and DG must also = 0); A = Ascendancy coefficient; when i is greater than j, A = 0; when i is smaller, then A = 1 (when $i = j$, then G = 0, and AG must also = 0); f = 0 when direct-line kin or half siblings are considered; f = 1 for all other kin.

row $i=1$ would have the same score on the unique component; those in row $i=2$ would all have the same score; and so on.

4. Like the Standard American model, Parentela Orders also has three components: the Canon Law factor $(G+R)$, the Civil Law contribution (R), and a unique factor. The unique component in Parentela Orders, which is defined in Table 9-2 as $m(AG+R)$, provides an equal weight to all kin descended from any particular ancestor of Ego (as well as from Ego himself). In Table 9-1, all relatives listed in a given column j would have the same score on this component. The exact weight for each class—i.e., an ancestor and his line of descendants—depends upon the generational distance G between Ego and the ancestor. The classification of ancestors and their sets of descendants corresponds precisely with the verbal description of the Parentela Orders conception in Chapter 1.

This series from Canon Law to Standard American and Parentela Orders models is described in terms of metaphors of social space—from concentric circles (from Ego) to categorical structure (from line of descent)—in Chapter 3. The concentric circles model rests upon the generation of gradients radiating from a single point; the categorical model is based upon a classification derived from a line of demarcation. The propositions examined in the Phoenix study are: (a) the spatial metaphors symbolized by the components of the kinship models are isomorphic with communal versus segmental distinctions in religious, ethnic, and socioeconomic settings in the social structure, and (b) these components are associated with particular kinship norms and values relevant to the communal-segmental dichotomy.

KINSHIP MODELS AND SOCIAL SETTINGS

If kinship structures are perceived as modes of organization which connect personal life to the general social structure, then we can interpret each pattern of collaterality as expressing a particular set of assumptions regarding the nature of this connection. The character of these assumptions is suggested by the kinds of social structure in which these patterns seem to have crystalized historically:

1. The Parentela Orders orientation appears to have emerged in pluralistic settings (e.g., the Jewish experience, classical Greece). The ideology upon which this orientation rests is that kinship is organized centripetally to promote the perpetuation of special political and/or religious interests embodied in the *mischpokheh*, the house, or the *oikos*.

2. The Standard American pattern of collaterality seems to have developed as Protestantism and family capitalism blossomed and the merchant class dominated economic and political life in Western society. The Standard American orientation appears to be associated with high achievement motivation and therefore with the perpetuation of special socioeconomic interests.

3. The Civil Law map represents a compromise in the Twelve Tables between the pluralism of the Patricians and universalism of the Plebes at the founding of the Roman Republic. Its principles thus seem to express a middle ground in pluralism versus universalism as ideologies.

4. The Canon Law measure evolved in its present form during the 12th century to express the aims of the Church toward universalism in spreading the faith over vast domains—with centralized authority and a common body of law. The main vehicles for the perpetuation of society were organized to promote the common interests of the entire social organism with centrifugal family and kinship ties providing the informal supports for the cores of authority and power.

5. The Genetic model, which has emerged in the 20th century with the development of population genetics, implies that the precise form of family organization is irrelevant to determining the mode of the larger social structure. Rather, again by implication, the ideal is the reverse—that "rational scientific" principles should guide governments and other major institutions in determining the character of family and kinship ties.

The above description of social contexts suggests that the models of collaterality express differing modes of kinship orientation along a continuum from centripetal to centrifugal norms and values. Theoretically, at least, centripetal kinship organization emerges (or is sustained) in a situation in which a special interest group is vying with other groups for economic, political, or religious "goods." Centrifugal kinship, however, is fostered when special interests are subordinated to broader concerns extending beyond the particular group. As a general rule, centripetally organized groups appear to be mobilized into tightly organized corporate structures that concentrate their efforts on promoting their special interests. In contrast, the centrifugal systems are organized in ways which place individual members under numerous cross-pressures and which serve to erase group boundaries (Farber, 1975).

Jewish and Catholic norms offer a sharp distinction between centripetal and centrifugal modes of organization. The contrast between the centripetal tendencies in Jewish kinship and the centrifugal forces in the Catholic kinship can be clarifed by a comparison of assumptions about social structure. According to Andrew Greeley's (1977) analysis, central to contemporary Catholic social theory is the existence of all-embracing Church that is directed at unifying the diverse segments of society. Although conflict and competition are everpresent, common interests deriving from the spirit of the Church outweigh divergent concerns in the maintenance of social order. The Church is regarded as the formal organization fostering unity and it sustains its effectiveness through the informal organization existing among localized groups (such as families, friendship networks, neighborhoods, and so on). The particularism and emphasis upon personal relationships (rather that mobilization of family and kinship ties into corporate entities) create a cohesion, based on cooperative norms, in these "dense and intimate interpersonal networks." But at the same time, Greeley (1977, p.262) informs us, "Catholic theory categorically rejects the notion that one can or should sacrifice the present for the future." Sacrifice ignores the mutuality of interests and, besides, a "benign future paradise cannot be counted on to appear (Greeley, 1977, p.262)." Instead, like the humanist, "The Catholic theorist is absolutely commited to the worth and dignity of the individual person (Greeley, 1977, p.265)." The "dense networks of overlapping commitments, relationships, loyalties, involvements" (Greeley, 1977, p.260) create a myriad of cross-pressures that undercut special interests of subgroups. What remains is a web of relationships expanding to envelop the entire collectivity. From the perspective of kinship, this web extends outward, with gradients interweaving with other webs. This centrifugal movement in reaching out to create webs of relationships is symbolized in Church lore by the Canon Law model of collaterality.

As opposed to Catholic views on social order, the Jewish vision assumes a merger of religious and familial obligations and minimizes the distinction between formal and informal organization. The kinship community itself is identified as a religious community; birth and endogamy even more than faith mark its boundaries. Parents and children, husband and wife, grandparent and grandchild, cousins, uncles and aunts, nieces and nephews are mobilized in an organization with numerous corporate aspects—homogenization of religious norms and values, sacrifice and benefice, household rituals, interest in ancestral "roots"—a historical mission for family and kinship. The persistence of Judaism is identified as inhering in family continuity and in Hasidic sects even rabbinic dynasties are established. It is primarily among Reform Jews that a sharp distinction emerges between formally organized religious institutions and informal family relationships, i.e., a gap between ties with Judaism and domestic existence; and it is primarily Reform Jews who often hold a Canon Law or Genetic conception of collaterality. Otherwise, the separatist tendencies in Judaism are expressed by the Parentela Orders model of kinship, which appears in the *Mishnah* and survives in modified form in Israeli law.

Both Jewish and Catholics are generally regarded as "familistic"—interested in family and kin. However, they appear to represent different approaches: Jews with their Parentela Orders perspective seem attuned to long-distance kinship interaction, while kinship contact among Catholics appears to be tied more to locale (as it is with other persons with a Genetic or Canon Law orientation). These different approaches apparently represent opposing "templates" in organizing the social existence of Catholic, Jew, Protestant, and humanist.

In this book, I have referred to the "corporate structure" of kinship in connection with the Parentela Orders model and to a lesser extent the Standard

American model. Obviously corporate structures in American kinship are shadowy as compared with the unilineal structures in African societies (Radcliffe-Brown and Forde, 1950). In those societies, membership is clearly demarcated by descent through males or females; units are named; offices are assigned; and rights and obligations are explicitly designated. In American kinship, all of these criteria are weakened. Yet, there are some signs of people treating their kinship structures as more than a collection of individuals: emphasis on line of descent extending to ancestors no longer alive and to descendants yet to come; a tendency to homogenize values within the group; recognition of general norms and values connected to kinship ties— priority in assisting relatives more than nonrelatives, maintenance of contact over long distances, obligations to see kin, and so on. Unfortunately, there is no English term that falls between aggregate (or network) of individuals and formal corporate group. Unless I resort to a word like semi-corporate structure, I am left only with the option of referring to "corporate aspects" of kinship.

Apparently, the absence of appropriate terms to express the corporate aspects of American kinship suggests to some observers that such structural elements do not exist. But such an omission seems legitimate since there is considerable variation in American society in the extent to which kinship connotes corporateness. As ethnographic reports show, this kind of oversight is not unique; basic social categories lack terminological indicators in many societies. For example, the patrilineal Chinese have no *he* or *she* pronouns. Similarly, the lexicon of classical Athens and of the Penan of Borneo have no word for *marriage* (Needham, 1974). Under such circumstances one would expect the meanings of other words to be stretched to incorporate phenomena for which vocabulary is missing and to rely upon contextual cues to signal intended usages. For instance, the modern German word for marriage (*Ehe*)is an extension of the Middle-High German term for law or statute (ēwe), and the English *marriage* and French *mariage* are derived from *maritus,* husband in Latin (Needham, 1974, p.43). The semantic stretch, which gives rise to multiple meanings, serves to transform categorical concepts into "odd-job" words (Needham, 1974). In American society, people have to rely upon *family, cousins, roots,* or a special term (e.g. tribe, *mishpokheh, Verwandtschaft,* clan) to express corporate aspects of kinship, but others may apply these same terms merely to identify aggregates. Consequently, as in any cultural analysis, one cannot expect that every significant element be unambiguously named (Schneider, 1968).

Nevertheless, the findings of the Phoenix study reveal a relationship between kinship orientation and corporateness in the structure of family and kinship ties. In marriage, this corporateness is seen in tendencies toward (a) regarding marriage as a sanctified institution; (b) homogenization of religious values of husband and wife; (c) low probability of a sense of disillusionment for self and spouse; and (d) a high degree of marital stability. In family life, corporateness is express by (a) priority given to domestic roles over occupation, (b) emphasis upon status placement functions, and (c) stability of fertility norms over generations. In kinship ties, corporateness is reflected in: (a) a greater tendency toward virilocal than uxorilocal residence (presumably an emphasis upon instrumental ties); (b) the presence of interest in kinship as a general principle; (c) the maintenance of frequent contact with kin over long distances as apparently expressing an "axiom of amity"; (d) a desire to increase contact with non-nuclear family relatives, in spite of competing interests, and (e) a hint of authority problems with paternal kin—perhaps tied to traditional patrilineal tendencies. The clustering of these attributes among persons in the Parentela Orders and to a lesser extent the Standard American categories suggests that these models of collaterality signify kinship structures with strong corporate components.

These findings can be interpreted in terms of the dimensions of the kinship models derived in the componential analysis in Chapter 4. At one extreme, the lineality component, expressed by the Parentela Orders and Standard American unique components, is overrepresented in segmental (or factional-type) settings, religious as well as socioeconomic, and it is related to the presence of "corporate" elements in kinship ideology. At the other extreme, the undifferentiated-distance component, expressed by the Canon Law and to lesser extent by the Genetics model, is associated with communal settings, and it is tied to individualistic kinship ideologies, which minimize classes of kin. The Civil Law model, expressing the lineal core component, lies between the extremes. Consequently, the findings in the Phoenix study can be construed as disclosing an isomorphism between these components as spatial metaphors and types of social settings.

KINSHIP MODELS AND OTHER PERSPECTIVES

In the final analysis, the contributions by the Phoenix study to knowledge about contemporary social structure and changes now occurring can be assessed only by an answer to the question: Does the analysis of American kinship ties in terms of models of collaterality yield insights that are absent from other conceptualizations? In this section I will discuss implications of the findings of the Phoenix study for comparing the kinship-model perspective with previous conceptualizations regarding American kinship. There are four subsections, each of them an independent essay dealing with a different topic. The subsections include: (a) Standard American versus middle-class kinship, (b) permanent availability and kinship orientation, (c) kinship orientation and communal structures, and finally (d) components in measures of collaterality.

STANDARD AMERICAN VERSUS MIDDLE-CLASS KINSHIP

One of the contributions of the Phoenix study is the serendipitous finding of the existence of the Standard American model of collaterality. This model, held by over 40 percent of the respondents, is prevalent among families with Protestant, "middle-class" attributes, and it appears least often among persons with the following characteristics: (a) blue-collar occupation of the male household co-head; (b) family income in 1977 under $10,000; (c) respondent not a high school graduate; (d) respondent's father born in Europe; (e) member of a racial minority group; and (f) respondent not in a traditional Protestant denomination (i.e., is instead neofundamentalist, Catholic, Mormon, or Jewish). Typically non-middle-class and non-Protestant characteristics are associated with non-standard-English linguistic codes in speech. Because of this analogy between kinship model and linguistic code, I have identified the serendipitous measure of collaterality as the Standard American paradigm.

In order to determine whether the Standard American model is a useful tool for understanding the workings of contemporary kinship, I shall compare findings pertaining to this model with those for other conceptualizations, notably those by Talcott Parsons, David M. Schneider, and Eugene Litwak. Prior to the comparison, I shall briefly outline their conceptualizations.

The Parsons Conception

Talcott Parsons (1954) characterizes the standard form of American kinship as an "open, symmetrically multilineal, conjugal system." The openness refers to the lack of restrictions on assortive mating (apart from limitations imposed by the incest taboo). Multilineality refers to the lack of distinction by sex among intermediate ancestors who intervene between a distant ancestor and any given descendant; as a consequence, there are numerous lines of descent—eight from the great-grandparents alone. Unlike its European forebears, the American system is symmetrical, giving no preference in solidarity to any one line. Conjugality refers to the fact that parents and children constitute an identifiable household unit that is regarded as a distinct collectivity. Thus, according to Parsons, the system is marked by "a maximum of dispersion of lines of descent and the prevention of the structuring of kinship groups on any other principle than the 'onion' principle, which implies proportionately increasing 'distantness' with each 'circle' of linked conjugal families (Parsons, 1954, p.182)."

Parsons proposes that deviations from the standard kinship system occur when solidarity with one line of descent is emphasized at the expense of another. Specifically, he mentions (a) tendencies in farm families to approach the pattern of the European stem family as described by LePlay, (b) strong patrilineal proclivities in the upper class, and (c) the powerful matrilineal ties in lower-class settings. In the urban middle class, however, neither line of descent is stressed, and instead one's "first kinship loyalty is unequivocally to his spouse and then to their children (Parsons, 1954, p.186)." Parsons stresses that, in the middle class, upon marrying, Ego "is by comparison with other kinship systems drastically segregated from his family of orientation, both from his parents and from his siblings" (Parsons, 1954, p.186). Parsons also attributes to the symmetrical multilineality the norm of sexual equality in family relationships.

For Parsons, conformity to the standard kinship system (or deviance from it) derives from the American occupational system. There is a "fit" between the "open, symmetrical multilineal conjugal family system" and the requirement of the occupational system for a high degree of social and residential mobility, unhampered by competing loyalties. The societal need for a highly mobile work force interferes with the maintenance of close kinship ties and unilineal solidarity. Litwak and others have criticized the Parsonian conception because of its emphasis on the isolation of the nuclear family as a kinship structure.

The Litwak Conception

In the years following World War II, family sociologists mustered sufficient data to launch an attack on Parsons' description of the American kinship system (Sussman, 1965; Sussman and Burchinal, 1962a and 1962b). The thrust of the criticism is that Parsons is too extreme in his depiction of the nuclear family unit as segregated from the family of orientation and other forebears. Research findings indicated to these sociologists that Parsons had underestimated the extent to which families share functions and resources despite their residential isolation from each other. In particular, Litwak's concept of the modified expended family calls attention to the fact that kinship ties may be valued despite residential distance and lack of day-to-day contact.

The classical extended family demands "geographical propinquity, occupational involvement, . . . nepotism, [and] . . . an hierarchical authority structure," while the modified extended family "consists of a series of nuclear families bound together on an equalitarian basis, with a strong emphasis on these extended family bonds as an end value (Litwak, 1960a, p. 10)." Litwak's paradigm for the classical exended family in the United States is the Italian family, and his model for the modified extended family is the Jewish family. He indicates that "the Italian family structure, relatively speaking, is still defined in terms of geographical and occupational proximity. In contrast, the Jewish extended family, for historical reasons, closely resembles the family structure considered to be prototypical of contemporary urban bureaucratic life."

But in contradiction to Litwak's analysis, Winch and his associates (1977) report that, as compared with Catholics and Protestants, Jews show higher occupational and geographic concentrations. They are "more entrepreneurial, less migratory, and more familistic than either Catholics or Protestants," and even when they do migrate, "they are much more likely to live in the spouse's home community (Winch, 1977, p. 32)." The contradictory statements by Litwak and Winch suggest that it is difficult to differentiate between a non-mobile modified extended family and a classical extended family. The features that Litwak attributes to Jewish kinship are generally confirmed by the Phoenix study, but they express the Parentela Orders orientation rather than the Standard American view.

Litwak proposes that the modified extended family is the most effective form of kinship organization in modern society in that it permits geographical and social mobility which simultaneously makes affectional and instrumental resources of close kin available to individual families. Yet, Litwak's own data (Table 5, 1960a) contradict the claim that the modified extended family is a more effective instrument than the isolated nuclear family in meeting the needs for most people. In his study, a majority of respondents in any occupational stratum conform to the "nuclear family orientation," and fewer than a fourth are classified as "extended family orientation." (See also Kerckhoff, 1965, Table 5-2.) Moreover, the major differences between upwardly mobile and stationary occupational classes are not in percentages of persons with an extended family orientaton but in the percentages who want nothing to do with "family" (with 34 percent of the stationary lower class classified an "non-family oriented" as compared with 23 percent of the upwardly mobile). These data from Litwak's investigation suggest that the modified extended family is more of a goal for social policy than a description of prevalent kinship norms. Although Litwak's work may have focused attention on a residue of kin ties in contemporary society, it does not appear to negate Parsons' notions about American kinship.

The Schneider Conception

The position taken by David M. Schneider is that standard American kinship exists only at the cultural level and that variations in American society result from the intrusion of influences from other domains upon the kinship domain. Actual relationships with kin are thereby governed by norms which are a compromise of the demands of the various domains. Hence, for Schneider, American kinship survives only as a set of general symbols pertaining to blood ties and general moral codes isolated from specific social contexts.

But Schneider's analysis of American kinship as a normative phenomenon —as compromised norms—does emphasize the significance of socioeconomic class in molding ties among relatives. Like Parsons, Schneider assigns primary weight to the occupational structure in the development of kinship norms: "One of the most important sets of forces affecting familial behavior is the relationship of individuals and families to the economic system (Schneider and Smith, 1973, p.197)" Yet, he weakens this assertion by indicating that, "The cultural orientation of the lower class can be found among people who are quite well off, just as there are many genteel poor of undoubted middle-class orientation (Schneider and Smith, 1973, p.67)." One must assume, therefore, that for Schneider and Smith orientation toward kinship is at least partly independent of social class.

Schneider and Smith (1973) characterize middle-class kinship by distinguishing it from norms associated with the lower class. For them, middle-class kinship has these characteristics:

1. Nuclear family self-sufficiency;
2. Nuclear family solidarity undifferentiated by sex (as opposed to separateness of men and women and solidarity of mother and children in the lower class);
3. The kindred as a chain of linked nuclear families (as opposed to person-to-person relationships in the lower class);
4. The rule of reason (with accompanying self-discipline and self-control) and expertise (i.e.,rationality) rather than status as basis for authority (as opposed to authority vested in males in lower class).

Comparison with Standard American Model

The analysis based on the Standard American collaterality model yields insights into the functioning of kinship in middle-class American that are not apparent in the Parsons, Litwak, or Schneider formulations. This section compares these conceptions with the Standard American model, first in their similarities and then in their differences.

The Standard American model provides a means for integrating the depictions of middle-class kinship by Parsons, Litwak, and Schneider: (a) sexual de-differentiation (Table 8-2); (b) significance of the marital tie (Table 4-7); (c) norms of equalitarianism in family relationships (Table 6-11); (d) facilitation of upward social mobility (Table 5-9); (e) fairly frequent contact with parents and siblings living at a distance (Table 8-6); and (f) interpretation of relatives as representatives of collectivities rather than simply persons (Table 8-3, 8-9, and 8-10). Like Litwak's concept of the modified extended family, the series of which the Standard American model is a part differentiates between distinctly kinship ties (regardless of residence) and the "segregated nuclear family" as a household unit. Nevertheless, along with integrating these attributes, the Standard American model generates additional insights about contemporary American kinship. Unlike other models of collaterality, the Standard American measure is associated with (a) emphasis upon ancestral line in conception of collateraltiy (Table 4-4); (b) connections among nativity, traditional Protestantism, and kinship orientation (Table 4-5); (c) the transmission of a norm of low fertility and consequently the production of small kindreds (Table 6-8, 6-9, 7-15, and 7-16); and (d) responsiveness to the changing status of women in American society (Tables 7-10 and 7-12). Significantly, the findings indicate that the Standard American model is not the only kinship orientation whose adherents show a propensity toward upward social mobility (Table 5-9).

Perhaps of most importance, the representation of Standard American kinship as a model of collaterality avoids logical difficulties in the Parsons, Litwak, and Schneider approaches. All three analysts—through their emphasis on functionality in a socioeconomic setting—face the problem first of deriving the attributes of "middle-class" kinship from the functional requirements of the American occupational structure and then of having to account for its existence in non-middle-class segements of society (as well as its absence in many middle-class families). The persistence of kinship structures that deviate from social class "needs" (or demands) prompts one to consider an alternate approach.

The analysis based on kinship models, however, rests upon an alternative set of assumptions. It begins with the notion that transcendant pluralist (or factionalist) ideologies stimulate groups to develop views about kinship that set them off over generations from other groups. I have suggested that the emergence of family capitalism (along with early Protestant ideas about worldly success and worthiness of ancestors among the Elect) accented the function of status-placement as a dominant family function. I have further proposed that this accentuation is symbolized in the Standard American model of collaterality. Certainly, families in relatively high socioeconomic positions are motivated to perpetuate their status—to continue to set themselves off from families with inferior resources and modes of existence. Such families tend to exhibit a Standard American conception of kinship over generations. But, in addition, similar ideologies may emanate in groups and movements in diverse parts of the social structure. For example, the data indicate that the Standard American model is especially prevalent among younger women, who apparently have been stimulated by the contemporary feminist movement and consequently exhibit high concentrations in the work force and in graduate level education (Table 7-9, 7-10, and 7-12). Hence, by conceiving of kinship orientations as cultural models, which are applicable to wide range of social conditions and economic systems, we can avoid the logical circularity of explaining the features of middle-class kinship by positing "needs" for such structures.

PERMANENT AVAILABILITY AND KINSHIP ORIENTATION

The fact that mode of kinship organization has an impact on norms pertaining to marriage is well documented in anthropological literature (e.g., Fox, 1967). But the nuances in marriage rules implied by the American kinship system have scarcely been explored. In 1964, in my book, *Family: Organization and Interaction* I suggested that, insofar as the multilineal system is associated with assortive mating, not only marital selection but also temporal aspects of marriage would be affected. Following Parsons' lead that kinship in the United States is organized as a symmetrical multilineal system, I reasoned along the following lines:

1. In a multilineal system, no recognizable descent group or line of ancestors has any exclusive claim on an individual's assests or abilities. (The nuclear family's claims are limited only to its life span; special claims of the family of orientation are dissipated as the individual marries. Any such claims that remain derive from personal relationships among family members rather than from familial status.)

2. Without such a claim, the kindred has no legitimate basis for any special rights or obligations pertaining to an individual and hence no special stake in that individual's destiny, particularly his marital destiny.

3. Without a special stake, there are no grounds for imposing restrictions on an individual's choice of spouse or mode of existence (i.e., family life style) following marriage.

4. Since the openness extends not merely to choice of marriage partner but also to home life afterwards, individuals are free to end marriages and begin new ones without the intrusion of parents or siblings.

5. As marital status assumes the identity of a potentially transitory relationship, individuals become aware that they are permanently available for a new marriage (or a new mate) regardless of their current marital status.

6. Whereas for some individuals, this permanent availability may become a positive value, for many people this awareness decreases the level of tolerance for enduring difficulties in a marriage. Moreover, it may sensitize people to focus on problems in their marriage in order to determine whether the critical point of toleration has been exceeded (or will soon be reached).

7. Permanent availability as a social reality has various implications for courtship and family norms:

   a. Since marriage is potentially a temporary relationship, the appropriate courtship process is not one of carefully sifting and narrowing a field of eligibles until one person is selected for lifetime mating. Instead the proper procedure would be to enter into a series of marital-like relationships. When one of these trial relationships is sufficiently satistying to call for stabilizing measures, marriages may then be formalized.

b. Inasmuch as the system assumes remarriage as a normal occurrence, there is no special virtue in maintaining virginity prior to marriage. Rather, appropriate socialization for permanent availability would call for early training in developing sexual competence.

c. Since marriages are not assumed to be permanent, there is no special virtue in delaying marriage or a quasi-marital tie. Formal marriage symbolizes a personal *desire* to stabilize the relationship rather than a *commitment* to do so.

d. Children serve as pledges to maintain the marital relationship. Nevertheless, there is no certainty that they will be effective in performing that task.

e. With the presupposition that marriages may be temporary, one is reluctant to break sentimental ties with one's parents and siblings. In the event of marital breakup, bonds to parents and siblings may resume their importance as sources of personal and financial assistance and emotional support. This view implies that a chasm exists whereby continued support is regarded as appropriate but parental controls are not. Controls are attributed to family ties of a corporate nature, whereas assistance is given on a personal basis (i.e. for love).

f. Even after marriage, because of the uncertainty of marital destinies, people (intentionally or inadvertently) remain in a state of readiness, with an emphasis on youthfulness, keeping attractive, and maintaining sociability with the opposite sex.

g. Because of the openness in choice of sequential marital partners, any given line of descent is highly vulnerable to the introduction of diverse norms and values; consequently permanent availability is associated with changes in family organization over time. The opposite of permanent availability is orderly replacement of family norms and values in any given line of descent from one generation to the next—as it might be symbolized by the Parentela Orders orientation.

Of the several kinship orientations, the Genetic and particularly the Canon Law models seem closest in approximating the conception of social space that fits the attributes of permanent availability. The Canon Law model is Ego-centered, with gradients extended outward. The members of the nuclear family occupy the innermost space and with each step away from the nuclear family in collateral or generational links, one degree of genealogical distance is added. Pictorially, the Canon Law model resembles the onion analogy applied by Parsons in his characterization of American kinship (Parsons, 1954).

In norms as well, the Genetic and Canon Law models approach the conditions of permanent availability. The findings in the Phoenix study reveal the following for respondents in the Genetic and Canon Law category:

1. *Openness in choice of marital partner:* Among Protestants, the persons with a Genetic or Canon Law orientation have the largest percentage of religious intermarriages of any of the kinship classifications (Tables 6-3 and 7-2).

2. *Prevalence of divorce:* The Genetic and Canon Law category has the largest percentage of divorced parents and siblings (Tables 6-1 and 6-2) and the preponderance of respondents themselves who have ever been divorced (Tables 7-6 and 7-7).

3. *Living together as part of courtship:* Canon Law and Genetic women, in particular, yield the largest percentage of persons who agree that "it is a good idea for a man and woman to live together for a while before they marry" (Table 7-14).

4. *Age at marriage:* Genetic and Canon Law women tend to marry at an early age (as in Table 6-5 for respondents' mothers and Table 7-8 for women respondents and wives of men respondents).

5. *Having children as a pledge:* Regardless of social background, women in the Genetic and Canon Law category (unlike others) want more children than men in that category do. Since it is generally the women who seek to stabilize cohabiting relationships, this finding is consistent with the view that children serve as a pledge to maintain the marital tie.

6. *Kinship ties:* Persons in the Genetic and Canon Law category have the largest percentage of close relatives residing in Arizona (Table 8-1) and see them frequently (Table 8-7), thereby keeping kin ties in readiness if the marital relationship proves inadequate.

7. *Sensitivity to tolerance limits:* The respondents in the Genetic and Canon Law classification are also most prone to perceive a high degree of general disillusionment (or "anomia") in their marriages (Table 7-4), and they tend to view their spouses as more profane than they themselves are (Table 7-5).

The findings thus point to a convergence between conditions for permanent availability and the Genetic and Canon Law models of collaterality. Despite this general convergence, the countervailing influence of religious controls cannot be ignored. It is true that among the parents of respondents, regardless of religion, divorce tends to be more prevalent in the Canon Law and Genetic category than for the total sample (Table 6-1). Nevertheless, for the respondents themselves, the relationship between prevalence of divorce and Genetic-Canon Law classification holds only for non-Catholics. Among Catholics, the percentage of persons currently in their first marriage (i.e., neither remarried nor now divorced) is equal to that for all Catholics in the sample (Table 7-7). But clearly, fewer Jews and Protestants with a Genetic or Canon Law orientation are still in their first marriages than is true of the sample totals in those religious groups (Table 7-7). Hence, Catholicism—with its canonical limitations on divorce—appears to counteract effectively the proclivities toward marital breakup and remarriage stemming from Genetic and Canon Law kinship orientations.

KINSHIP ORIENTATION AND COMMUNAL STRUCTURES

The distinction between associational and communal structures has been fruitfully applied in the analysis of religious and ethnic correlates of family life. Over a decade ago, Gerhard Lenski (1963, p.356) suggested that American Judaism faces an uncertain future because "the weakening of the associational side of Judaism [by which he meant the hold of the synagogue or temple] may make the subculture of that group more vulnerable to environmental influences." Since a communal subculture seems to rest, at least in part, on family and kinship ties, it would seem that the persistence of American Judaism as an identifiable entity requires a strong commitment to traditional family and kinship obligations.

The Lenski "communal" position places much emphasis on those factors that have been found in sociological research to affect family ties: extent of mobility, residential scatter, and personal contact (or to use Robert Winch's (1974) term, functionality). These are the elements that sustain commitment to the informal networks of relationship required for the persistence of a subculture. However, the "associational" position taken by Herberg (1960) and by Glazer and Moynihan (1974) opposes that of Lenski. Whereas Lenski sees ethnic survival as a consequence of a balance between associational and communal elements, the associational proponents suggest that the persistence of Jewish and other ethnic groups depends more upon religious and/or secular collective action than upon the peculiar functionality of the family and other communal institutions. This position leads to the expectation that degree of commitment to Judaism and its familial concomitants rests primarily upon participation in formal, specialized structures—extent of synagogue attendance and ritual observance and membership in Jewish organizations (e.g., B'nai B'rith, Hadassah, Organization for Rehabilitation through Training).

Andrew Greeley (1976) made a comparable distinction with regard to Catholics—ecclesiastical Catholicism versus communal Catholicism. Although Greeley's dichotomy is stated in political terms—the sources of leadership and authority in Catholic praxis—essentially it too rests upon assessing the role of associations in the persistence of Catholicism as an identifiable collectivity, despite its considerable ethnic diversity in America. Ecclesiastical Catholicism refers to the influence of Church institutions on the lives of people, that is, the impact of the organized church and the various institutions under its control (Greeley, 1976, p.2) By contrast, communal Catholicism refers to "other power centers within the collectivity that have an independent influence of their own, not necessarily in opposition to the religious institution but distinct and separate from it (Greeley, 1976, p.104)." These must grasp "the considerable heterogeneity of family structures, role expectations, and values concerning intimate behaviour that can be found among the diverse communities that constitute our society."

Further light on this dichotomy is shed by a study of Jews living in Kansas City in 1976. That analysis discloses two patterns of participation in the Jewish community. One segment of the community participates association-ally—by formal and ritual means and reliance on formal institutional arrange-ments for its involvement. This group, which shows the greatest inclination toward membership in Jewish organizations, synagogue (or temple) attend-ance, and ritual observation, tends to conform to kinship models that disre-gard line of descent in partitioning of relatives (i.e., Genetic and Canon Law models). There is, however, another segment that participates communally. This second group consists of people who tend to be more active in Jewish matters than their parents, live in Jewish areas of the city, disapprove of religious intermarriage, and are concerned with the persistence of Jewish identity. The communally oriented Jews conform more often to the Parentela Orders model (Farber, 1979).

The connection found between kinship model and communal (as opposed to associational) ties to the Jewish community, it seems, can be generalized to Catholics and Protestants as well. Both Lenski (1963) and Greeley (1976) suggest that Catholics convey many communal ties in organizing their daily lives. Indeed, Greeley (1976) proposes that, despite the official theoretical position, as skepticism about Church teachings grows, Catholics are becom-ing increasingly communally oriented in their approach to social ethics. There are, therefore, two questions to be asked about communal-versus-associa-tional ties: (a) Do American Catholics continue to show greater communal inclinations than Protestants do (and less than Jews)? (b) What role does kinship orientation play in associational-versus-communal organization?

Drawing from the Kansas City findings cited above, let us assume that the Parentela Orders model expresses a communal mode of organization. The regression analysis in the Phoenix study indicates that in a general population the Civil Law model is associated with associational ties. (See Appendix A). Then for any particular religion, the extent to which the proportion of respon-dents in the Parentela Orders category outweighs the proportion in the Civil Law category describes the degree to which that religious group can be depicted as communal in its kinship organization. A computation based on Table 5-1 shows that the ratio of Parentela-Orders to Civil-Law respondents for the various religious groups is as follows:

Jewish	1.75
Catholic	1.37
Neofundamentalist Protestant sects	1.33

Reformation Era Protestant denominations	0.77
Pietistic Protestant denominations	0.83
Mormon (Latter Day Saints)	0.37

The dependence among Protestant denominations upon formal institutional ties for their coherence as social entities is apparent in the list of ratios above. Except for the sectarians, who set themselves apart communally, Protestants, as in Lenski's earlier analysis, remain associational in orientation. Moreover, while Catholics appear to be highly communal in outlook, Jews are even more so.

Table 9-3 summarizes the data presented in previous chapters pertaining to kinship characteristics relevant to the communal-associational distinction. Presumably, a communal orientation rests upon kinship relations that (a) inhibit divorce; (b) foster religious unity in the family; and (c) encourage frequent contact with close kin. The table discloses that, for both the respondents and their parents, kinship characteristics expressing communalism are generally most prevalent among Jews, next among Catholics, and least prevalent among Protestants. Moreover, within religious groups, persons in the Parentela Orders category display more evidence of communalism than do those with a Civil Law orientation. The data therefore offer support for the "stickiness" of kinship sources of communal organization among religious groups in American society. The tenacity of kinship ideologies that foster autonomous group identities seems to complement socioeconomic characteristics in structuring religious collectivities.

COMPONENTS IN MEASURES OF COLLATERALITY

In the past, analysis of kinship terminology has provided anthropologists with numerous insights into the mechanics of social structure. Nevertheless, when they have sought to apply conventional linguistic procedures to American kinship, they have faced two major problems;

1. Past research and speculation have indicated that changes in kinship nomenclature occur long after other modifications have taken place in norms governing kinship ties (Naroll, 1970). In those societies in which changes in social structure accrue slowly, the study of kinship terms offers many clues to the factors that give the society its form. In modern, rapidly-changing society like the United States, however, terms may lag far behind current family and kinship usages. Consequently, an analysis of American kinship terminology per se may reveal more about the family and kinship structure of "our founding fathers" than it might about contemporary arrangements. For example, in their analyses, several anthropologists have concluded that

Table 9-3. Summary of Family and Kinship Characteristics Relevant for Communal-Associational Distinction, by Religion and Kinship Orientation of Respondents

Source table	Family and kinship characteristics and kinship orientation	Jewish	Catholic	Protestant
6-1	Prevalence of divorced parents of respondents[a]			
	Parentela orders (%)	6.7	15.8	22.4
	Civil law (%)	11.8[b]	26.7	20.8
7-6	Percent of respondents now in their first marriage (i.e., neither remarried or currently divorced) (%)	74.1	69.3	64.9
6-3	Parents who intermarried across religious groups[c]			
	Parentela orders (%)	—	9.7	22.7
	Civil law (%)	—	25.9	31.2
7-3	Religious intermarriages which remain "mixed"[a]			
	Parentela orders (%)	37.5	63.9	52.2
	Civil law (%)	100.0	73.4	83.6
6-4	Respondents' siblings are all in the same religion[a]			
	Total sample (%)	85.7	72.9	54.6
	Parentela orders (%)	—	86.7	52.9
	Civil law (%)	—	71.4	58.8
	Respondents' children are all raised in the same religion (%)	97.5	88.6	82.9
8-8	Close relatives living in Maricopa County who are seen at least weekly			
	Mother (%)	93.3	77.4	73.6
	Father (%)	84.6	65.2	65.0
	Brother closest in age to ego (%)	75.0	44.9	40.7
	Sister closest in age to ego (%)	77.8	64.0	42.3
	Brother second closest in age to ego (%)	—	46.9	36.0
	Sister second closest in age to ego (%)	—	67.3	43.4

[a] By religion in which respondent was raised.

[b] Because of small number of cases, Genetic and Canon Law category combined with Civil Law category.

[c] By religion in which mother was raised.

the traditional American-English terminology still reflects the structure of the "typical" conjugal family in the United States, that is, a family in which husband and wife and their children share a household (Brown, 1974; Casson, 1973; Schneider, 1968). Yet, for decades U.S. Census data, papers in law journals, research on kinship and family life styles, and court decisions have described a shift in both legal and community norms toward an increasing conceptual separation between (a) family and kinship as *social entities* and (b) family and kinship as *residential and ecological arrangements*. Obviously, the conventional analysis of traditional nomenclature cannot discern this change in American culture.

2. A second deficiency in the past research on American kinship terminology has been its failure to take into account the heterogeneity of family and kinship structures in American society. Unlike most societies studied by anthropologists, American society consists of a multitude of peoples with different ethnic and religious backgrounds. The countless waves of immigration that occurred throughout American history have introduced diverse and often contradictory ideas about kinship into the United States. Each ethnic group has imported those conceptions of kinship prevalent in its native land. But despite this heterogeneity, the ideal of Americanization has, in the past, made it incumbent upon immigrants and their children to use American-English as a vehicle of communication in all domains, including kinship. However, the use of the English language does not imply that the newcomers and their descendants have automatically assimilated norms and values which molded English kinship nomenclature. Rather, it seems plausible that standard English terminology has been stretched to accommodate the diversity of kinship usages current in the various ethnic and religious groups. To the extent that the United States remains a pluralistic society, one would expect this heterogeneity to persist in spite of the common use of English to describe kinship statuses.

Empirical investigation by anthropologists has indeed revealed that people apply disparate semantic models in their categorizations of kin statuses (e.g., Sanday, 1968; Wexler and Romney, 1972; Brown, 1976). An analysis of the models of collaterality in the Phoenix study has demonstrated that each model expresses a unique component in kinship classification. These components are described in the last column of Table 9-2 (i.e., componential emphasis). The Canon Law component stresses gradients of kin from Ego; the Genetic component is intermediate between the Canon Law and the Civil Law models; the Civil Law component is based upon a minimal lineal core consisting of Ego, his parents, and his children; Standard American component emphasizes the role of lineality in categorizing kin; and the Parentela Orders component places relatives in classes based upon their lines of descent.

This brief review of the componential analysis indicates that the kinship models differ in their emphasis upon distancing, lineality, and generational differentiation. But it also reveals that each model of collaterality produces additional information about dimensions applied in the structuring of American kinship ties.

The first point to be made in the discussion of the components concerns the Civil Law model. As Chapter 2 indicated, the Civil Law model emerged as a form of accommodation between the Plebians and Patricians in formulating the Twelve Tables when the Roman Republic was founded. In the Phoenix study, the Civil Law model is overrepresented where accommodation between social classes might be most prevalent—in the lower-middle class. This class is characterized by the following combination of attributes; (a) families of clerical, sales, and craft workers (Tables 5-7 and 5-8); (b) high school graduates who have not attended college (Table 7-10); (c) non-minority families with a relatively high income (Tables 5-4 and 5-6); (d) persons in Protestant denominations, particularly Mormons and Neofundamentalists (Table 5-1); and (e) individuals with a history of frequent church attendance (Table A-1). As for kinship structure, the data disclose that the Civil Law model represents conventional views we normally associate with relatively affluent, stable lower-middle-class family life: (a) intergenerational stability in social status (Table 5-9); (b) low prevalence of marital breakup (Table 7-6); (c) utrolocality in marital residence (Table 8-2); (d) a high percentage of religious intermarriages that remain "mixed" afterwards (Table 7-3); (e) a tendency to disapprove of premarital cohabitation (Table 7-14); (f) a tradition of maternal employment—to maintain income level (Table 6-7), and (g) the maintenance of strong ties with close relatives (particularly siblings) living in Arizona (Table 8-8). These findings suggest that there is a distinct pattern of kinship prevalent in lower-middle-class American society, which differs from both the upwardly mobile professional and managerial class and the lower blue-collar class. This mode of kinship organization, structured by the principle of an abbreviated lineal core (i.e., Ego, parents, and children), seem to have escaped the attention of sociologists and anthropologists studying modern kinship.

A second point evoked by the data in the Phoenix study, especially by the uncovering of the Standard American model, pertains to the application of the concept of generation in American kinship. Wexler and Romney (1972) have identified generational distance of relatives from Ego as a major dimension in the semantics of American kinship terminology. But unlike Wallace and Atkins (1960), they have dismissed the concept of ascending versus descending generations as a central cognitive principle in partitioning kin. Instead, the diagram provided by Wexler and Romney gives priority to generational distance from Ego over the ascending-descending distinction. Supporting Wallace and Atkins, the componential analysis of collaterality models shows that the Standard American and Parentela Orders models (each of which has its own norms and social correlates) assign differential weights to Ego's kin in ascending generations as opposed to those in descending generations. Since the Standard American model is the most prevalent one in the Phoenix study, the omission of this cognitive dimension from a listing of primary principles in the semantics of American kinship terms appears to be a serious deficiency.

A BRIEF EPILOGUE: MODELS OF COLLATERALITY AND SECULAR IMMORTALITY

In the past decades, the American family has undergone many changes at all stages of the life course. Yet, of the normative shifts that have occurred, most have taken place among young adults—those persons under 40. These changes have included fluctuations in (a) age at first marriage, (b) the popularity of marriage, divorce, and remarriage, (c) the prevalence of one-parent families and concomitantly young parents living apart from their children, (d) the entrance of married women in childbearing years into the labor force, (e) the decline in fertility, and (f) the widespread phenomenon of households consisting of unmarried couples (Glick, 1979). Many people have interpreted this proliferation of alternative life styles as a broadening of normative options over the life span. Although these options have obvious consequences that follow people into their old age, nevertheless, they derive from choices made in youth.

Despite the long-run effects of these early decisions, the ideas that people hold about kinship and its significance seem to shift as they mature. Data from a 1976 Kansas City study, which includes the elderly, supplement the findings of the Phoenix investigation in disclosing a trend in patterns of kinship orientation. Table 9-4 shows the age distribution of kinship models in a survey of the Kansas City Jewish community. The table describes a dramatic drop in Genetic and Canon Law responses after 40, with a corresponding increase in Parentela Orders and Standard American conceptions. Whereas the percentage for persons with a Parentela Orders orientation is similar to that of persons classified as Genetic or Canon Law (about 25 percent) in the age category of 40 or under, there is a large gap between them in the 65 or over age group—35 percent for Parentela Orders and only 12

Table 9-4. Kinship Orientation of Respondents in 1976 Kansas City Study of Jewish Community, by Age

	Age of respondent			
Kinship Orientation	40 years or under	40–64	65 years of over	Total
Parentela orders (%)	27.3	34.6	35.3	33.5
Ratio to total	.81	1.03	1.05	
Standard american (%)	36.4	38.8	43.1	39.6
Ratio to total	.92	.98	1.09	
Civil law	12.1	11.2	9.8	11.0
Ratio to total	1.10	1.02	.89	
Genetic model and canon law	24.2	15.3	11.8	15.9
Ratio to total	1.52	.96	.74	
N	33	98	51	182

Data recomputed to accommodate Standard American model. See Farber (1979) for description of the study.

percent for Genetic and Canon Law. Thus, the data for Kansas City extend the trends apparent in the Phoenix study on the relationship between age and model of collaterality.

But what is the significance of the age trend for social policy? The findings in Chapter 7 on children's ages and residence (Table 7-11) suggest that stages in the life course have little impact on kinship orientation. But the data for both men and women do show that as individuals ripen into later maturity, they increasingly regard kinship as a secular means for perpetuating themselves—symbolically as well as biologically. (See Table 7-9). It is plausible that the trend over the life course toward the Parentela Orders conception of collaterality expresses this continually growing concern with secular immortality. While the data permit alternative interpretations, they do not rule out secular immortality as an explanatory concept. (Cf Craig, 1979; Farber, 1971, on symbolic family estates; and Needham, 1974, on definition of "kinship.")

The age shift in kinship orientation toward an increasing concern with secular immortality evokes questions about the adequacy of basing family policies upon a single kinship perspective. As the predominant conception, the Standard American paradigm probably should be applied to establish criteria for defining familial rights and obligations. Characteristics of Standard American kinship are in accord with current trends in public policy. Consistent with the Standard American model, proposals have been made by legal scholars and students of public policy that: (a) in intestacy law, the entire estate should devolve upon the surviving spouse, with its residue eventually trickling downward to the children (Table 4-8); (b) in fertility, small families should be encourged by law and regulatory agencies (Table 7-16); (c) in educational and occupational matters, active participation of married women should be facilitated by an extension of affirmative-action and child-care programs (Tables 7-10 and 7-12); (d) finally, measures should be taken to make early marriage difficult (Table 7-8). Thus, insofar as there is a movement toward a comprehensive family policy in the United States, it appears to follow guidelines consistent with the Standard American model.

But there is another problem. One of the principles buttressing recent legal views is that the law should not impose a single family life style upon the entire population. Instead, it should admit a wide range of religious and ethical systems in its application. Despite this libertarian principle, however, the data of the Phoenix study suggest that the Standard American model most readily accommodates a Protestant, upper-middle-class population segment and serves religious, ethnic, and racial minorities least. (See Table A-1.) Less than half of the Phoenix sample conforms to this kinship perspective. Therefore, one can construe use of the Standard American model as a basis for social policy as favoring the family norms and values of one religious group and one social class over others.

The problem to be solved in public policy is how to accommodate a diversity of kinship ideologies associated with age, religion and ethnicity when (a) the dominant kinship ideology itself is overrepresented in a single religious and socioeconomic class and (b) even the least restrictive version of kinship ideology itself is expressed by a particular kinship model (i.e., Canon Law collaterality) held by only a small minority in the society. A dedication to pluralism logically involves granting a measure of legal autonomy to religious, racial, and ethnic communities—a state of affairs that the Enlightenment dispelled. Perhaps, all that can be hoped for is a continued dialectic between pluralist and universalist doctrines in the creation of eclectic public policies, a dialectic that would involve cognizance of the full range of concern with secular immortality in kinship ideologies.

Appendix A
Multiple
Regression
Analysis

Tabular presentations of percentages are useful in that they communicate information in a straightforward manner with minimal loss of important details. Unlike more complex forms of analysis, they permit much flexibility in selecting subsamples for display; they accommodate nonlinear relationships readily; and they are easily comprehended. Their greatest deficiency is that they place limits upon the extent to which the interactions among a large series of variables can be taken into account in an analysis. Consequently, use of tabular analysis based on percentages may produce spurious interpretations of a set of data. In order to avoid this danger, it appears advisable to supplement the tabular analyses of percentages with a multivariate procedure.

This appendix consists of three sections. First, the procedure followed in the multivariate analysis is described. Then, the findings are discussed, and finally conclusions are offered.

THE MULTIVARIATE PROCEDURE

A stepwise multiple regression analysis was undertaken to monitor the interpretations yielded by the tabular analyses in the various chapters of the book. The regression procedure weights the contribution of each independent variable on the basis of a linear relationship to the kinship orientations, and it accommodates a large number of independent variables in computation. The regression analysis thereby allows for simultaneous treatment of many variables whose direct influence on one another may not have been anticipated.

Table A-1 reports the results of four regression analyses—one for each kinship orientation (with Genetic and Canon Law treated as a single category). The dependent variable in each case is a dummy variable in which a given kinship orientation is assigned a value of *one* and all others are given a *zero* value. A single set of independent variables is used for all four analyses. Inasmuch as the main purpose of the regression analysis is to avoid spurious interpretations regarding the relationship between the kinship orientations and the social structure, questions pertaining to opinions or subjective states pertaining to family and kinship are omitted. The items selected as independent variables thus consist of the more objective types of information presented in the tables of the monograph. Except where dummy variables have been constructed, the range of categories for these items is described in those tables. The variables in the regression analyses include the following:

A. Social and demographic background variables
   1. Occupational status of male co-head of household
   2. Educational level of respondent
   3. Family income in 1977
   4. Minority-group status
   5. Religion: dummy variables for General Protestants, Reformation Era Protestant denominations, Pietistic Protestant denominations, Neofundamentalist Protestants, Catholics, Mormons, and Jews
   6. Size of community in which respondent was raised
   7. Was respondent raised in Arizona?
   8. Age of respondent
   9. Male respondent = 1; female respondent = 0

B. Family and Kin of Orientation
   10. How well the respondent knew each grandparent while growing up:
       10a. Father's Father
       10b. Father's Mother
       10c. Mother's Father
       10d. Mother's Mother
   11. Nativity of Father's Father (U.S. = 1; Other = 0).
   12. Were parents divorced?
   13. Number of respondent's siblings
   14. Is mother living in Arizona?
   15. Actual contact with mother
   16. Actual contact with father
   17. Desired contact with mother
   18. Desired contact with father

C. Self and Family of Procreation
   19. Is this the respondent's first marriage?
   20. Is respondent now divorced?
   21. Number of children born to respondent
   22. Frequency of church or synagogue attendance
   23. Importance of religion to respondent

An examination of Table A-1 indicates that the Beta coefficients, as well as explained variance (R-square), are small. The use of dummy variables as the dependent variables tends to attenuate both the regression coefficients and the explained variance. Moreover, the incorporation of 32 independent variables (including dummy variables) into the equation itself has a depressing effect on the individual Beta coefficients, though not on the explained variance. However, the purpose of this regression analysis is not to produce a statistical model but to institute a check for spuriousness of interpretations based upon the indivudual tables. Consequently, my concern is only whether those items with the largest Betas (arbitrarily those exceeding .05) correspond to the factors that I have concluded are important for kinship orientations.

The regression analysis utilizes the 772 cases in the Phoenix study. As pointed out in Appendix B, the criteria for inclusion in the sample are (a) permanent residence in the city of Phoenix, (b) 18-45 age range, and (c) now or previously married. There are two subsamples: one of them, consisting of 723 respondents, was obtained by use of probability sampling procedures, and the other 49 cases are Jewish persons in a convenience sample. In order to retain all 772 cases in the regression analyses, when data for specific items are missing for any individual respondent, mean values for the total sample are applied.

FINDINGS

Table A-1 presents standardized regression coefficients (Betas) in stepwise multiple regression equations where the kinship orientations are the dependent variables. Only those Betas of .05 or over are displayed and those items for which there are no Betas of that magnitude are omitted. The independent variables are classified under three rubrics: (a) social and demographic background variables, (b) family and kin of orientation, and (c) self and family of procreation.

Social and Demographic Background

The Beta weights in the multivariate analyses reveal the following results with regard to the respondents' social and demographic background:

1. By themselves, several items have little influence on kinship orientation. Those variables with no Beta weights of .05 or over include: (a) family income, (b) Catholic religion, (c) size of community in which the respondent was raised, and (d) whether or not the respondent was raised in Arizona. Their interaction with other variables in the analyses dissipate their effect on kinship orientation. In particular, much of the variance in kinship orientations explained by family income is reduced by correlations with education ($r = .36$), occupation ($r = .33$), Jewish religion ($r = .26$), minority group status ($r = -.24$), and currently divorced ($r = -.24$).

2. The data in Table A-1 indicate that diverse kinds of variables are associated with the various orientations. But this diversity is consistent with interpretations in the text. Table A-2, which compares the results of the multiple regression analyses with the tabular presentations, shows a strong confirmation of the tabular findings based on percentages. The major revision in interpretation pertains to family income and minority-group status.

Table A-1. Standardized Regression Coefficients (Beta) of .05 or Over in Multiple Regression Equations, with Kinship Orientations as Dependent Variables[a]

Independent variables	Parentela orders	Standard american	Civil law	Genetic or canon law
Social and demographic background variables				
Occupational status		.060		
Educational level		.073	−.060	
Minority-group status	−.061		−.134	.126
Religion				
General Protestant		.049		
Reformation Era Protestant		.054		
Pietistic Protesant		.046	.058	
Neofundamentalist Protestant	.049			−.074
Mormon (LDS)	−.045		.079	
Jewish	.056	−.070		
Age	.078	−.085		
Male gender	.062			−.061
Family and kin of orientation				
How well respondent knew grandparent while growing up:				
Father's father		.099		−.098
Father's mother	−.051			.080
Parents divorced				.050
Number of siblings	.052	−.108		.080
Mother living in Arizona		−.047	.079	−.046
Actual contact with mother			−.067	.124
Actual contact with father		.057		−.093
Desired contact with mother				−.048
Desired contact with father	−.055			.095
Self and family of procreation				
Is this the respondent's first marriage?		.053		
Is respondent now divorced?			−.067	.076
Number of children born to respondent				−.116
Frequency of church or synagogue attendance			.112	
Importance of religion, to respondent			−.068	
Multiple R	.23	.25	.21	.30
R-square	.05	.06	.05	.09

[a] Only those independent variables with at least one Beta of .05 or over are listed in this table. All smaller Beta weights are omitted. The complete variable list used in the stepwise regression analysis appears in the text of Appendix A. Except for dummy variables, the categories of the independent variables are those found in the various tables throughout the monograph. Kinship orientations are dummy variables derived from the classification procedure described in Chapter 4.

218

TABLE A-2. Comparison of Results of Multiple Regression Analyses with Tabular Presentations

Specific regression analysis: Kinship orientation	Variable	Overrepresentation (+) or underrepresentation (−) of variable: Sign of beta	Relevant table in text	Comparison with table
SOCIAL AND DEMOGRAPHIC BACKGROUND VARIABLES				
Parentela orders	Jewish	(+)	5-1	Confirms
	Neofundamentalist Protestant	(+)	5-1	Confirms
	Mormon	(−)	5-1	Confirms
	Age	(+)	7-9	Confirms
	Male gender	(+)	7-9	Confirms
	Racial minority-group status	(−)	5-5	Clarifies ambiguity
Standard american	Occupational status	(+)	4-5	Confirms
	Educational level	(+)	4-5	Confirms
	Protestantism:			
	Reformation-Era	(+)	4-5	Confirms
	General	(+)	4-5	Confirms
	Pietistic	(+)	4-5	Confirms
	Age	(−)	7-9	Confirms
Civil law	Racial minority-group status	(−)	5-5	Confirms
	Educational level	(−)	7-10	Confirms
	Pietistic Protestant	(+)	5-1	Confirms
Genetic or canon law	Racial minority-group status	(+)	5-5	Confirms
	Male gender	(−)	7-9	Confirms
FAMILY AND KIN OF ORIENTATION				
Parentela orders	Number of siblings	(+)	6-8	Confirms
	Knew father's mother	(−)	5-12	Clarifies
	Desired contact with father	(−)	8-7	Confirms
Standard american	Knew father's father	(+)	5-12	Confirms
	Number of siblings	(−)	6-8	Confirms
	Mother living in Arizona	(−)	8-1	Confirms
	Contact with father	(+)	8-7	Confirms
Civil law	Mother living in Arizona	(+)	8-1	Confirms
	Contact with mother	(−)	8-7	Confirms

(continued)

TABLE A-2 *(continued)*

Specific regression analysis: Kinship orientation	Variable	Overrepresentation (+) or underrepresentation (−) of variable: Sign of beta	Relevant table in text	Comparison with table
Genetic or	Number of siblings	(+)	6-8	Confirms
cannon law	Parents divorced	(+)	6-1	Confirms
	Contact with mother	(+)	8-7	Confirms
	Contact with father	(−)	8-7	Disconfirms
	Knew father's father	(−)	5-12	Confirms
	Knew father's mother	(+)	5-12	Clarifies
	Desired contact with:			
	Father	(+)	8-7	Clarifies
	Mother	(−)	8-7	Confirms

SELF AND FAMILY OF PROCREATION

Parentela orders

Standard american	Is this respondent's first marriage?	(+)	7-6	Clarifies
Civil law	Is respondent now divorced?	(−)	7-6	Confirms
	Frequency of church attendance	(+)	7-1	Clarifies
	Importance of religion to respondent	(−)		Not reported
Genetic or	Is respondent now divorced?	(+)	7-6	Confirms
canon law	Number of children	(−)	7-15	Confirms

[a] The following variables did not yield any Beta coefficients of .05 or over: (a) Family income in 1977; (b) Size of community in which respondent was raised; (c) Was respondent raised in Arizona?; (d) Respondent's religion is Catholic; (e) How well respondent knew Mother's Father while growing up; (f) How well respondent knew Mother's Mother while growing up; and (g) Nativity of Father's Father.

Whereas the analyses based on Tables, 5-5 and 5-6 yields the conclusion that income outweighs minority-group status in affecting kinship orientations, the regression analysis demands the reverse judgment.

Family and Kin of Orientation

As shown in Table A-1, the regression coefficients for items referring to parents, siblings, and grandparents indicate that:

1. When interactions among variables are taken into account, nativity of paternal grandfather and having known maternal grandparents are inconsequential for the development of kinship orientations.

2. The comparisons in Table A-2 show that the regression analysis tends to confirm the tabular interpretations of the role of the family of orientation in the development of kinship ideology. In addition to supporting the pervasive findings that number of siblings is associated with kinship orientation, the regression findings also reveal negative weights for paternal kin in Parentela Orders (in contrast to Standard American kinship) and a strong female skew in kin ties in the Genetic and Canon Law models.

Self and Family of Procreation

The Beta weights in Table A-1 clarify the following tendencies about the respondents and their families of procreation:

1. Parentela Orders and Standard American models, with one exception, do not have any regression coefficients exceeding .05 among items pertaining to families of procreation.
2. The Civil Law model is characterized not only by high marital stability but also by frequent church attendance (though not religiosity).
3. The data on Genetic-Canon Law emphasize the precariousness of marriage in these orientations.
4. Table A-2 indicates that the family-of-procreation interpretations based on the tables in the text are generally confirmed.

CONCLUSIONS

Overall, the data provided in Tables A-1 and A-2 strongly buttress the interpretations in the text. Moreover, the findings of the regression analyses tend to clarify some of the ambiguities of the tables that report percentages. For example, in contrast to the tables, the regression equations show that (a) minority-group status is more salient than income in influencing kinship orientation; (b) Civil Law orientation is expressive of associational tendencies in religion; and (c) there may be some resentment of the frequent contact among Genetic-Canon Law respondents with their mothers.

Perhaps the major contribution of the regression analyses is revealed in the distribution of Betas of .05 or over among the different categories of independent variables. In Table A-3, the Beta coeffients displayed in Table A-1 are classified as either Social and Demographic (SD) or Family Variables (F) (which includes the items pertaining to family of orientation and to family of procreation). The bottom row of Table A-3 presents ratios of the number of "high" Betas in the Social and Demographic category to those in the

Table A-3. Number of Beta Coefficients .05 or Over for Variables Classified as Social and Demographic Background or as Family Variables, by Kinship Orientation

Classification of variables	Parentela orders	Standard american	Civil law	Genetic or canon law
Social and demographic (SD)	6	7	4	3
Family variables[a] (F)	3	5	5	11
Ratio (SD)/(F)	2.00	1.40	.80	.27

[a] Includes variables classified as Family and Kin of Orientation and as Self and Family of Procreation.

Gamma = .51

Family Variables category [(SD)/(F)]. As one proceeds along the columns from Parentela Orders to Genetic-Canon Law, the size of the ratios decreases regularly. My interpretation is that this decrease expresses a shift in the comparative influence of pluralistic (in contrast to universalistic) ideologies. Parentela Orders and Standard American models reveal effects on kinship organization derived from class-membership in the larger institutional structure of society (e.g., religion, socioeconomic grouping), whereas the more Ego-centered kinship orientations are shaped by a communal outlook and they stress the character of familial interactions. Thus, the overall pattern of Betas provides additional support for the theoretical position taken here.

Appendix B
Method of
Data Collection
Morris Axelrod and
Edward A. Greenberg

This appendix describes the method by which the data were collected for the Phoenix kinship study. In order to limit the population to those persons for whom the questions were most meaningful in terms of the immediacy of their experience, the target group consisted of residents of Phoenix, Arizona, who had been married and who were now between the ages of 18 and 45. These restrictions were instituted (1) to preclude asking elderly respondents about their parental household during adolescence and (2) to avoid querying persons about marriage and family norms when they had never been married.

The 772-case sample, yielding the data upon which the analysis is based, consists of two components—a probability sample of Phoenix and a supplementary sample of Jewish households. The first part of this appendix describes the technique by which the probability sample was selected. The sample frame consisted of all households within the city limits of Phoenix that (1) are served by a telephone and (2) contain at least one permanent resident, between 18 and 45 years of age, inclusive, who is either now or has once been married. Respondents were selected in two steps: First, a random-digit-dialing (RDD) telephoning procedure was applied to screen for eligible households. Next, within each household that contained at least one person eligible for a household interview, a respondent was randomly selected from among all eligible persons. Since the probability sample would yield too few cases for ethnic and religious comparative analysis of Jewish households, it was decided to augment the sample with cases drawn from an available list of Jewish households. Telephone screening procedures similar to those used for the probability sample were followed to select cases for the supplement. The second part of the appendix depicts the procedure for selecting respondents in the Jewish supplementary sample.

The final section discusses the field procedures applied in the telephone screening and household interviews. It touches on the variety of interviewing techniques, required to elicit the data for analysis, and presents an enumeration of topics included in the questionnaires.

PHOENIX PROBABILITY SAMPLE

To eliminate ineligible persons, we screened potential respondents by telephone before investing heavily in household interviews. According to the U.S. Census, 84 percent of Phoenix households are served by at least one telephone (United States Bureau of the Census, 1970); so the biasing effects of non-subscribership are assumed to be minimal. (Cf. Tuchfarber and Klecka, 1976.) Additionally, the use of random-digit-dialing (RDD) allows us to reach unlisted and unpublished as well as listed telephone numbers.

The telephone informant at each randomly selected number was asked several Telephone Contact Questions to determine whether the number served a residence in Phoenix. If the telephone number was associated with a Phoenix residence, a Telephone Screening Interview was used to ascertain the composition of the household and the eligibility of the household for inclusion in the final sample. In addition, several attitudinal items of current interest were included in the telephone interview. These served to gain the cooperation of the informant, establish rapport, and provide some topical data about the community. The following sections report the sample selection procedure and the analysis of response rates.

Sample Selection Procedure

The telephone sampling procedure was based on a design suggested by Waksberg (1976) and elaborated on by Groves (1977). This technique consists of dividing the entire list of possible telephone numbers in a community into clusters, choosing a sample of clusters, and then determining which of these clusters are likely to contain households with specified characteristics. If the first number called in a cluster is eligible, chances are that the cluster contains a greater-than-average proportion of eligible households, and that cluster is retained in the sampling frame. The probability that a cluster is kept in the sample is directly proportional to the number of eligible households in that cluster (Waksberg, 1976). The procedure thus raises the percentage of productive calls above that yielded by a simple random sample.

The cluster technique was applied in the following manner: for Phoenix, the total hypothesized telephone coverage was divided into clusters of 100 numbers each. Particular clusters were then selected for inclusion in the sample as a result of a call to a single randomly selected telephone number in each cluster. If the number reached was assigned to a residence in Phoenix, the entire cluster was considered to be in the sample and n additional numbers within the cluster were called. (In this study, $n = 5$.) If any of these were non-sample, they were replaced by other numbers from the same cluster until *n* eligible households are identified. The specific steps in the selection of the sample are graphically presented in Figure B-1 and are detailed below.

Step 1. Determining the range of telephone numbers. The city of Phoenix is served by telephones with 63 different prefixes (the first three digits of the telephone numbers). These include 46 prefixes specifically designated as Phoenix prefixes and 17 prefixes that jointly serve Phoenix and neighboring communities. If every number for each of these prefixes were in use, there would be 10,000 numbers for each prefix (e.g., 555-0000 through 555-9999). Thus, there are $63 \times 10,000 = 630,000$ possible Phoenix telephone numbers. Of course, not all of these numbers are in service. In addition, many of the working numbers are assigned to telephones outside the Phoenix city limits or to non-residential telephones.

Step 2. Division into clusters. The next step in the telephone survey was to determine which of the 630,000 possible numbers are likely to be both in Phoenix and residential. Each "bank" of 10,000 numbers was divided into 100 groups, or clusters, of 100 numbers each. The numbers 555-0000 through 555-0099 constitute one such cluster, as do the numbers 555-0100 through 555-0199, and so on. There are 6300 clusters of 100 numbers each in our population of telephone numbers.

Step 3. Selection of cluster sample. We wrote a computer program to generate a random number from each cluster. That number was designated the "primary" number for its cluster. At random, 2750 of the 6300 primary numbers were selected for contact. If, on the basis of the Telephone Contact Questions, a primary number was found to be both in Phoenix and residential, the cluster was included in our sample. If the primary number was ascertained to be not in service, out of Phoenix, or non-residential, the entire cluster was dropped from the sample.

Step 4. Contacting primary numbers. The primary numbers were used only to determine whether a cluster remained in or was excluded from the sample (via the Telephone Contact Questions). Telephone Screening Interviews were not taken at the primary numbers. The 2750 selected primary numbers were called during a seven-week period from October to December, 1977. Of these, 975 primary numbers (35.5 percent) were in Phoenix and residential; 1775 numbers (64.5 percent) were non-residential, not in service, or outside Phoenix city limits.

Step 5. Selection of numbers for Telephone Screening Interviews. We estimated that about half of Phoenix households would contain a respondent

Step	Retained	Eliminated	
1. Prefixes serving PHX	63		
Numbers per prefix	x 10,000		
Numbers serving PHX	630,000		
2. Numbers per cluster	÷ 100		
Clusters in PHX	6,300		
3. Clusters screened	2,750 (43.7%)	3,550 (56.3%)	Unused clusters
4. In-Sample clusters (In=PHX, residential)	975 (35.5%)	1,775 (64.5%)	Non-Sample clusters
5. Clusters selected for Telephone Screening Interviews	406 (41.6%)	569 (58.4%)	Unused clusters
Telephone numbers selected for contact in each cluster	x 5		
Telephone sample n	2,030		
6. Completed interviews	1,826 (90.0%)	204 (10.0%)	Non-Interviews
7. Households containing an eligible respondent	916 (50.2%)	907 (48.8%)	Households containing no eligible respondent
8. Address ascertained	868 (94.8%)	48 (5.2%)	Address not ascertained
9. Selection of a respondent in each household	868		
10. Completed Household Interviews	716 (82.5%)	152 (17.5%)	Non-Interviews

Figure B-1. Disposition of cases in selection of Phoenix probability sample eligible for a Household Interview (i.e., 45 or under and ever-married). Our projected sample size was 800. Allowing for nonresponse in both telephone screening and household interviewing, we felt it necessary to screen about 2000 telephone numbers.

We decided to take Telephone Screening Interviews at five "secondary" numbers selected from each cluster retained in the sample. We therefore needed to select about 400 clusters from the 975 clusters (from Step 4) to yield 2000 numbers for screening. In fact, 406 clusters were selected, for a sample of 5 × 406 = 2030 telephone numbers serving residences in Phoenix.

Step 6. Telephone Screening Interviews. A total of 1826 Telephone Screening Interviews were taken from November, 1977 through May, 1978, when a 90.0 percent response rate was achieved. During this period, another 1844 numbers were ascertained to be non-working, non-residential, or outside the Phoenix city limits. Each of these 1844 numbers was replaced with a randomly chosen number from the same cluster.

Step 7. Determining eligibility for home interview. In order to determine whether a family member was eligible for inclusion in the Household Interview sample, we asked the telephone informant during the Telephone Screening Interview to report the household composition by age, sex, marital status, and relationship to the informant. If the household contained a person between 18 and 45 who was ever married, it was considered eligible for a household interview. Of the 1826 households at which a Teleopone Screening Interview was taken, 916 contained at least one eligible respondent. The remaining 910 households contained only persons who were over 45 years of age or who had never been married.

Step 8. Ascertaining address of eligible households. If a household contained a person eligible for a Household Interview, the telephone informant was asked to provide a name and an address to which a letter outlining the project and requesting an interview could be sent. Addresses were obtained for 868 of the 916 eligible households (or 94.8 percent). A few informants declined to divulge their names, but they were willing to provide an address to which a letter could be sent.

Step 9. Selection of respondent. The next step was to select a respondent randomly from among eligible persons in each of the 868 households for which we had an address. The procedure used was developed by Kish (1949). According to this technique, for every household, eligible adults of each sex are numbered in order of decreasing age. A series of 12 selection tables is used to designate a respondent in each household, so that every eligible adult in each household has an equal chance of being chosen. At the beginning, one table is chosen at random, and the tables are then used in sequence with each succeeding household.

Step 10. Interviewing the respondents. After the selection of respondents, the cases were assigned to household interviewers. The interviewers were not permitted to substitute other household members for designated respondents; instead, they were instructed to make as many callbacks or appointments as feasible within the field period in order to complete the interview with the respondent-designate.

The last page of the Telephone Screening Interview served as the cover sheet for the household questionnaire. It contained a listing of household members (including the designation of the selected respondent), the surname of the family (if given), the telephone number, and address. When each completed interview was received, the cover sheet was removed from the household questionnaire in order to ensure confidentiality of the interviews. Of the 868 households for which we had an address, household interviews were completed at 716.

Response Analysis

Response rates to the Telephone Screening Interviews and household interviews are summarized in Table B-1. The response rate for the probability sample is a product of three stages in the interviewing procedure. The first factor affecting the response rate was the sample loss due to failure to obtain a telephone screening interview. It is obviously not possible to determine whether those persons who declined at this point were eligible for a household interview. The Telephone Screening Interview (T) response rate is:

$$T = \frac{\text{Completed Interviews}}{\text{Completed Interviews} + \text{Non-Interviews}} = \frac{1826}{2030} = 90.0\%$$

The second factor affecting the response rate was the ability to obtain an address of households found to hold an eligible respondent. The address (A) response rate among households containing an eligible respondent is:

$$A = \frac{\text{Households with addresses}}{\text{Eligible households}} = \frac{868}{916} = 94.8\%$$

The final factor governing the response rate was the respondent's decision to take part in the Household Interview. This decision can be evaluated on the basis of two different denominators: (a) households for which addresses are known (H_1) and (b) households with eligible respondents (H_2).

The response rate for households for which addresses were obtained (H_1) is:

$$H_1 = \frac{\text{Completed Household Interviews}}{\text{Households with addresses}} = \frac{716}{868} = 82.5\%$$

The eligible Household Interview response rate (H_2) equals the number of household interviews completed divided by the number of households in the sample that contain eligible persons, that is:

$$H_2 = \frac{\text{Completed Household Interviews}}{\text{Households with eligible persons}} = \frac{716}{916} = 78.2\%$$

An overall, adjusted Household Interview response rate incorporates the response rate for Household Interviews and the response rate for the Tele-

Table B-1. Survey Response Analysis

Response category	Probability sample		Jewish supplement	
	Stage I: Telephone screening	Stage II: Household interviews	Stage I: Telephone screening	Stage II: Household interviews
Sample n	2030	916	425	58
Interviews				
Eligible for household interviews[a]	(916)	(716)	(58)	(49)[b]
Ineligible for household interviews	(910)	—	(118)	—
Total	1826	716	176	49
Non-interviews	204	200	100[c]	9
Non-sample	1844[d]	—	149	—
Response rate[e]	.900	.782	.638	.845

[a] Households containing at least one person between the ages of 18 and 45 and ever married.

[b] Seven interviews taken in the Jewish household supplementary sample were discovered to be non-Jewish. These seven were used to replace non-interviews and were combined with the 716 interviews from the probability sample to increase the number of cases to 723 for analysis. The seven added cases were excluded from the computation of response rates.

[c] Non-interviews for this phase of the study included 44 households which were found to be eligible for a household interview. In addition, there were 86 for which eligibility was not ascertained (ENA). It is assumed that the proportion of non-sample households to sample households is the same for ENA cases as for the remainder of the sample. Thus, 35 percent of the ENAs (30 households) were considered to be non-sample and were added to the known non-sample cases (30 + 119 = 149). Similarly, 65 percent of the ENAs (56 households) were treated as non-interviews and were added to the actual non-interviews (44 + 56 = 100). Since most of the ENAs are probably in fact non-sample, the non-interview estimate is a conservative one.

[d] In the random-digit dialing sampling procedure, a telephone number classified as non-sample (i.e., outside Phoenix and/or non-residential) is replaced by a new randomly-selected number from the same cluster.

[e] Response rate $= \dfrac{\text{Completed interviews}}{\text{Completed interviews} + \text{Non-interviews}}$.

phone Screening Interviews. The adjusted Household Interview response rate, which takes into account telephone screening non-interviews, withholding addresses, and household non-interviews is the product of the Telephone Screening Interview response rate (T) and the eligible Household Interview response rate (H_2), or:

$$T \times H_2 = 90.0 \text{ x } 78.2 = 70.3\%$$

JEWISH SUPPLEMENTARY SAMPLE

Previous analysis has shown a relationship between the Parentela Orders model and Judaism (Farber, 1977). For this reason, it was considered desirable to select a supplementary sample of Jewish respondents to be interviewed. This supplement was necessary to augment the small proportion of interviews with Jews in Phoenix yielded by the telephone probability sample (approximately 2 percent). The probability sample produced fewer than 20 Jewish households, too few for analysis. We elected to supplement the probability sample by selecting Jewish households from available lists.

The response analysis for the Jewish Supplementary Sample is described in Table B-1. We began with a list of 425 names of potentially eligible households (i.e., containing at least one Jewish, ever-married person between the ages of 18 and 45). Telephone numbers were available for some of the names on the list, but not all. For those whose telephone numbers were not provided, other sources (in particular, the Phoenix Telephone Directory) were used to ascertain the number when possible.

For the Supplementary Sample, telephone numbers were obtained for 339 of the original list of 425 households. These numbers were telephoned and the Telephone Screening Interview was administered. Of the 339 numbers, Telephone Screening Interviews were completed for 176. One hundred of these numbers yielded non-interviews (refusals, incomplete interviews, address not ascertained, etc.), and 149 numbers were found to serve non-sample households (outside Phoenix, non-residential, or non-Jewish). Of the completed Telephone Screening Interviews, 58 yielded households that contained at least one eligible respondent who met the age, marital status, and religious criteria. Household interviews were taken at 49 of the 58 eligible households (or 84.5 percent). Although the Jewish Supplementary Sample was selected on the basis of availability, it is believed to be reasonably representative of the known Jewish community.

An additional adjustment was made to the set of completed Household Interviews after the data collection for the supplementary sample was completed. Seven interviews taken at households selected from this sample frame did not contain an eligible Jewish respondent. These interviews were taken with respondents who were in most respects similar to the Phoenix probability sample with respect to religion, marital history, family size, and other characteristics. These interviews were retained as replacements for non-interviews in the probability household sample. In summary, the final set of completed household interviews consists of:

Probability Sample	716
Jewish Supplementary Sample	49
Non-Jewish from supplementary sample	7
Total Interview	772

FIELD PROCEDURES

The interviewing for the Phoenix kinship study was done in two major stages: (a) Telephone Screening Interviews were conducted with a sample of Phoenix households selected by random digit dialing; (b) face-to-face interviews were conducted with selected eligible respondents in their homes. Household interviewing took place from January through July, 1978. On the average, the interviewing staff consisted of about 20 persons at any one time.

Because the telephone interviewing was done on our premises, we had close, continuous contact between project staff and interviewers. This contact extended interviewer instruction informally on a regular basis after the initial training periods, and it permitted the interviewers to gain a heightened understanding of the total project. As a result, they were well equipped for the subsequent household interviewing.

The forms used in the household interviews were intended to elicit information in a variety of areas, and several techniques were applied. The household questionnaire was rather complex in that it used charts, self-administered forms, "map games," and many sets of questions that were contingent upon marital status, number of children, number of siblings, and so on. For the most part, however, the interview consisted of a straightforward face-to-face oral administration of a questionnaire, with the interviewer recording the responses on the form. The orally administered sections pertained to material on the following:

a. Respondent's and spouse's children—vital statistics, religion, residence, and marital and parental status.
b. The respondent's brothers and sisters—vital statistics, religion, and marital and parental history.
c. Teenage values—a series of questions aimed at ascertaining the role expectations in the respondent's family of orientation.
d. The respondent's parents—vital statistics, marital history, religious background, educational and occupational backround.

e. Views about family and society—questions on topics relevant to family relationships (including views on abortion, unmarried couples living together, obligations to relatives, religion and the family, and comparative loyalty to home versus work) and the Srole Anomia scale. The respondent's speculations about the spouse's views were also solicited.

f. Respondent's and spouse's background—demographic information and marital histories.

A second series of questions was included in a self-administered written form on closeness of kin. Responses to these questions were used to classify respondents according to kinship orientation. This form also referred to acquaintanceship with relatives prior to adulthood.

A third segment of the interview involved a card-sorting technique. In this segment, the respondent placed cards, on which were written specific relatives, on maps to indicate where kin were born and where they now live. In another series of card sorts, the respondent showed how much contact there is with these relatives and how much contact is desired.

The Household Interviews averaged about an hour in length. Despite the apparent complexity, we were able to develop a questionnaire form that was virtually self-guiding for the interviewer and proved to be effective in eliciting the necessary information with little error or confusion.

References

Ackerman, Charles
 1963   Affiliations: Structural Determinants of Differential Divorce Rates. *American Journal of Sociology* 69: 13–20.

Adams, Bert N.
 1968   *Kinship in An Urban Setting*. Chicago: Markham.
 1970   Isolation, Function, and Beyond: American Kinship in the 1960's. *Journal of Marriage and the Family* 32: 575–597.

Alsop, Stewart
 1968   The New American Family—II: It Wasn't Born Yesterday. *Saturday Evening Post* 241, issue 15, July 27.

Altheim, Franz
 1938   *A History of Roman Religion*. London: Methuen and Company.

Anderson, Michael
 1971   *Family Structure in Nineteenth Century Lancashire*. New York: Cambridge University Press.

Aristotle
 1942   *The Student's Oxford Aristotle*. Edited by W.D. Ross. New York: Oxford University Press. Vol. V, Ethics.

Arizona
 1975   *Arizona Revised Statutes*. St. Paul: West Publishing Company. (Pocket Supplement, 1979).

Atkins, John R.
 1974   On the Fundamental Consanguineal Numbers and Their Structural Basis. *American Ethnologist* 1: 1–31.

Augustine
 1966   *The City of God Against the Pagans*. Cambridge, Massachusetts: Harvard University Press. Vol. 4.

Babchuk, Nicholas
 1965   Primary Friends and Kin: A Study of the Associations of Middle-Class Couples. *Social Forces* 43: 483–493.

Bahr, Howard M.
 1976   The Kinship Role. In Ivan F. Nye, ed., *Role Structure and Analysis of the Family*. Beverly Hills, California: Sage Publications. Pp. 61–79.

Beale, Howard K.
1964 Family Culture and Genealogy. In Edward N. Saveth, ed., *American History and the Social Sciences.* New York: Free Press.

Blau, Peter
1964 *Exchange and Power in Social Life.* New York: Wiley.

Bogardus, Emory S.
1959 *Social Distance.* Los Angeles: Published by author.

Brown, Cecil H.
1974 Psychological, Semantic, and Structural Aspects of American English Kinship Terms. *American Ethnologist* 1: 415–436.
1976 An Examination of the Ordinary Use of American English Kin Terms and Kin Term Bound Forms: "Semantics" as Necessary Meaning. *Anthropoligical Linguistics* 18: 129-156.

Buchler, Ira R. and Henry A. Selby
1968 *Kinship and Social Organization.* New York: Macmillan.

Burgess, Ernest W.
1973 *On Community, Family, and Delinquency.* Chicago: University of Chicago Press.

Burgess, Ernest W., Harvey J. Locke, and Mary Margaret Thomes
1963 *The Family: From Institution to Companionship.* New York: American Book Co.

Burgess, Ernest W. and Leonard S. Cottrell
1939 *Predicting Success or Failure in Marriage* New York: Prentice Hall.

Burgess, Ernest W. and Paul Wallin
1953 *Engagement and Marriage.* New York: Lippincott.

Burr, Wesley R.
1973 *Theory Construction and the Sociology of the Family.* New York: Wiley.

Campbell, Bruce L. and Eugene E. Campbell
1976 The Mormon Family. In Charles H. Mindel and Robert W. Habenstein, eds., *Ethnic Families in America.* New York: Elsevier. Pp. 379–412.

Carr, Leslie G.
1971 The Srole Items and Acquiescence. *American Sociological Review* 36: 287–293.

Casson, Ronald W.
1973 An Equivalence Rule Analysis of American Kinship Terminology. *Anthropological Linguistics* 15: 189–202.

Chodorow, Stanley
1972 *Christian Political Theory and Church Politics in the Mid-Twelfth Century.* Berkeley and Los Angeles: University of California Press.

Church Educational System
1976 *Achieving a Celestial Marriage.* Salt Lake City: Department of Seminaries and Institutes of Religion, Church of Jesus Christ of Latter-day Saints.

Coser, Lewis
1974   *Greedy Institutions: Patterns of Undivided Commitment.* New York: Free Press.

Craig, Daniel
1979   Immortality through Kinship: The Vertical Transmission of Substance and Symbolic Estate. *American Anthropologist* 81: 94–96.

Cruz-Coke, Ricardo
1977   A Genetic Reform of the Civil Law Computation of the Degrees of Relationship in Families. *Social Biology* 24: 93–99.

Danby, Herbert (translator)
1933   *The Mishnah.* New York: Oxford University Press.

Dizzard, Jan
1968   *Social Change in the Family.* Chicago: Community and Family Study Center, University of Chicago.

Durkheim, Emile
1915   *Elementary Forms of Religious Life.* New York: Macmillan.

Durkheim, Emile and Marcel Mauss
1961   Social Structure and the Structure of Thought. In Talcott Parsons, Edward Shils, Kaspar Naegele, and Jessee R. Pitts, eds., *Theories of Society.* New York: Free Press. Pp. 1065–1068.

Ehrenberg, Victor
1946   *Aspects of the Ancient World.* New York: William Salloch.

Eisenstadt, Shmuel N.
1977   Sociological Theory and an Analysis of the Dynamics of Civilizations and of Revolutions. *Daedalus* 106: 59–78. (Discoveries and Interpretations: Studies in Contemporary Scholarship, Volume II.)

Ekeh, Peter
1975   *Social Exchange Theory and the Two Sociological Traditions.* Cambridge, Massachusetts: Harvard University Press.

Epstein, Isadore (ed.)
1935   *The Babylonian Talmud.* London: Soncino Press. Volume 2.

Farber, Bernard
1964   *Family: Organization and Interaction.* San Francisco: Chandler.
1971   *Kinship and Class: A Midwestern Study.* New York: Basic Books.
1972   *Guardians of Virtue: Salem Families in 1800.* New York: Basic Books.
1973   *Family and Kinship in Modern Society.* Glenview, Illinois: Scott, Foresman.
1975   Bilateral Kinship: Centripetal and Centrifugal Types of Organization. *Journal of Marriage and the Family* 37: 871–888.
1977   Social Context, Kinship Mapping, and Family Norms. *Journal of Marriage and the Family* 39: 227–240.
1979   Kinship Mapping Among Jews In A Midwestern City. *Social Forces* 57: 1107–1123.

Farber, Bernard, Charles H. Mindel, and **Bernard Lazerwitz**
1976   The Jewish American Family. In Charles H. Mindel and Robert W. Habenstein, eds., *Ethnic Families in America*. New York: Elsevier. Pp. 347–378.

Feng, Han-yi
1937   The Chinese Kinship. *Harvard Journal of Asiatic Studies* 2: 141–274.

Firth, Raymond
1956   *Two Studies of Kinship in London*. London: Athlone Press.

Fortes, Meyer
1969   *Kinship and the Social Order*. Chicago: Aldine.

Fox, Robin
1967   *Kinship and Marriage*. Baltimore: Penguin.

Freedman, Ronald, Paul K. Whelpton, and **Arthur A. Campbell**
1959   *Family Planning, Sterility, and Population Growth*. New York: MacGraw-Hill.

Glazer, Nathan and **Daniel P. Moynihan**
1974   Why Ethnicity. *Commentary* 58: 33–39.

Glick, Paul C.
1979   The Future of the American Family. *Current Population Reports: Special Studies*. Series P-23, No. 78. U.S. Bureau of the Census.

Glock, Charles Y. and **Rodney Stark**
1965   *Religion and Society in Tension*. Chicago: Rand McNally.

Gluckman, Joel R.
1976   Intestate Succession in New Jersey: Does It Conform To Popular Expectations? *Columbia Journal of Law and Social Problems* 12: 253–294.

Goffman, Erving
1956   *Presentation of the Self in Everyday Life*. Edinburgh: Social Sciences Center, University of Edinburgh.

Goode, William J.
1960   A Theory of Role Strain. *American Sociological Review* 25: 483–496.
1962   Marital Satisfaction and Instability: A Cross-cultural Class Analysis of Divorce Rates. *International Social Science Journal* 14: 307–526.
1963   *World Revolution and Family Patterns*. New York: Free Press.

Goody, Jack
1976   *Production and Reproduction*. Cambridge: Cambridge University Press.

Gordon, Michael
1977   Primary-Group Differentiation in Urban Ireland. *Social Forces* 55: 743–752.

Greeley, Andrew M.
1976   *The Communal Catholic, A Personal Manifesto*. New York: Seabury Press.
1977   *The American Catholic, A Social Portrait*. New York: Basic Books.

Groves, R.M.
1977   An Empirical Comparison of Two Telephone Sample Designs. Unpublished report of the Survey Research Center of the University of Michigan, 1977.

Harrison, Alick R.W.
1968   *The Law of Athens, Family and Property.* New York: Oxford University Press.

Haskins, George Lee
1960   *Law and Authority in Early Massachusetts.* New York: Macmillan.

Health Resources Administration
1974   Teenagers: Marriages, Divorces, Parenthood, and Mortality. *Vital and Health Statistics.* Series 21, Number 23. Washington, D.C.: U.S. Government Printing Office.

Heitland, W.E.
1923   *The Roman Republic.* Cambridge, England: Cambridge University Press.

Herberg, Will
1960   *Protestant, Catholic, Jew.* New York: Anchor.

Hertz, J.H. (ed.)
1960   *The Pentateuch and Haftorahs.* London: Soncino Press. Second Edition.

Hill, Daniel
1977   Labor Force Participation Decisions of Wives. In Greg Duncan and James N. Morgan, eds., *Five Thousand American Families - Patterns of Economic Progress, Volume V.* Ann Arbor: Institute for Social Research, University of Michigan.

Horst, Paul (ed.)
1941   *The Prediction of Personal Adjustment.* New York: Social Science Research Council.

Hoyt, Homer
1933   *One Hundred Years of Land Values in Chicago.* Chicago: University of Chicago Press.

Huebner, Rudolf
1968   *A History of Germanic Private Law.* New York: Augustus M. Kelley Publishers. (Published originally in 1918.)

Joffe, Natalie F.
1949   The Dynamics of Benefice Among East European Jews. *Social Forces* 27: 238–247.

Johnson, E.L.
1969   *An Introduction to the Soviet Legal System.* London: Methuen and Company.

Jolowicz, H.F.
1967   *Historical Introduction to the Study of Roman Law.* Cambridge, England: Cambridge University Press.

238

Kerckhoff, Alan C.
1965   Nuclear and Extended Family Relationships: A Normative and Behavioral Analysis. In Ethel Shanas and Gordon F. Strieb, eds., *Social Structure and the Family: Generational Relations*. Englewood Cliffs, New Jersey: Prentice-Hall. Pp. 93–112.

Kish, L.
1949   A Procedure for Objective Response Selection within the Household. *Journal of the American Statistical Association* 44: 380–387.

Klatzky, Sheila R.
n.d.   *Patterns of Contact with Relatives*. Washington, D.C.: American Sociological Association.

Köhler, Wolfgang
1947   *Gestalt Psychology*. New York: Liveright.

Laumann, Edward O.
1966   *Prestige and Association in an Urban Community*. New York: Bobbs-Merrill.
1973   *Bonds of Pluralism: The Form and Substance of Urban Social Networks*. New York: Wiley.

Leichter, Hope J. and **William E. Mitchell**
1956   *Kinship and Case Work*. New York: Russell Sage Foundation.

Lenski, Gerhard E.
1963   *The Religious Factor*. New York: Doubleday.

Lenski, Gerhard E. and **John C. Leggett**
1960   Caste, Class, and Deference in the Research Interview. *American Journal of Sociology* 65: 463–467.

Lévi-Strauss, Claude
1963   *Structural Anthropology*. New York: Basic Books.
1966   *The Savage Mind*. Chicago: University of Chicago Press.
1969   *The Elementary Structures of Kinship*. Boston: Beacon Press.

Lewin, Kurt
1936   *Principles of Topological Psychology*. New York: McGraw-Hill.

Lewis, Oscar
1967   Further Observations on the Folk-Urban Continuum and Urbanization, with Special Reference to Mexico City. Cited in Elliot Liebow, *Tally's Corner*, pp. 204–205.

Liebow, Elliot
1967   *Tally's Corner*. Boston: Little, Brown.

Litwak, Eugene
1960a Geographic Mobility and Extended Family Cohesion. *American Sociological Review* 25: 385–394.
1960b Occupational Mobility and Extended Family Cohesion. *American Sociological Review* 25: 9–21.

1965   Extended Kin Relations in an Industrial Democratic Society. In Ethel Shanas and Gordon F. Streib, eds., *Social Structure and the Family:Generational Relations*. Englewood Cliffs, New Jersey: Prentice-Hall. Pp. 290–325.

Locke, Harvey J.
1951   *Predicting Adjustment in Marriage: A Comparison of a Divorced and a Happily Married Group*. New York: Holt.

Lopata, Helena Znaniecki
1973   *Widowhood in an American City*. Cambridge, Massachusetts: Schenkman (General Learning Press).

Maimonides, Moses
1963   *The Guide of the Perplexed*. Chicago: University of Chicago Press.
1967   *Mishneh Torah*. New York: Hebrew Publishing Company.

Maranda, Pierre
1974   *French Kinship, Structure and History*. The Hague: Mouton.

McFarland, David D. and **Daniel J. Brown**
1973   Social Distance as a Metric: A Systematic Introduction to Smallest Space Analysis. In Edward O. Laumann, ed., *Bonds of Pluralism: The Form and Substance of Urban Social Networks*. New York: Wiley. Pp. 213–253 (Appendix A).

Miller, Delbert C.
1977   *Handbook of Research Design and Social Measurement*. New York: David McKay.

Model, Otto
1964   *Testamentsrecht*. Berlin: C.H. Beck'she Verlagsbuchhandlung.

Modell, John, Frank F. Furstenberg and **Douglas Strong**
1978   The Timing of Marriage in the Transition to Adulthood: Continuity and Change, 1860–1975. In John Demos and Sarane Spence Boocock, eds., *Turning Points*. Chicago: *American Journal of Sociology*, Supplement 84: S120–S150.

Mommsen, Theodor
1905   *The History of Rome*. New York: Charles Scribner's Sons.

Morgan, D.H.J.
1975   *Social Theory and the Family*. London: Routledge & Kegan Paul.

Morgan, Lewis Henry
1871   *Systems of Consanguinity and Affinity of the Human Family*. Washington, D.C.: Smithsonian Institution.

Murdock, George Peter
1949   *Social Structure*. New York: Macmillan.
1970   Cross-sex Patterns of Kin Behavior. *Ethnology* 9: 359–368.

Naroll, Raoul
1970   What Have We Learned from Cross-Cultural Surveys? *American Anthropologist* 72: 1227–1288.

240

Needham, Rodney
1974 *Remarks and Inventions: Skeptical Essays about Kinship*. London: Tavistock Publications.

Paige, Jeffery M.
1974 Kinship and Polity in Stateless Societies. *American Journal of Sociology* 80: 301–320.

Parsons, Talcott
1949 The Social Structure of the Family. In Ruth Nanda Anshen, ed., *The Family: Its Function and Destiny*. New York: Harper. Pp. 241–274.
1954 The Kinship System of the Contemporary United States. In Talcott Parsons, ed., *Essays in Sociological Theory*. New York: Free Press. Pp. 177–196.

Radcliffe-Brown, A.R. and **Daryll Forde**
1950 *African Systems of Kinship and Marriage*. New York: Oxford University Press.

Radin, Max
1915 *The Jews Among the Greeks and Romans*. Philadelphia: Jewish Publication Society of America.

Rainwater, Lee
1960 *And the Poor Get Children*. Chicago: Quadrangle Books.

Reiss, Paul J.
1960 The Extended Kinship System in The American Middle Class. Ph.D dissertation, Harvard University.

Rheinstein, Max
1955 *The Law of Decedents' Estates*. Indianapolis: Bobbs Merrill (Second edition).

Romney, A. Kimball and **Roy G. D'Andrade**
1964 Cognitive Aspects of English Kin Terms. *American Anthropologist* 66: 146–170.

Rosenberg, George S. and **Donald F. Anspach**
1973 *Working Class Kinship*. Lexington, Massachusetts: Lexington Books.

Rosenfeld, Jeffrey P.
1974 Inheritance: A Sex-Related System of Exchange. In Rose Laub Coser, ed., *The Family, Its Structures and Functions*. New York: St. Martin's Press. Pp. 400–411.

Sahlins, Marshall
1965 On the Sociology of Primitive Exchange. In Michael Banton, ed., *The Relevance of Models for Social Anthropology*. New York: Frederick A. Praeger. Pp. 139–236.

Sandars, Thomas Collett
1874 *The Institutes of Justinian*. London: Longmans, Green (Fifth Edition).

Sanday, Peggy R.
1968 The "Psychological Reality" of American–English Kinship Terms: An Information-Processing Approach. *American Anthropologist* 70: 508–523.

Saveth, Edward N.
1963 The American Patrician Class: A Field of Research. *American Quarterly* 15 (Summer Supplement): 235–252.

Schlesinger, Benjamin
1974 The Jewish Family and Religion. *Journal of Comparative Family Studies* 5: 27–36.

Schneider, David M.
1968 *American Kinship: A Cultural Account.* Englewood Cliffs, New Jersey: Prentice-Hall.

Schneider, David M. and **Calvert B. Cottrell**
1975 *The American Kin Universe: A Genealogical Study.* Chicago: Department of Anthropology, University of Chicago.

Schneider, David M. and **Raymond T. Smith**
1973 *Class Differences and Sex Roles in American Kinship and Family Structure.* Englewood Cliffs, New Jersey: Prentice-Hall.

Schulz, Fritz
1951 *Classical Roman Law.* London: Oxford at the Claredon Press.

Selden, John
1636 *De Successionibus in Bona Defuncti, ad Legis Ebraeorum.* London: Richard Bishop.
1640 *De Jure Naturali et Gentium, Juxta Disciplinam Ebraeorum.* London: Richard Bishop.

Sherman, C. Bezalel
1964 Demographic and Social Aspects. In Oscar I. Janowsky, ed., *The American Jew: A Reappraisal.* Philadelphia: Jewish Publication Society. Pp.27–52.

Shils, Edward
1975 *Center and Periphery, Essays in Macrosociology.* Chicago: University of Chicago Press.

Simmel, Georg
1911 How Is Society Possible? *American Journal of Sociology* 16: 372–391.

Simon, Rita J., William Rau, and **Mary Louis Fellows**
1980 Public Versus Statutory Choice of Heirs: A Study of Public Attitudes about Property Distribution at Death. *Social Forces* 58:1263–1271.

Skolnick, Arlene S. and **Jerome H. Skolnick**
1971 *Family in Transition.* Boston: Little, Brown.

Smelser, Neil J.
1976 *The Sociology of Economic Life.* Englewood Cliffs, New Jersey: Prentice-Hall

Smith, Charles Edward
1940 *Papal Enforcement of Some Medieval Marriage Laws.* Baton Rouge: Louisiana State University Press. (Reissued in 1972 by Kennikat Press, New York.)

Sorokin, Pitirim A.

1959 *Social and Cultural Mobility.* New York: Free Press.

Srole, Leo

1956 Social Integration and Certain Corollaries: An Exploratory Study. *American Sociological Review* 21: 709–716.

Staples, Robert

1971 *The Black Family, Essays and Studies.* Belmont, California: Wadsworth

Stone, Lawrence

1975 The Rise of the Nuclear Family in Early Modern England: The Patriarchal State. In Charles E. Rosenberg, ed., *The Family in History.* Philadelphia: University of Pennsylvania Press. Pp. 13–57.

Sussman, Marvin B.

1965 Relationships of Adult Children with their Parents in the United States. In Ethel Shanas and Gordon F. Streib, eds., *Social Structure and the Family: Generational Relations.* Englewood Cliffs, New Jersey: Prentice-Hall. Pp. 62–92.

Sussman, Marvin B. and **Lee G. Burchinal**

1962a Kin Family Network: Unheralded Structure in Current Conceptionalizations of Family Functioning. *Marriage and Family Living* 24: 231–240.

1962b Parental Aid to Married Children: Implications for Family Functioning. *Journal of Marriage and the Family* 24: 320–332.

Sussman, Marvin B., Judith N. Cates, and **David T. Smith**

1970 *The Family and Inheritance.* New York: Russell Sage Foundation.

Swanson, Guy E.

1967 *Religion and Regime.* Ann Arbor: University of Michigan Press.

1969 *Rules of Descent: Studies in the Sociology of Parentage.* Anthropological Papers, No. 39. Ann Arbor: Museum of Anthropology, University of Michigan.

Tedeschi, Guido

1966 *Studies in Israeli Private Law.* Jerusalem: Kiryat Sepher.

Terman, Lewis

1938 *Psychological Factors in Marital Happiness.* New York: McGraw-Hill.

Tuchfarber, A.J. and Klecka, W.R.

1976 *Random Digit Dialing: Lowering the Cost of Victimization Surveys.* Washington, D.C.: The Police Foundation.

Ullmann, Walter

1955 *The Growth of Papal Government in the Middle Ages.* Ithaca, New York: Cornell University Press.

1975 *Law and Politics in the Middle Ages.* Ithaca, New York: Cornell University Press.

United States Bureau of the Census.
1970   *Census of Housing: Vol. 1, Housing Characteristics for States, Cities, and Counties, Part 4, Arizona.* Washington, D.C.: U.S. Government Printing Office.

Waksberg, J.
1976   Sampling Methods for Random Digit Dialing. Unpublished report. Rockville, Maryland: Westat, Inc.

Wallace, Anthony F.C. and **John R. Atkins**
1960   The Meaning of Kinship Terms. *American Anthropologist* 62: 58–80.

Waller, Willard and **Reuben Hill**
1951   *The Family.* New York: Dryden.

Watson, Alan
1971   *The Law of Succession in the Later Roman Republic.* London: Oxford at the Clarendon Press.

Weber, Max
1961   *General Economic History.* New York: Collier Books.

Weigert, Andrew J. and **Ross Hastings**
1977   Identity Loss, Family, and Social Change. *American Journal of Sociology* 82: 1171–1185.

Westoff, Charles F. and **Norman Ryder**
1977   *The Contraceptive Revolution.* Princeton, New Jersey: Princeton University Press.

Wexler, Kenneth N. and **A. Kimball Romney**
1972   Individual Variations in Cognitive Structures. In A. Kimball Romney, Roger N. Shepard, and Sara Beth Nerlove, eds., *Multidimensional Scaling* (Vol. 2, *Applications*). New York: Seminar Press. Pp. 73–92.

Winch, Robert F.
1974   Some Observations on Extended Familism in the United States. In Robert F. Winch and Graham B. Spanier, eds., *Selected Studies in Marriage and the Family.* New York: Holt, Rinehart, and Winston. Pp. 147–160.

1977   *Familial Organization, A Quest for Determinants.* New York: Free Press.

Wypyski, Eugene M.
1976   *The Law of Inheritance in All Fifty States.* Dobbs Ferry, New York: Oceana.

Index